THE CIVILIZATION OF THE AMERICAN INDIAN SERIES

Indians & Pioneers

The Story of the American Southwest

Before 1830

By Grant Foreman

Revised Edition

Norman: University of Oklahoma Press

To the Memory of
My Father and Mother

PREFACE

WHEN early writers told of the West and Southwest, they were, with few exceptions, writing of a region east of the Mississippi River. As the country enlarged after the Mexican War and the discovery of gold, the West suddenly expanded to the Pacific, and the Southwest of that period was the region colored by the romantic atmosphere of Spain. The Northwest had its Lewis and Clark, its Astoria, and the Oregon Trail. Historians and novelists have reaped harvests from the fertile soil between Westport and the Pacific with narratives of the covered wagon, the pony-express, and the cow-horse. The adventures of explorers and military expeditions, the saga of white settlement and pioneering in this boundless domain have been celebrated in volumes without number.

For years scholars have been bringing into view thousands of manuscripts from the opulent archives of Spain and Mexico, to contribute to the history of our Spanish domain; and "Southwest" came to suggest the land of Texas, Arizona, New Mexico, and California, of the cliff dweller, the pueblo, and the Spanish mission.

But there was another Southwest that has remained in eclipse. Between the Mississippi River and New Spain was a region little known. That part of the original Missouri Territory which afterward became Arkansas Territory, southern Missouri, and southern Kansas, has held for the historian only fugitive interest. When the state was erected out of Arkansas Territory, the remaining domain extending westward to the Spanish possessions was held as an Indian country, and until modern times was not opened up for settlement by white people; and thereby it missed much of the romance of white pioneering. Before the Civil War the Government made several abortive efforts to set up an Indian state here, where many indigenous and immigrant tribes were to be combined under a government in which they would all participate. This interesting experiment was never put into operation as the plans of the Government were invariably rejected by the Indian owners of the soil, though they were at the time engaged in building up an interesting civilization here.

When the state of Oklahoma was admitted to the Union, with four times as many people as there were in the next largest state at the time of its admission, it began with a degree of literacy exceeding that of most pioneer states. Unlike other young states, its civilization was to a great extent the civilization of the aborigines. The Indian owners of this land had erected orderly constitutional governments, and established schools patronized by them with a zeal unequaled by most frontier white settlements.

These and other interesting characteristics peculiar to this region developed from an equally interesting early history that distinguished it from the surrounding territory. While most of the writers of books have passed it by in quest of the white man's adventures, this American Southwest was not wanting for chroniclers of early conditions and events. More than one hundred years ago army officers, Indian agents, factors, traders, and missionaries, matter-of-fact observers of this virgin country from the Mississippi to the Spanish possessions, in the discharge of routine duties began recording and forwarding their accounts to the East. These documents accumulated in the dust-covered files of official storerooms, appeared in early prints, or in more recent years drifted into the archives of historical societies.

This documentary material designed for a limited number of readers, and for temporary information and service, contains all that is known or ever can be known about much of the Indian warfare and other matters of interest on this southwestern frontier. And in the aggregate it constitutes a very great preponderance of all the recorded history of this American Southwest for the early decades of the nineteenth century.

This material is but little known to the historian and still less to the general reader; so that in the writing of this book it is my privilege to put in print for the first time the contents of many documents depicting phases of history of this region not otherwise available. I am hopeful that in assembling these hitherto unpublished accounts I shall have contributed materially to a definite history for this period and region about which so little is known. And I trust that the bibliography will help the student to a knowledge of the few books that contain fragmentary accounts of the subject.

Different observers of the same events contributed from their various sources of information. In some cases the letters of an army officer, an Indian agent, a missionary, and a trader supplied different items of information about the same Indian battle or massacre, to be further supplemented by accounts in one to half a dozen newspapers; so that pursuit of details has led for months and years through widely separated archives and newspaper files in many states, in order to piece together the accounts of some of the incidents set down in this book.

The fascination of this employment has relieved it of much of its drudgery, and the courtesy and helpfulness of the staffs in charge of the archives have done much to promote the work and make my labor more effective. It would be impossible to mention the large number of persons to whom I am indebted through the years I have been engaged in assembling the material for this book. And if the effort were made, I would inevitably fall into errors of omission that would make me appear ungrateful to some. But I cannot forbear making acknowledgment here to a few to whom I am under the greatest obligation.

In the War Department, Adjt. Gen. Charles H. Bridges has very courteously facilitated my research. Dr. Harlow R. Street, in charge of the Old Files Division, Mr. Fred C. Burrus, formerly in charge, and Mr. Gustav A. Kolbe of the staff, both of whom have since died, Maj. John E. Brooks of the Old Records Division and his assistants have been most helpful. In the

Quartermaster General's old files in the Hall of Records, Miss
M. D. Sabotka, Mr. Joseph W. Griffin, and Mr. Thomas J.
Crawford took great pains and very efficiently aided in my
search for desired manuscripts. In the department of the Corps
of Engineers, the officers have been uniformly courteous and
helpful. And I am much obligated to Mr. J. William De Grange
in charge of the historical records of that department for his
assistance.

In the Office of Indian Affairs, Mr. C. F. Hawke, chief clerk,
has accorded me facilities for examining documents in which I
am interested; and Mr. W. L. Simpson in charge of the Old
Files in that department has given much of his time and contributed without stint from his extensive fund of information to
facilitate my work. In the Library of Congress, Mr. John C.
Fitzpatrick, while assistant chief in charge of the manuscript
division, and his successor, Dr. T. P. Martin, have been most
helpful.

For assistance in examining an extensive collection of documents related to early Arkansas Territory now in the Department of State at Washington, I am indebted to Mr. Tyler
Dennett, chief of the Division of Publications, and Dr. Newton
D. Mereness, archivist of the Conference of State Historical
Agencies of the Mississippi Valley, who has been in charge of
the collection of these territorial records for publication under
a recent act of Congress.

On the occasions of my many visits to the Missouri Historical Society, Mrs. Nettie H. Beauregard, the archivist, and Miss
Stella M. Drumm, librarian, have cheerfully given of their
time and information to assist me in an adequate examination
of the priceless and well-arranged collections of manuscripts
belonging to that society. I am also indebted to Mr. Floyd C.
Shoemaker, secretary of the State Historical Society of Missouri. Dr. Joseph Schafer, Dr. Louise Phelps Kellogg, and
Miss Iva A. Welsh of the State Historical Society of Wisconsin assisted me in examining and securing copies of manuscripts

and newspapers in the extensive collections of that society. Mr. W. E. Connelley, secretary of the Kansas Historical Society at Topeka, kindly allowed me to make extracts from the invaluable diaries and other manuscripts of Isaac McCoy.

I am under obligations also to Dr. Ernest W. Winkler, librarian, and Mrs. Mattie Austin Hatcher, archivist of the University of Texas, and to Mr. Dabney in charge of the extensive newspaper files of the University, for their helpful assistance. Miss Harriet Smithers, state archivist of Texas, assisted me in finding important manuscripts. Dr. Herbert I. Priestly, librarian of the Bancroft Library at the University of California, facilitated my examination of interesting manuscripts in his library. In the same manner Capt. Reginald B. Haselden, in charge of the manuscript division in the Huntington Library in California, made my work easier and more effective.

United States Senator Elmer Thomas and his secretary, Mrs. M. E. Pool, Representative W. W. Hastings and his secretary, Mr. C. A. Cowper, have for a number of years aided me in many ways, for which I am particularly grateful. For the large amount of valuable historical material I have been allowed to extract from the missionary manuscripts, I am indebted to the courtesy of the officials of the American Board of Commissioners for Foreign Missions in Boston, and to Miss Grace H. Knapp, librarian. Since the book went to press, these early missionary records have been removed from the Congregational House in Boston, and are now deposited in the Andover-Harvard Theological Library at Cambridge, Massachusetts.

For permission to quote from H. E. Bolton's *Athanase de Mézierès and the Louisiana-Texas Frontier* and from R. G. Thwaites's *Early Western Travels,* and to use material from my own *Pioneer Days in the Early Southwest,* thanks are due to the publishers, the Arthur H. Clark Company of Cleveland, Ohio.

More than all, I am indebted to the patient, unremitting, and intelligent assistance of my wife, Carolyn Thomas Foreman, who has shared with me the search into all the archives and libraries explored whether fruitful or not, and who has labored long hours in making notes and extracts from the manuscripts used. And it was she who translated into English all the French accounts in books, newspapers, journals, and manuscripts that have been drawn upon in writing this book.

GRANT FOREMAN

Muskogee, Oklahoma

January, 1930

CONTENTS

ILLUSTRATIONS

INDIANS AND PIONEERS

I

FRENCH AND SPANISH EXPLORATIONS BEFORE THE LOUISIANA PURCHASE

AGES before white men saw that section of the American Southwest which eventually became Oklahoma, it bore the impress of certain natural characteristics that influenced if they did not determine its destiny as an Indian state, aptly named to identify it as the home of the Red Man.

It formed part of the vast expanse of prairies and plains which was the habitat of innumerable thousands of buffaloes, moving like a hairy tide from south to north and south again with the succession of the seasons. Wintering in the benign climate of the Red River, the Brazos, and Rio Grande, they traveled northward in the springtime when the succulent grass appeared, and enjoyed Nature's first offering as they made their way through Oklahoma, Kansas, and Nebraska to the Missouri River. When winter approached they retraced their pilgrimage, leaving as they moved over the prairies a wake of dust and dried grass from which all nourishing herbage had been cropped.

The buffaloes did not travel alone on these migrations. They were followed by bands of Indians who found in the herds food, raiment, and fuel—the essentials of life itself for these primitive people. The Indians had established themselves in the country contiguous to winter pastures near the Red River in western Oklahoma and Texas. They included the Comanche, Kiowa, Tawehash, Wichita, and other tribes, who exercised arrogant sovereignty over the territory in which they lived and challenged other Indians and white men venturing into their hunting grounds. They presented for many years a barrier to colonial expansion; and this region lying between the outposts of their countries remained practically a *terra incognita* to the French and Spaniards, who watched each other across it with greedy hostility.

A few of their hardy adventurers traversed part of this beautiful and rich expanse of Oklahoma, but it was not the object of their enterprises; its rivers and pastures furnished only the means of communication with more remote regions. Spanish advances from the southwest, partly military and partly religious, had established a frontier extending northwest through Texas to Santa Fe and Taos. While Coronado in 1541 and other Spaniards in later years penetrated beyond this limit[1] across Oklahoma, into eastern Kansas, no territory was held beyond the Spanish frontier.

Though a Spaniard discovered and crossed the Mississippi,[2] it remained for the French to explore it[3] and to establish themselves upon its shores. From their vantage points along this river, their *voyageurs, chasseurs,* and traders essayed the long journey to New Mexico, which they regarded with covetous eyes; to these adventurers the Spanish country appeared a land of gold and silver, which offered rich profits in trade. But those who attempted that distant and hazardous adventure were opposed by the jealousy of the Spaniards and the fiercer

---

[1] Hubert Howe Bancroft, *History of the North Mexican States,* I, 85. In his account Prof. A. B. Thomas details five Spanish expeditions in the seventeenth century and twelve in the eighteenth (A. B. Thomas, "Spanish Explorations of Oklahoma," *Chronicles of Oklahoma,* VI, 186-213).

[2] "The River S. Louis .... is named by some Savages of the North *Meact Chassipi,* which signifies literally *old Father of Rivers,* from which the French .... have made that of Mississippi; other natives .... towards the lower part of the River, named it Balbancha; finally the French .... have named it River St. Louis" (Antoine S. le Page du Pratz, *Histoire de la Louisane* [Paris, 1758], I, 141). "Balbancha" is the name the Choctaw gave the Mississippi, signifying a large body of flowing water; because it is located on that river they gave the same name to New Orleans (authority of Peter J. Hudson, Oklahoma Historical Society).

[3] La Salle in 1682; Montigny in 1699; LeSueur in 1699; Gravier in 1700 (John Gilmary Shea, *Early Voyages Up and Down the Mississippi* [Albany, 1861]).

hostility of the Indians who barred the way on the Red, Canadian, Arkansas, and Missouri river routes.[4]

Arkansas Post was established in 1686 on the Arkansas River, fifty miles above the mouth, by members of La Salle's party; the French maintained a garrison there for many years, and it remained a small but important outpost. It was not until 1718 that the French began to build the village which was to be called New Orleans. The same year young Pierre Duque Boisbriant, the newly appointed commandant of French military affairs in Illinois, arrived at Kaskaskia with instructions to erect a fort on the Mississippi; and he completed the construction of Fort Chartres in 1721.[5] In 1719 Du Tisné visited the Osage Indians on the Osage River, and pushed on southwest to the Arkansas River where, to facilitate the passage of traders to Santa Fe, he made an alliance with the Pawnee Indians, bought horses from them, and left them a French flag.[6] The same year Bernard de la Harpe established a post among the Cadodacho on the Red River above Natchitoches. He continued his expedition to the Tawakoni[7] near the mouth of the Canadian River, where he proposed to establish a post as a base for trade with the Comanche and Arikara.[8]

The Spaniards, alarmed at the activity of the French on the Mississippi, determined to prevent them from crossing the intervening country to New Mexico. In June, 1720, an expedition started from Santa Fe, under the command of Lieutenant Colonel Pedro de Villasur, composed of about sixty soldiers

[4] H. E. Bolton and T. M. Marshall, *The Colonization of North America* (New York, 1920), p. 285.

[5] John W. Monette, M.D., *History of the Discovery and Settlement of the Valley of the Mississippi*, I, 232.

[6] Anna Lewis, "Du Tisné's Expedition into Oklahoma 1719," in *Chronicles of Oklahoma*, III, 319; *French Interests and Activities in Oklahoma, idem*, II, 253.

[7] H. E. Bolton, *Athanase de Mézières and the Louisiana-Texas Frontier*, I, 45. These Indians, called by La Harpe "Tauacara," and other Wichita tribes then living within Oklahoma, were afterward forced by the Osage to remove south of Red River (*Handbook of American Indians*, II, 702).

[8] Bolton and Marshall, *op. cit.*, p. 283.

and traders, seventy Indians, and two priests. They proceeded
northeast from Santa Fe; but before they had accomplished
their object, nearly all of them were massacred on August 11.
Indians subsequently appeared at Fort Chartres decorated with
chasubles, stoles, maniples, and surplices taken from the chap-
lains who accompanied Villasur, and gave Boisbriant an account of the massacre.[9]

La Harpe was sent in 1721 to explore the Arkansas River
with the idea of developing Indian trade, preventing Spanish
encroachment, and opening commerce with New Mexico.[10] He
ascended that stream about halfway to the Canadian River,
and on his return recommended the establishment of posts at
Little Rock, the mouth of the Canadian River, and the Tawakoni villages.[11]

Having heard that the Spaniards were preparing to return

[9] From information gained by the French, it was related that Villasur had
planned to visit the Osage and incite them to destroy the Missouri Indians, the
allies of the French; but the Spaniards fell in with the Missouri and, mistaking
them for the Osage, revealed their plans; whereupon the Indians fell upon and
killed nearly all of them. This version of the affair was related by N. Bossu,
Travels through That Part of North America Formerly Called Louisiana; Le
Page du Pratz, *op. cit.,* II, 236; Louis Dubroca, *Itinerary of the French in Louisiana* (Paris, 1802), p. 55; Francois Xavier Martin, *History of Louisiana,* p. 128;
Maj. Amos Stoddard, Dr. John W. Monette, and numerous other writers, who
probably copied from them. Recently, however, part of a notebook kept by the
Spanish officer of the massacred party, which had been delivered by the Indians
to Boisbriant, has been discovered in Paris in the archives of the Hydrographic
Service of the Marine and of the Minister of War; it was published (*Journal de
la Société des Américanistes de Paris* [nouvelle série], XIII, 239), with introduction, notes, and text contributed by Baron Marc de Villiers. This was subsequently translated by Addison E. Sheldon and published (*Nebraska State Historical Society Publications,* Vol. VI, No. 1). Villiers concludes that the massacre
was committed by the Oto Indians, at the junction of the Loup fork with the
Platte River in Nebraska. Other students do not agree on the location, Prof. A.
B. Thomas placing it at a point in Colorado east of Pueblo (*ibid.,* Vol. VII, No.
3, "The Massacre of the Villasur Expedition at the Forks of the Platte River
August 12, 1720," by A. B. Thomas).

[10] Bolton and Marshall, *op. cit.,* p. 283.

[11] *Idem;* La Harpe had in his company twenty-five men, including M. Dumont, an engineer, who wrote: "....In 1721 some visionaries having assured

to avenge the massacre of Villasur's expedition and occupy the country, the French sent Etienne Veniard de Bourgmond[12] from Mobile to the Missouri River to forestall them; in 1723[13] he began the establishment of a post on an island in that river above the mouth of the Osage, within what is now Carroll County, Missouri, which he named Fort Orleans.[14] The next year he took one hundred Missouri, sixty-four Osage, and a number of Kansa and other Indians, and a quantity of merchandise, and set out to visit the Oto and Iowa; afterward going southwest to visit towns of the Comanche.[15]

The French traders found profit in smuggling merchandise into the Spanish possessions and in trading with the western

the company that there was an emerald rock on the Arcanzas River, Captain de la Harpe was sent to look for it .... we ascended the river for more than 250 leagues, without being able to discover this pretended treasure, probably because it existed only in imagination; we even advanced nearly fifty leagues further by land into the country, till complaints arising in the troop, the Sieur de la Harpe, who apprehended a fate similar to La Salle's, resolved to retrace his steps and return to the capital" (M. Dumont, *History of Louisiana, Translated from the Historical Memoirs of* ——, Historical Collections of Louisiana [New York, 1853], V, 35).

[12] "Such seems to be the true spelling of his name, written often Bourgmont or Bourmont. He belonged to an old bourgeois family of Normandy, and his father, Charles de Veniard .... was a physician" (Baron Marc de Villiers, *La Découverte de Missouri et l'histoire du Fort D'Orleans (1673-1728)* [Paris, 1925], p. 41, No. 1).

[13] "The expedition of the Spaniards in 1720 showed the necessity of occupying the Missouri .... Boisbriant, commandant of the country of the Illinois, had intended to ascend the Missouri in 1720, but he announced the fifth of October, 'that the want of ammunition and merchandise prevented him from executing this enterprise which would have been very useful'...." (Villiers, *op. cit.*, p. 71). "Thanks to the aid of the Missouri, who came to Illinois to meet Bourgmond, the convoy composed of three large barques, of canoes, and of forty French arrived the 5 November, 1723, at the village of the Missouri, situated 450 kilometres from the Mississippi. The site of the post was determined the 15 of November ...." (*idem*, p. 84).

[14] Bolton and Marshall, *op. cit.*, p. 284; John O'Hanlon, *Life and Scenes in Missouri* (Dublin, 1890); Le Page du Pratz, *op. cit.*, I, 324.

[15] Le Page du Pratz, *op. cit.*, III, 161 ff.; Le Page du Pratz says that on the twenty-fourth of July, at six in the morning, this little army set out, consisting of three hundred warriors including the chiefs of the Kansa, three hundred

Indians from whom they received furs, skins, Indian captives, and mules stolen from the Spaniards. The successful expedition in 1739 of the Mallet brothers who passed through the Comanche country and some of whom returned down the Canadian and Arkansas rivers, encouraged others; in 1741 Governor Bienville sent Fabre de la Bruyère, with members of the Mallet party, to open a trade route up the Canadian River.[16] Though they never reached New Mexico, they made a treaty with the Comanche, a few years later, that stimulated other French adventurers; and for some years after 1748, several French trading expeditions succeeded in reaching· Santa Fe, where the Spaniards treated them with great harshness.[17]

These expeditions could maintain themselves against hostile Indians only by traveling in large parties, and made no permanent settlements. After nearly one hundred years of tentative and hazardous adventuring across this vast region, at the time of the Louisiana Purchase, the same lines of French and Spanish outposts continued to mark their boundaries, and between them for hundreds of miles there were no settlements by either nation. Only the nomenclature of that region gives some record of the adventures and explorers of the two countries, mountains and streams on the east bearing French names and those on the west, Spanish names.

Friendship for one nation aligned the Indians against the other. Thus, in 1758, a large force of Comanche, Wichita, and

women, about five hundred young people, and at least three hundred dogs. The women carried considerable loads to the astonishment of the French, unaccustomed to such a sight, and the dogs were made to trail a part of the baggage. To facilitate the opening up of a route to New Mexico, Bourgmond made peace between the Indians who accompanied him, and the Comanche, and arranged to send traders to the latter.

[16] On *The First Part of Captain Pike's Chart of the Internal Part of Louisiana* is the notation, "At the mouth of the Canadian River the Ensigns armorial of France were buried in a leaden Box at the feet of a Great Oak in 1742" (Elliott Coues, *The Expeditions of Zebulon Montgomery Pike* [New York, 1895]).

[17] Bolton and Marshall, *op. cit.*, p. 286.

Caddo allies of the French destroyed the Spanish San Saba Mission and killed several Spaniards. To repel the expected reprisal, the Indians fortified themselves in a settlement of Taovayas[18] on the south side of the Red River, opposite Jefferson County, Oklahoma. Don Diego Ortiz Parrilla, at the head of six hundred Spanish and Indians, marched from San Antonio de Béxar in August, 1759, and attacked the fortified force that they found surrounded by a stockade over which flew the French flag. The defenders sallied forth and attacked the enemy, repulsing them with the loss of their baggage and two cannons.[19] This fort was said to consist of a palisaded embankment about four feet high, with deep ditches at its east and west ends, to prevent approach on horseback. Inside the enclosure were four subterranean chambers or cellars for the safety of noncombatants.[20] The cannons left by Parrilla were not recovered until De Mézières went among the Wichita nearly twenty years later.[21]

Both the French seeking to open up trade routes to New Mexico, by way of the streams of Oklahoma, and the Spaniards opposing them relied upon the assistance of the Indians whose friendship they cultivated to their conflicting purposes; and the influence of these associations persisted as long as the Indian was a factor in the Southwest, and even afterward. For many years the powerful Osage were probably more active than any other force in maintaining a state of warfare throughout Oklahoma and preventing its peaceful occupation by either red or white men. They challenged practically all tribes of Indians they encountered on the prairies and east to the Mississippi, but they were long the allies of the French.[22]

[18] Tawehash or Pani Piqué.
[19] H. E. Bolton, *Athanase de Mézières*, I, 49.
[20] Frederick W. Hodge, ed., *Handbook of American Indians*, II, 705.
[21] Bolton, *op. cit.*, p. 50.
[22] "The relations between the French and the Missouris and Osages were, at this epoch, excellent, since these Indians went, in 1712, to the relief of Du Buisson, besieged at Fort Detroit by the Renards [Fox]" (Villiers, *op. cit.*, p. 39).

The isolation of this buffalo-Indian country was favored by the proximity of a hostile Spanish and a succeeding weak Texan government on the south. After the Louisiana Purchase, the Spaniards, claiming sovereignty over most of Oklahoma, prevented exploration by the United States of the Spanish-American boundaries. The expedition under Colonel Thomas Freeman sent up the Red River by President Jefferson in 1806, to explore the country traversed by that stream, was turned back by an armed force of Spaniards at a point near the southeast corner of Oklahoma.[23] Another Spanish expedition under Lieutenant Don Facundo Malgares, was dispatched from Santa Fe in 1806 to intercept the exploring tour of Lieutenant Zebulon M. Pike:

> .... They descended the Red River 233 leagues; met the grand band of the Tetaus, and held council with them; then struck off N.E., and crossed the country of the Arkansas, where Lieutenant Malgares left 240 of his men with the lame and tired horses, while he proceeded on with the rest to the Pawnee republic. Here he was met by the chiefs and warriors of the Grand Pawnees; held councils with the two nations, and presented them with the flags, medals, etc., which were destined for them. .... Malgares took with him all the traders he found there from our country.[24]

However, he failed to meet Pike, who did not reach that country until the next year, when he substituted American flags for

Soon after the conclusion of the French and Indian War, a conference was held at Kaskaskia between Lieut. John Ross, an officer of the new English rulers of the country bordering the Mississippi, and the representatives of the Missouri, Osage, and Illinois Indians. Tamaroa, chief of the Kaskaskia, in the name of all the Illinois nations requested the English to leave; the Osage and Missouri assured the English that they would always look to the French as the sovereigns of the country they occupied; told them that the Indians did not wish the English on their soil and demanded that they leave and never come back (Letter from M. Aubry, May 16, 1765, Paris, Arch. Nat. Colonies, C 13 A. 45, 1765-68, Library of Congress, Manuscript Division).

[23] Isaac J. Cox, "The Exploration of the Louisiana Frontier, 1803-1806," *Report for 1904* (Washington: American Historical Association, 1904), p. 173.

[24] Elliott Coues, *op. cit.*, II, 413.

those of Spain over the lodges of the Pawnee. But when Pike reached a point in what is now southeastern Colorado, he was taken prisoner by the Spaniards and carried to Chihuahua.

This Spanish hostility kept the United States in ignorance of its southwestern limits long after the treaty of 1819 with Spain; and it was not until 1852 that the Red River boundary was explored.[25] Having no outlet to the west until after the Mexican War, this region was a *cul-de-sac* that lacked the inducement to settlement and commerce offered by the Northwest. But it was primarily the hostility of the Indians that intimidated intercourse and restricted commerce with the Spanish country, and prevented settlement in the intervening region.

[25] The influence of Spanish and Indian hostility that prevented the United States from acquiring definite knowledge of this boundary, continued until modern times; it was instrumental in invoking the jurisdiction of the United States Supreme Court in recent years to determine controversies growing out of that lack of information (Grant Foreman, "Red River and the Spanish Boundary in the United States Supreme Court," in *Chronicles of Oklahoma* [Oklahoma City, 1924], II, 298).

II

THE OSAGE TERRORIZE THE SOUTH-
WEST, 1770-1810

BEFORE the Louisiana Purchase[1] the Mississippi River formed the western boundary of the United States. Indian owners had been forced out from lands desired by white settlers, but were still living in restricted areas in the states and territories east of that stream. Here in the populated sections the whites were already rubbing elbows with Indians living on their ancestral possessions; and in more remote regions where the pioneers had ventured, the Indians challenged their right of possession, and bloody contests resulted.

Of all the Indian tribes within those limits, those destined to maintain their rights with the greatest tenacity, to present the most obstinate and intelligent resistance to the aggressions of the whites, and to raise a great national issue on the subject of their wrongs, were the Indians who in later years became known as the Five Civilized Tribes—the Choctaw, Chickasaw, Cherokee, Creek, and Seminole. These were southern Indians who occupied a great domain from which the states of Tennessee, Georgia, Alabama, Mississippi, Florida, and parts of the Carolinas were formed. Cessions had been obtained from them prior to 1802; and in that year, in the adjustment of a dispute with Georgia involving the title to the land from which the present states of Alabama and Mississippi were formed, and providing for the establishment of a government in the Mississippi Territory, the United States entered into a compact with Georgia.[2] By this agreement the Federal Government promised to extinguish at its own expense the Indian title within the re-

[1] The Louisiana Purchase was negotiated in 1803.
[2] *American State Papers,* "Public Lands," I, 125.

served limits of Georgia as soon as it could be done "peaceably and on reasonable terms." This measure was afterward used effectively by Georgia to drive the Government into a partnership in the oppression of the Indians within the state and in the execution of so-called treaties providing for their removal.

The Louisiana Purchase, that great domain stretching to an unknown extent westward from the Mississippi, was early looked to for relief from the irritating contact of whites and Indians in the East. This idea was in the mind of Jefferson himself during the negotiation of the Purchase, and he prepared an amendment to the Constitution authorizing, among other things, an exchange of land in this region with the Indians east of the Mississippi. This amendment, however, was never voted on for adoption.[3] Jefferson submitted to Congress on February 19, 1806, a report made to him by Meriwether Lewis concerning the Indians west of the Mississippi, giving information derived on the memorable Lewis and Clark Expedition that Jefferson launched.[4] He reported on the tenure by which many of them held the land where they were found, and their disposition to remain there, all bearing on the possibility of removing Indians from the East to that country. For example, he noted the removal of nearly half of the Osage from the Osage River to the Arkansas in 1802, and added his opinion that two other villages of Osage could be induced to follow them and ". . . . the Kansas higher up the Missouri, thus leave a sufficient scope of country for the Shawanese, Delawares, Miamies, and Kickapoos."

Congress passed an act[5] on October 31, 1803, authorizing the President to take possession of the Louisiana Purchase[6]

[3] Annie Heloise Abel, Ph.D., "The History of Events Resulting in Indian Consolidation West of the Mississippi River," *Annual Report for 1906* (Washington: American Historical Association, 1908), I, 241.

[4] *American State Papers,* "Indian Affairs," I, 706.

[5] *U. S. Statutes at Large,* II, 245.

[6] By authority of this act the President appointed Maj. Amos Stoddard to take possession of Upper Louisiana under the treaty of cession, which he did in

and on March 26, 1804, adopted a general act[7] for the government of that vast empire. Section 15 of the Act provided:

> The President of the United States is hereby authorized to stipulate with any Indian tribes owning lands on the east side of the Mississippi, and residing thereon, for an exchange of lands, the property of the United States, on the west side of the Mississippi, in case the said tribes shall remove and settle thereon, but in such stipulation the tribes shall acknowledge themselves to be under the protection of the United States, and shall agree that they will not hold any treaty with any foreign power, individual or state, or with the individuals of any state; and that they will not sell or dispose of said lands, or any part thereof, to any foreign power, except the United States, nor to the subjects or citizens of any other sovereign power, nor to the citizens of the United States.

It was many years, however, before the Government took steps to carry this proposal into effect. Jefferson suggested removal to the Chickasaw in 1805 and to the Choctaw in 1808,[8] but he did not insist and nothing came of it. But even if an effort had been made there were for many years insuperable obstacles to the removal of the eastern Indians to the west of the Mississippi. Foremost among these, of course, were lack of public interest and of information and total want of capacity for effecting such a huge undertaking. Many years of experimenting with the removal of Indians on a small scale were required, before the Indian Removal Bill of 1830 was enacted and the effort was made on a comprehensive plan to carry it into effect. But among the difficulties confronting the Government in its efforts to plant the eastern Indians west of the Mississippi was the hostility of the Indians already occupying that country; if they did not present the most serious obstacle, they at least made a picturesque one which colored the history of the region for many years.

March, 1804 (Amos Stoddard, *Sketches, Historical and Descriptive of Louisiana* [Philadelphia, 1812]).

[7] *U. S. Statutes at Large*, II, 277.   [8] Abel, *op. cit.*, p. 252.

The country adjacent to the west bank of the Lower Mississippi was the home of the Caddo tribe that had been weakened by the continued struggle between the French and Spaniards. As Louisiana was claimed by the whites and Texas was Spanish territory, there was no territory south of the Red River that offered a home for the eastern Indians, although a few of them were living there. Between the Red River and the Arkansas, the Quapaw were recognized as the owners of the land for a distance of several hundred miles west of the Mississippi. At the time of the Louisiana Purchase they had dwindled to a weak tribe of a few hundred members who lived near the mouth of the Arkansas River; but although they were not strong enough to hold the country against new arrivals, the Government in 1818 by treaty[9] recognized their ownership.

North of the Arkansas River, however, was the home of the Osage, a warlike, aggressive tribe of Indians who ranged over the country from the Missouri to the Red River and from the Mississippi to the Rocky Mountains on their hunting and marauding expeditions. The Osage were first known historically in 1673 on the Osage River where they were placed, until recent years, by all subsequent writers.[10] Thence they extended their activities to remote places. They had few friends, among whom were the Illinois. At Cahokia[11] in 1756, the French officer Bossu[12] saw some Osage bearing as their *manitou,* or false deity, a "dried serpent of a monstrous size" and heard a romantic tale of its capture. Le Page de Pratz[13] says that in 1757 the Osage lived near the Missouri River on a tributary bearing their name. From their earliest known history the Osage were at war with most of the surrounding peoples, and

[9] Charles J. Kappler, ed., *Indian Affairs,* "Laws and Treaties," II, 112.

[10] *Handbook of American Indians,* II, 157.

[11] In the present state of Illinois, across the Mississippi from St. Louis, Missouri.

[12] N. Bossu, *Travels through That Part of North America Formerly Called Louisiana,* trans. by J. R. Forster (London, 1771).

[13] *Op. cit.,* II, 245.

La Harpe bears witness to the terror in which they were held by the Caddoan tribes.[14] They were, in fact, the scourge of all the tribes within hundreds of miles.

The Osage were traditional enemies of the Caddo and Hasínai Indians; this attitude, together with the hostility of the Apache in the West through the eighteenth century and even later, formed a constant factor in the policy of tribal balance pursued alike by France and Spain.[15] The Osage were described by De Mézières as insolent and proud. They had aided Spain in her war against England and made the Spaniards feel the obligation that assistance entailed. He said in 1772 that the Osage lived in two principal villages on the Missouri River, and that they numbered one thousand men.[16] De Mézières reported[17] in May, 1770, that the Tonkawa, Tawakoni, Kichai, and Yscanis had suffered so from outrageous robberies and bloody encounters at the hands of the Osage that in despair they had retreated toward the south and located near San Antonio and other presidios in that part of modern Texas.[18]

By July, 1772, these Indians had formed an alliance to resist the aggressions of the Osage and Apache;[19] and De Mézières recommended[20] to Baron de Ripperda, Governor of Texas, who approved, the construction of a presidio for their protec-

[14] *Handbook of American Indians,* II, 157.

[15] Bolton, *op. cit.,* I, 22.

[16] Bolton, *op. cit.,* I, 304; "They are not more than seven regular days' journey from Los Ylinuezes, where we are established on the west bank of the Micissipi River, opposite the English, who occupy the other bank" (*ibid*). Reprinted by permission of the publishers, The Arthur H. Clark Company.

[17] *Ibid.,* I, 167.

[18] *Loc. cit.* Throughout the two volumes of Professor Bolton's interesting and valuable collection of documents from French and Spanish archives concerning both sides of the Red River, reference is frequently made to the tremendous difficulties caused by the hostilities of the Osage.

[19] *Ibid.,* I, 289.

[20] *Ibid.,* I, 97, 302.

[21] Athanase de Mézières was appointed Lieutenant Governor of Natchitoches in 1769, and until 1779 he was chief executive of affairs on the Louisiana-Texas border.

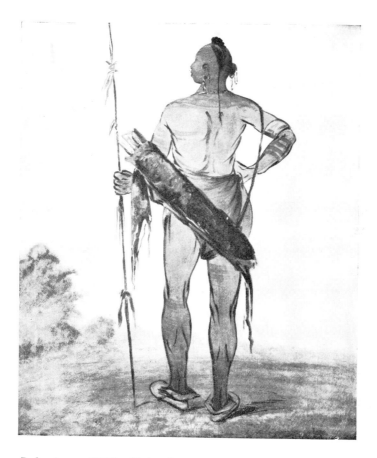

Pahuska or White Hair the younger. Painted by George Catlin, 1834. Courtesy of Smithsonian Institution, Bureau of American Ethnology.

tion on the north.[21] This was to be employed as a bulwark for
the Indians against the Osage, though the Spaniards and
French also secretly intended it to resist the encroachments of
English traders.

Five traders were reported killed by the Osage, on the Washita River in 1773[22] and similar outrages were related from time
to time by De Mézières, such as the murder of Caddo men and
women and the theft of their horses, and a raid on the hunters
on Arkansas River near Arkansas Post when seven Frenchmen
were killed. Gruesome accounts of these affairs were given in
detail.[23] The Osage made peace with the Arkansas[24] in 1777,
a fact which the Spaniards greatly deplored since it would facilitate aggressions against the Indians of the Red River; but in
the same year the Panis-maha or Skidi, in dread of their Osage
neighbors, left the Missouri River with eight hundred warriors[25] and moved south to the Red River where they could
unite with their new neighbors, the Taovayas or Tawehash,[26]
Caddo, and others in resisting the aggressions of the Osage.

The situation had then become so intolerable that De Mézières suggested[27] to his chief, Galvez, under date of September
14, 1777, a plan to resist and punish the Osage. He proposed
to enlist 1,270 warriors from ten tribes of Indians living within
his jurisdiction, including the Caddo, Nacogdoches, Comanche,
Panis-maha, Tonkawa, and Tawehash. "The Indians of this
district who may be desired and regarded of service, will come
and enlist at the slightest suggestion, without asking for a sti-
pend, and solely to satisfy their hatred." He planned to leave
Natchitoches in the spring, ascend the Red River in canoes to

[22] Bolton, *op. cit.*, II, 118 n.

[23] *Ibid.*, II, 122 n., 130, 131, 138.

[24] *Ibid.*, II, 130.

[25] *Ibid.*, II, 122 n.

[26] The Tawehash were a principal tribe of the Wichita confederacy, distinct
from the Wichita proper, although the terms are now used as synonymous
(*Handbook of American Indians*, II, 705).

[27] Bolton, *op. cit.*, II, 143.

the villages of the Caddo, then go overland to the villages of the Tawehash.[28] This was to be the rendezvous of the warriors, who were to join the army here for their march on the Osage. He said he was informed that the village of the Osage contained eight hundred warriors. "Their houses being built of straw, with a narrow street between them, they will easily burn, by making use of arrows, tinder, and the aid of wind. This will deliver to the knife those who attempt to flee from the flames." It is doubtful whether this proposed campaign was realized, as there is no account of it; and the next year De Mézières wrote[29] of ".... the large and indomitable tribe of Osagues" that continued to harass ".... the inhabitants of Lusiana, in whose territories, principally those bathed by the Arcanzas and Natchitoches [Red] Rivers, they become more notorious each day on account of their treachery and rapine." And in 1779 he wrote[30] to Galvez that the Caddo nation was much enfeebled by the continual warfare of the Osage.

Constant jealousy prevailed between the Osage chiefs; and at a very early day a lawless band of warriors had broken from the tribe and ranged over the country, committing depredations on white hunters and settlements. De Villemont sent by M. Bogy[31] to August Chouteau a letter dated "aux Arkansas"[32] in 1769, telling of the killing by the Osage of a hunter on the

28 The Tawehash were then located on both sides of Red River in what are now Jefferson County, Oklahoma, and Montague County, Texas (*ibid.*, I, map).

29 Bolton, *op. cit.*, II, 176.

30 *Ibid.*, II, 250.

31 Joseph Bogy, a Frenchman, had a trading house at Arkansas Post whence he trafficked by keelboat with the Indians up the Arkansas River as high as the Three Forks and probably higher (Grant Foreman, *Pioneer Days in the Early Southwest* [Cleveland, 1926], pp. 72, 73; *U. S. Senate Document No. 23*, Twenty-fourth Congress, first session).

32 This French phrase "aux-Arkansas," i.e., "at the Arkansas" ("at Arkansas Post" probably) is here in the process through shortening to "aux Arca" or "aux-arcs," of forming the name "Ozark"; in the early days the names "Arkansas" and "Ozarks" were used interchangeably and were applied to the Arkansas River, its drainage basin, the mountains north of it, and the post near its mouth (Carl O. Sauer, *The Geography of the Ozark Highland of Missouri*, p. 5, n. 1).

Arkansas River below the mouth of the Poteau and the theft of fifty-four of his horses. Later, four Frenchmen having been killed on that river, the Osage under their chiefs Clermont, Jean Lafon, and others were called to St. Louis where on August 16, 1787, officials demanded the surrender of some of their chiefs to be delivered at New Orleans as hostages for their future good behavior.[33] But the Osage continued their depredations.

August Chouteau wrote on May 18, 1794, to the Spanish Governor, Carondelet, in New Orleans, that the Great and Little Osage, who numbered 2,200 warriors, by increasing raids and rapine had much disturbed the interior provinces, the "settlements of Ilinoa, Nuevo Madrid, Acanzas and even Natchitochez." He proposed to erect, with his brother Pierre, a fort in the Osage country whereby the Indians could be controlled, in consideration of a grant of the monopoly of the Osage trade until the end of the year 1800. Carondelet accepted the proposal and the contract was carried into effect the same year, by the construction of a fortified establishment[34] overlooking the Osage village, of which Pierre Chouteau[35] was made commandant.

Still the Osage continued their raids; and Villemont wrote on January 12, 1795, that trappers coming home reported they

[33] Library of Congress, Manuscript Division, Journal of a Council at St. Louis between the Chiefs of the Great Osage, August Chouteau, and French officers, August 16, 1787, Papeles Procedentes de la Isla de Cuba, Legajo 200.

[34] "Legended 'Chouteau's' on the map . . . . Pierre Chouteau's place was known in Spanish records as Fort Carondelet, and was built . . . . at what is now called Halley's Bluff named for Col. Anselm Halley. It was an actual fortification with mounted swivels, which Lieutenant Wilkinson speaks of in his report . . . . but it was only maintained for a few years. The post is twice noticed in the Hist. of Vernon Co., 1887 . . . . " (Elliott Coues, *The Expeditions of Zebulon Montgomery Pike* [New York, 1895], p. 384 n.). The location referred to is on the south bank of the Osage River.

[35] Chouteau to the Governor and Intendant-General, *Archives of the Indies, Papers from the Island of Cuba* (Louis Houck, *The Spanish Régime in Missouri,* II, 100 ff.).

had been robbed by the Osage 150 leagues above Arkansas Post, probably above the Poteau. The French and Spanish traders at Arkansas Post, St. Louis, and New Orleans were much alarmed by these hostilities, for the terrified hunters and trappers refused to venture into the forest to secure the furs so much desired for shipment to market; Chouteau was urged to use his influence with the Osage to prevent a repetition of such outrages. Villemont wrote a similar letter the next May, at "Ft. Estevan de Arkansas."[36] The Spanish *Intendente* gave permission for White Hair to attack and destroy the outlaw band of Osage, who had recently killed a man and a boy on the Meremec; but they came into St. Louis to make atonement and instead, on August 29, 1800, a peace conference took place.[37]

With the confirmation of the Louisiana Purchase, the Osage

[36] St. Louis Mercantile Library, Chouteau Manuscripts, Nos. 14, 20, and 21. In the Manuscript Division of the Library of Congress, is the *Chronological List of Transcripts and Facsimiles from Cuban Papers in the General Archives of Indias, Seville.* Here are a number of letters and reports written from 1777 to 1800 concerning robberies and murders committed by the Osage Indians on Arkansas River and in the district of Natchitoches; Legajo 16, 2358, 2360, and 2364. About 1795 a war party of Osage attacked the white settlers on Canteen Creek about twelve miles above St. Louis on the east side of the Mississippi River. This was afterward known by the settlers as the "Battle of the Canteen."

[37] Louis Houck, *History of Missouri,* II, 301. The leader of these wanderers was called LeChenier and his followers were called by the French, Osages of the Oaks, or *Osages des Chênes.* "This cognomen is a translation of his French name, Le Soldat du Chêne, given, it is said, on account of a desperate fight with several assailants, during which he sheltered himself behind an oak. His portrait, painted upon the occasion of a visit to Washington in 1805 or 1806, is published in McKenney, *Indian Tribes,* II, 169" (*Early Western Travels,* ed. R. G. Thwaites [Cleveland, 1906], XVI, 266).* Osage Agent Graham says Clermont's village was "called the Chêne from its being situated in an Oak Grove" (Richard Graham, "Graham Papers," November 12, 1821, Missouri Historical Society). At the council held in St. Louis in 1787, these wandering outlaws were designated as the chiens (dogs). The reader is thus offered the choice of three theories as to the origin of the name Cheneers by which this section of the tribe was known. Soon after the Louisiana Purchase these Arkansas Osage were known to the traders and trappers as Chaneers and Shaineers (Office of Indian Affairs, Retired

* Reprinted by permission of the publishers, The Arthur H. Clark Company.

became a problem for the United States. In 1802 the monopoly of the Osage River trade was taken from the Chouteaus and given to Manuel Lisa and other traders; but Pierre Chouteau, having great influence with the Indians, circumvented his rivals by inducing a considerable part of the tribe to remove to the Three Forks, the junction of the Verdigris, Grand, and Arkansas rivers. This location, with which they had long been familiar on their hunting expeditions, had many advantages. It was in the midst of a fine hunting region, at the head of navigation of the Arkansas River, whence furs could be shipped to New Orleans, and provided a location for the receipt of supplies by return voyages; it was a beautiful country, and included a celebrated saline spring that supplied the Indians and whites with salt for many years.

Chouteau employed these daring outlaws on the Arkansas River as the nucleus for his settlement at the Three Forks; he selected for their chief an influential Osage named Cashesegra or Big Track or Big Foot[38] who led a large number of his tribe from the Osage River to the Arkansas; but though Cashesegra was the nominal leader, their most influential warrior and leader was Clermont,[39] the lawful sovereign of the Osage tribe,[40] whose hereditary right was usurped by Pahuska or White Hair [Cheveux Blancs], while Clermont was yet an infant. White Hair, in fact, was a chief of Chouteau's creating, as well as

Classified Files [referred to hereafter as OIA, RCF], "Special File" 191). This band was also called Santsukhdhin (*Handbook of American Indians*, II, 462).

[38] Elliott Coues, *The Expeditions of Zebulon Montgomery Pike*, II, 557; *American State Papers*, "Indian Affairs," I, 708; Foreman, *op. cit.*, p. 25.

[39] This interesting chief was also called Clermo and Clamore and by Americans his name was corrupted into Claremore, whence came the name of the town of Claremore in Oklahoma, built near the site of Clermont's Town. He died in May, 1828, and was succeeded by a son named Clermont, also a man of great force, a warm friend of the army officers at Fort Gibson and of Col. A. P. Chouteau, a trader at the mouth of the Verdigris; this second Clermont died in 1838. Jean Lafon or Wa-tcha-wa-ha, the son-in-law of White Hair, was second chief.

[40] Coues, *op. cit.*, p. 558.

Cashesegra.[41] Soon after the arrival of the Osage on the Arkansas one of the principal chiefs visited the commandant at Arkansas Post and obtained permission for his people to settle, hunt, and occupy the country on the Arkansas above the Canadian River, which from that time the whites regarded as the boundary line between the Osage and the Quapaw, although the latter had not consented to the location of their new neighbors[42] and the Osage did not observe this limit to their activities.

These Osage on the Arkansas included in their band all the lawless members of the tribe, and the Government directed Pierre Chouteau to bring them back to their old home at the Grand Village;[43] Chouteau promised to do so[44] but, Pike said

[41] Pahuska derived his appellation of "White Hair" from a gray wig, or scratch, which he had taken from the head of an American at the disastrous defeat of General St. Clair. "He had grasped at the wig's tail in the *melée* of the battle, supposing it the man's hair, and that he should have him by that hold. The owner fled, and the scratch to his astonishment remained in his hand. It instantly became in his mind a charmed thing, a grand medicine. Supposing that in a like case it would always effect a like deliverance, he afterwards wore it, as a charmed thing, rudely fastened to his own scalp" (Timothy Flint, *Recollections of the Last Ten Years in the Valley of the Mississippi*, p. 155). White Hair died in 1808 (Louis Houck, *History of Missouri*, I, 193); he was buried near the junction of the Osage and Marmiton rivers (Coues, *op. cit.*, II, 389 n.). His successor, young White Hair or Pahuska, died in 1833.

[42] Statement of late Spanish commandant at Arkansas to Gov. William Clark, June 5, 1816 (Adjutant General's Office, Old Records Division, War Department Files [referred to hereafter as AGO, ORD, WDF]).

[43] Upon his appointment to this new post the Secretary of War wrote to Chouteau: "The President of the United States having appointed you an Agent of Indian Affairs for upper Louisiana .... you will be particularly attentive to our friends the Osage nation .... you will take the earliest opportunity for healing the breach between the Osage nation and the party under Big-track, and endeavor to prevail on the latter with his partizans to return to the nation and live in harmony.

"You will take the necessary measures for obtaining permission of the Big-track and his party for the safe passage of any party which may be sent by the President of the United States to explore the sources of Arkansas river and the interior country generally bordering on the waters of red river, the Arkansa and the Southwestern branches of the Missouri .... Your compensation to be $1500 per year, Noel Mongrain interpreter ...." to have one dollar per day

.... the other villages are much more likely to join the Arkansaw band, which is daily becoming more powerful, than the latter is to return to its ancient residence. For the Grand and Little Osage are both obliged to proceed to the Arkansaw every winter, to kill the summer's provision; also, all the nations with whom they are now at war are situated to the westward of that river, whence they get all their horses.[45] These inducements are such that the young, the bold, and the enterprising are daily emigrating from the Osage Village to the Arkansaw Village.[46]

The Osage had long been at war with the Sauk and Fox Indians who lived on the upper Mississippi; on November 3, 1804, these tribes made a treaty[47] at St. Louis with the United States in which they agreed, at the instance of William Henry Harrison, the United States Commissioner, to ".... put an end to the bloody war which has heretofore raged between their tribes and those of the Great and Little Osages" and to meet

(Secretary of War to Chouteau, July 17, 1804, OIA, RCF; also found in Department of State, "Department of Publications," copies of old Territorial Records, Louisiana, 3323-3493). On March 7, 1807, the Secretary of War limited Chouteau's field as follows: "Considering the extent of our Indian relations in the Territory of Louisiana, and your particular acquaintance with the great and little Osages, the President of the United States has thought it advisable to confine the duties of your agency to their Nations, and their several detachments; and to appoint William Clark Agent to all the other Indian Nations within said territory."

[44] Coues, *op. cit.*, II, 530.

[45] The Osage in common with nearly all western Indians secured their horses by stealing them from other tribes; horse-stealing raids formed a considerable part of the normal activities of these Indians; a man's skill as a horse thief advanced him in the esteem of his fellows.

[46] Coues, *op. cit.*, II, 530. "The village on the Arkansaw serves as a place of refuge for all the young, daring, and discontented; added to which, they are much more regularly supplied with ammunition, and should not our government take some steps to prevent it they will rule the Grand village as they are at liberty to make war without restraint, especially on the nations who are to the west, and have plenty of horses. The chief says he was promised, at Washington, that these people should be brought back to join him; but, on the contrary, many of his village are emigrating there" (*ibid.*, p. 582).

[47] Charles J. Kappler, ed., *Indian Affairs* "Laws and Treaties," II, 54.

the chiefs of the Osage at St. Louis, adjust their differences, and establish peace.

At the request of President Jefferson, William Dunbar of Natchez in 1804 headed an exploring party on a tour up the Red, Black, and Ouachita rivers to the celebrated hot springs, now in Arkansas. His interesting report, subsequently deposited with the American Philosophical Society and later published,[48] contained much valuable information touching on the character of the country and the inhabitants in the Louisiana Purchase. One subject to which he referred frequently, as bearing on the availability of the southwestern country, was the hostility of the Osage Indians.[49]

The Caddo, he said, who lived between the Washita[50] and Red rivers, were unable to defend themselves against the Osage of the Arkansas, who came down to their country and plundered them of their horses and other effects, for this band of Osage was a lawless gang of robbers making war on the whole world. Hunters refused to venture north or west of the hot springs for fear of encountering the dread Osage. A considerable band of the Arkansas Osage had recently been on a marauding expedition to the Red River and on the way had descended the Little Missouri[51] as far as Fourche d'Antoine;[52]

[48] Thomas Jefferson and William Dunbar, *Documents Relating to the Purchase and Exploration of Louisiana* (Boston, 1904); *American State Papers*, "Indian Affairs," I, 731.

[49] Jefferson and Dunbar, *op. cit.*, pp. 65, 68, 73, 157, 164, 166. When President Jefferson gave instructions to William Dunbar for his western explorations, he said: ".... Your observations on the difficulty of transporting baggage from the head of Red river to that of the Arcansa with the dangers from the seceding Osages residing on the last river, have determined me to confine the ensuing mission to the ascent of the Red river to its source and to descend the same again" (Library of Congress, Manuscript Division, Jefferson Papers, Vol. CL, Jefferson to Dunbar, May 25, 1805).

[50] On modern maps this stream in Arkansas is spelled Ouachita; it is not to be confused with the Washita of Oklahoma, called Fausse Washita and False Washita.

[51] A stream in western Arkansas flowing into the Ouachita.

there they met a hunting party of Cherokee, of whom they killed four. The Arkansas [Quapaw], Choctaw, Chickasaw, and Shawnee had organized a war party of eight hundred who were going to march against the Arkansas Osage with the intention of destroying them and obtaining possession of the fine lands (now in Oklahoma) over which they held dominion. Early in December, 1804, a war party of White Hair's town had plundered all the hunters and traders on the Arkansas River. The other tribes, Dunbar said, spoke of the Osage with abhorrence and called them a barbarous and uncivilized race.

At this period the Great and Little Osage made their temporary hunting camps on the Salt Fork which falls into the Arkansas River near Ponca City, Oklahoma; when very cold weather came they would retire to "Grosse Isle on the Verdigris or Wasetihoge" and in the spring would return to their villages on the Little Osage River.[53] Lieutenant Wilkinson visited their hunting villages on Salt Fork on November 30, 1806, to see their chief, Tuttasuggy or The Wind, who, being very ill, had sent for him. To reach the camp, Wilkinson was obliged to travel thirty miles across the prairies.[54] After passing the mouth of the Cimarron, in his descent of the Arkansas, he came to the hunting camp of Cashesegra or Big Foot.[55]

While the Osage, who possessed some firearms,[56] carried terror among the tribes of the South and West, who relied upon bows and arrows and lances, they were not a match for those

[52] This stream joins the Little Missouri at the southeast corner of Pike County, Arkansas.

[53] Coues, *op. cit.*, II, 555.

[54] *Ibid.*

[55] This was somewhere between Tulsa and the mouth of the Verdigris.

[56] Pike reported (Coues, *op. cit.*, II, 590-91), that in 1806 in the Grand Osage Village there were 1,909 individuals; in the Little Osage, 926; and the Arkansas numbered 1,700, making 4,535 in all, with a total of 1,252 warriors, among whom were 1,209 arms. They were at war, he said, with the "Tetaus, Potowatomies, Arkansaws, Cherokees, Chickasaws, Choctaws, Creeks, Padoucas and Caddoes." In 1816 Governor Clark reported that there were 1,600 of the Great Osage on Osage River three miles west of the line lately run; 1,800 "Little Osage on a

of the North and East who also used firearms, such as the warlike Sauk and Foxes and Potawatomi. Pike relates[57] that in the autumn of 1805 a war party of Potawatomi penetrated the Osage country on the river of that name and attacked an Osage camp, from which the men were absent on a hunting expedition. A number of the women and children were killed and about sixty taken prisoners. Forty-six of the prisoners were afterward recovered by the United States and with the deputation of ten Osage chiefs lately returned from Washington, in the summer of 1806, were delivered to Captain Pike when he started on his exploring tour of the Arkansas River. He conveyed them up the Missouri to their home on the Osage River. They proceeded in terror of the Potawatomi, who were known to be hunting in the vicinity.

Before they reached the Osage towns, Pike received word that a war party of the Little Osage had marched against the Kansa, and another party of the Grand Osage had started against the whites living or hunting on the Arkansas.[58] White Hair, it was said, did everything he could to prevent the attack on the whites, but he could not restrain the young warriors. When Pike's party reached the Osage towns, they learned that a boat ascending the Arkansas had been fired on and that two men had been killed and two wounded.[59]

Wilkinson reported[60] that when he visited Cashesegra or Big Foot, the chief expressed his desire for the Government to erect

fork of the Arkansas called the Neozho"; and that part of the Great Osage known as the Arkansas Osage on the Verdigris had increased to 2,600; one-fourth of the total were warriors (William Clark, Report on Indians in Missouri Territory, November 4, 1816, OIA, RCF). In 1825 there were said to be 5,200 Osage (*American State Papers,* "Indian Affairs," II, 544). In 1822 the Great Osage abandoned their village on Osage River and removed to the neighborhood of the Little Osage on the Neosho River. The Harmony Mission established a branch mission with them (*Arkansas Gazette* [November 20, 1822], p. 3, col. 3).

[57] Coues, *op. cit.,* II, 531.

[58] *Ibid.,* pp. 381, 576.

[59] *Ibid.,* II, 387.

[60] *Ibid.,* p. 556.

a factory[61] on the point of land between the Verdigris, Grand, and Arkansas rivers near his village; Wilkinson suggested that if this were done it might restore harmony between the Osage and the eastern tribes, and it would "prevent the Osages making excursions into the country of the poor and peaceably disposed Caddoes, and might have some effect on confining the Spaniards to their own territorial limits."

[61] A factory was a trading post operated by the Government, where Indians could exchange furs and skins for such articles of merchandise as they requested. Factories were established by the Government for the purpose of driving the British traders out of the United States by fair competition, and thus ending their troublesome machinations with the Indians (*American State Papers,* "Indian Affairs," I, 65). In 1822 the factories were abolished.

III

EASTERN INDIANS AS TENTATIVE
IMMIGRANTS, 1796-1817

THE idea of removing the eastern Indians to the West was doubtless promoted by the fact that some of them were already familiar with that country. One of the earliest accounts of the crossing of the Mississippi by the Cherokee is as follows: Shortly after the treaty of Hopewell in 1785, a few of the Cherokee who were dissatisfied with the terms of this instrument embarked in pirogues, and, descending the Tennessee, Ohio, and Mississippi rivers, reached and ascended the St. Francis, then in the Spanish province of Louisiana; there they formed a settlement, whence in later years they removed to a more satisfactory location on White River where they were joined by subsequent emigrants.[1]

In February, 1794, William Scott, James Pettigrew, and John Pettigrew were traveling from Williamsburgh, South Carolina, to Natchez, where Scott had previously located. They were accompanied by three other white men, three women, four children, and twenty-one slaves with a quantity of hardware and other goods. As they were passing down Tennessee River in their boat, they were attacked at Muscle Shoals on June 9 by a number of Cherokee under the leadership of The Bowle;[2]

---

[1] Charles C. Royce, *The Cherokee Nation of Indians*, p. 204.

[2] A different version of this affair is that the whites first made the Indians drunk and then swindled them out of all their annuity money with which they were just returning from the Indian Agency at Tellico; when they became sober, they asked for the return of their money, and the whites attacked and killed two of them; they then retaliated and killed all the whites except the women and children. These with their property and slaves the Indians escorted down the Tennessee, Ohio, and Mississippi as far as the St. Francis River, where they stopped. They then sent the women and children in their boat farther south to

all the white people were killed, and the negroes and goods carried away.[3]

Though it was claimed the white men were the aggressors, the Cherokee tribe disavowed the act of The Bowle and his followers who, fearing capture and punishment, fled to the west of the Mississippi and located on the south side of the Arkansas River, within what is now the state of Arkansas. With subsequent additions to their settlement they remained there many years.

In the years 1795 and 1796, first the Delaware and afterward the Cherokee made application to the Quapaw for leave to settle and hunt on the tract of country above them on the Arkansas River; this request was denied by the Quapaw, who would permit neither whites nor Indians to occupy the country above them. Upon word of this refusal, the governor of Orleans directed the commandant at Arkansas Post to permit the Cherokee to settle and hunt on the St. Francis River and the Delaware on White River.[4]

Soon after the Louisiana Purchase, the officials at Washington made inquiries concerning that part of the Cherokee tribe who were located west of the Mississippi,[5] and their warfare

---

their destination, where they arrived safely with their property (Cephas Washburn, *Reminiscences of the Indians* [Richmond, 1869], pp. 75 ff.; Houck, *History of Missouri*, I, 221).

[3] *American State Papers*, "Claims," p. 309.

[4] Statement of late Spanish commandant at Arkansas Post to Gov. William Clark, June 5, 1816, AGO, ORD, WDF. Certain Indians in American territory, angered by the terms of the Jay Treaty, began to show their dislike for the United States even before any posts had been delivered or any steps taken to run the boundary line fixed by its terms. One hundred and seventy Cherokee applied to the commandant of New Madrid asking for lands; while the chief of the Alibamu in the name of 394 of his tribe applied to the governor at New Orleans for a similar concession, and they were permitted to settle near the Opelousa. Morales, Intendente of Louisiana, regarded these immigrants as potential allies against the Americans in the event of hostilities (Morales to Ulloa, March 31, 1797, in Mattie Austin Hatcher, "Background of Colonization of Texas," *Southwestern Historical Quarterly*, XXIV, 187).

[5] "A scarcity of grain on the eastern side of the Mississippi has lately induced

with the Osage. Colonel Return J. Meigs, Cherokee agent in Tennessee, wrote to his chief, Henry Dearborn, in 1805, that the Cherokee had been in the habit for many years of hunting west of the Mississippi where clashes with the Osage were frequent; and that the winter before, a war party had gone against the Osage to avenge the death of one of their hunters.[6]

The Choctaw and Chickasaw Indians also ranged over the country west of the Mississippi. "In 1795 or 1796 a party of Chiakasaw warriors attacked Arkansas Post (consisting of a subaltern's command, six pieces of cannon and eight swivels) and killed ten soldiers of the command, and soon after concluded peace with the Spaniards."[7] As early as 1777 a Choctaw village on the Ouachita River in what is now Arkansas was known to the Spaniards.[8] Andrew Ellicott relates[9] that in 1797

a number of Cherokees, Choctaws, Chichasawa &c to frequent the neighborhood of the Arkansas, where game is still in abundance; they have contracted marriages with the Arkansas, and seem inclined to make a permanent settlement and incorporate themselves with that nation.

"On the river St. Francis, in the neighborhood of New Madrid, Cape Girardeau, Riviere a la Pomme, and the environs, are settled a number of vagabonds, emigrants from the Delawares, Shawnees, Miamis, Chichasaws, Cherokees, Peorias, and supposed to consist in all of five hundred families; they are at times troublesome to the boats descending the river, and have even plundered some of them, and committed a few murders. They are attached to liquor, seldom remain at any place, many of them speak English, all understand it, and there are some who even read it" (Berquin-Duvallon, *Travels in Louisiana and the Floridas in 1802* (New York, 1806), p. 98, footnote by translator). In 1805 the governor of Louisiana Territory who was under orders to remove intruding whites living on the St. Francis River, wrote: ". . . . I may find some difficulty (I fear) in dislodging eight families which have taken refuge with a strong tribe of Cherokee Indians, high up the same river" (Department of State, 3382 B.R.L. Wilkinson to Secretary of State, September 21, 1805.).

[6] Meigs to Dearborn, May 31, 1805, OIA, RCF.

[7] Gilbert Imlay, *A Topographical Description of the Western Territory of North America* (London, 1797), p. 428.

[8] Bolton, *op. cit.*, II, 100.

[9] *The Journal of Andrew Ellicott, Late Commissioner on Behalf of the United States during Part of the Year 1796, the Years 1797, 1798, 1799, and Part of the Year 1800, for Determining the Boundary between the United States and the Possessions of His Catholic Majesty in America*, p. 113.

while he was in Natchez, a body of Choctaw Indians crossed the Mississippi to make war upon the Caddo; they were very successful, and returned in June with a number of poles filled with scalps. Dr. John Sibley in 1804 was appointed agent for Orleans Territory and was stationed at Natchitoches; he prepared a historical sketch[10] in 1805 in which he accounts for eighty permanent Choctaw residents on the Red River, who raised corn there, and indicates that there were hunting parties of Choctaw and Cherokee all over Louisiana.

Dr. Sibley submitted a report[11] in 1807 in which he speaks of the Alibamu and Koasati of the Creek Federation, who were within his jurisdiction, some of them living on the Red River where they raised corn; on one occasion[12] they returned to their village with five Osage scalps they had taken in an encounter with members of that tribe. The Alibamu and Apalachicola had crossed the Mississippi forty-two years before. Part of the Kanchati[13] crossed the Mississippi, he said, in the latter part of the eighteenth century and spread over much of East Texas as far as the Trinity River; in 1812 there were 600 of them on the Sabine River, and in 1820, 350 lived on the Red River, 50 on the Neches, and 240 on the Trinity.[14] Dr. Sibley says that Spanish emissaries in 1807 induced these Indians to remove from Orleans Territory (afterward Louisiana) into Texas, then Spanish territory, where it was planned to organize them in hostilities against the United States. In the spring of 1807, he

[10] *American State Papers, "Indian Affairs,"* I, 725.

[11] Abel, *A Report from Natchitoches in 1807, by Dr. John Sibley* (New York: Museum of the American Indian, 1922).

[12] *Ibid.,* p. 15.

[13] "South of the San Antonio road in the counties of Nacodoches and Liberty live the Conchatees, Alabamas, Baluxies, and Muskogees, and the three former of about 50 and the latter of about 3 years residence in Texas, all originally from the 'Creek Country' of the U.S. They speak a similar dialect, are about 150 warriors in number, mostly Hunters" (Texas State Library, *Report of Texas Senate Committee on Indian Affairs,* October 12, 1837).

[14] *Handbook of American Indians,* I, 719; Rev. Jedidiah Morse, *A Report to the Secretary of War on Indian Affairs* (New Haven, 1822), p. 373.

says,[15] a party of Cherokee came in two pirogues to his post (at Natchitoches) to barter skins they had taken higher up the Red River. They told him of a difficulty with the Caddo growing out of the accidental killing of a Cherokee, seven or eight years before in the Caddo country.

In response to Dr. Sibley's request, two hundred chiefs and head men of the Choctaw living west of the Mississippi, assembled at Natchitoches[16] in 1807 under their newly elected Chief, Tombolin, for the purpose of making peace with the Caddo who were about to go to war against them for the murder of two Caddo women on Sabine River, committed by a party of Choctaw hunters, under a leader named Stamelachee.

> While the Chactas remain'd here a large Party of Pascagolas came to play a Match at Ball with them, there were twenty four players of a side they made high Betts, & even the Women bet with one Another every rag of Cloathing they had, and the Winer Stript the Looser immediately On the ground, the Men Bet their Horses, Guns, Jewelry &c—the first day the Chactas Beat the Pascagolas, they play'd again two days After Changing the Match a little by leaving out Some & taking in Others & the Pascagolas Beat.[17]

In the autumn Dr. Sibley was visited also by a party of Chickasaw warriors under their Chief, John Homo; they had been hunting higher up on the Red River where they had been robbed by the Koasati of 160 deerskins and two horses, of which they complained to the Indian agent.[18] Dr. Sibley reported[19] that in October, 1807, a delegation of Ietan and Pani came to him to complain of the depredations of the Osage, who, being armed, were very formidable, and to endeavor to secure arms so they might be able to resist the Osage.

---

[15] Dr. John Sibley, *op. cit.*, p. 16.
[16] *Ibid.*, p. 26.
[17] *Ibid.*, p. 29.
[18] *Ibid.*, p. 68.
[19] *Ibid.*, p. 74.

I asked, what had become of her parents? When one of them went to his sack and took from it TWO SCALPS! "Here" said he "they are"; holding them in his hand before me.—Frontispiece from The Little Osage Captive.

A war party of Choctaw Indians under the famous Chief Pushmataha came in 1807 all the way from their own country in Mississippi to the mouth of the Verdigris[20] to attack the Osage.[21] John Jamison, Indian agent for the Red River Agency at Natchitoches, reported in 1816 that within his jurisdiction in Louisiana there were fifteen hundred Choctaw in various settlements, one hundred Chickasaw, one hundred Cherokee, and one hundred Alibamu.[22]

A delegation of chiefs from the upper Cherokee towns waited on President Jefferson in May, 1808, and told him they wished to become farmers, to establish fixed laws, and a regular government,[23] and to have their territory marked off separately from the people of the lower towns who preferred to follow the lives of hunters. The President told them he would consider their requests but, removal of the Indians being foremost in his mind, added that "it may facilitate the settlement among yourselves to be told that we will give to these leave to go if they choose it, & and settle on our lands beyond the Mississippi where some Cherokees are already settled and where game is plenty."[24] The next January, Jefferson told the Cherokee of the lower towns that when they had found a suitable tract of land in the West, the Government would arrange its exchange for a portion of the country they had left.[25]

The country west of the Mississippi referred to by the Presi-

[20] The Verdigris was called by the Osage, "Was-su-ja," according to Captain Bell (Thwaites, *op. cit.*, XVI, 281). To Lieutenant Wilkinson's ear the name was "Wasetihoge" (Coues, *op. cit.*, p. 555).

[21] Foreman, *op. cit.*, p. 73. *U.S. Senate Document No. 23,* Twenty-fourth Congress, first session. Petition of Joseph Bogy praying for compensation for spoliation by Choctaw Indians while on a trading expedition on the Arkansas River.

[22] Jamison to Secretary of War, November 20, 1816, OIA, RCF.

[23] *American State Papers,* "Indian Affairs," II, 485.

[24] Thomas Jefferson to chiefs of the Upper Cherokee, May 8, 1808, OIA, RFC.

[25] *American State Papers,* "Indian Affairs," II, 125. The deputation of the Upper and Lower Towns was composed of John Walker, the Seed, Skinkee, Touchalee, Quotequeskee, and the Ridge (Jackson Papers, No. 6579).

dent was, however, claimed by the Osage, traditional enemies of the Cherokee who could not move into it until some arrangement had been made with its savage owners. Since this country had passed by the Louisiana Purchase from their friends the French to American control, the lawless Osage had increased their hostilities toward the whites. They raided the settlers, plundered them of their horses and other property, and subjected the frontier to a reign of terror. White Hair or Pahuska, the chief of the Great Osage, who had come to St. Louis, told Governor Lewis in 1808 that he was unable to restrain the warriors of his band from these acts of violence; and the Governor, for lack of a better method of controlling the situation, gave his consent to a large war party of Shawnee, Delaware, and other tribes, who were organizing for the purpose, to attack the Osage.[26]

Then directions came from the Secretary of War to select a site for a factory in their country and to try to make peace with the Osage. A large quantity of supplies such as the Indians needed was sent to their country, this being the surest way to interest the Indian and win his friendship. This store of supplies was taken by George C. Sibley,[27] escorted by a company of troops under Captain Eli. B. Clemson, to Fire Prairie on the south bank of Missouri River near the site of the present Kansas City, Missouri, where a post was established, afterward called Fort Clark and Fort Osage. General William Clark[28] arrived there on September 4 with a detachment of militia;

[26] Library of Congress, Manuscripts Division, Senate Files, 3454; *American State Papers,* "Indian Affairs," I, 765.

[27] Sibley was appointed agent to conduct the "trading post at Saint Louis in the territory of Louisiana" in 1805 (Secretary of War to George C. Sibley, August 17, 1805, State Department, Territorial Records). On March 18 of that year John B. Treat was appointed to manage the trading post at Arkansas Post (*ibid*).

[28] William Clark, brother of George Rogers Clark, was born in Virginia in 1770; while a lieutenant in the army, he was appointed a member of Captain Lewis' expedition to the mouth of the Columbia River in 1804. The success of the expedition was largely due to his knowledge of Indian habits. He was after-

from there Captain Nathan Boone was sent with an interpreter to all their towns, to notify the Osage that they would be protected by the United States if they would come to the fort and deliver up the horses stolen from the whites. On the twelfth Boone returned with some of the chiefs, with whom a council was held. They expressed their pleasure that a trading post was to be established in their country, and under this influence and the threat of withholding supplies from them altogether, General Clark induced them to enter into a treaty ceding to the United States an extensive tract of country.[29] When this treaty was brought to St. Louis, other Osage chiefs[30] came there and objected to it; and since it had not been accepted by a representative gathering of the Indians; it was decided to prepare a new treaty covering the same ground. This was accordingly taken by Pierre Chouteau to Fort Clark, where on November 10, 1808, the Great and Little Osage agreed to it;[31] and the next summer a deputation of the principal chiefs and warriors of the Arkansas Osage came to St. Louis where they also approved the treaty.[32] The most important feature of this

ward made brigadier general for the territory of Upper Louisiana; in 1813-20 he was governor of Missouri Territory. From 1822 he was superintendent of Indian Affairs in St. Louis, where he died September 1, 1838.

[29] *American State Papers,* "Indian Affairs," I, 765. "In consequence of the measures which were taken last spring in relation to the Osage nations, they were reduced in the course of a few months to a state of perfect submission without bloodshed; this has in my opinion, fairly proven the superiority which the policy of withholding from the Indians, has over the chastisement of the sword, where their local situation is such as will enable us to practice it.

"In this state of humiliation Gen'l Clarke found them in September last when he established the post at Fire Prarie; he very properly seized this favorable occasion to enter into a treaty with them which he effected on the 14th September" (Gov. Meriwether Lewis to the President, December 15, 1808, Library of Congress, Manuscript Division, Senate Files, 3454).

[30] Seventy-four Osage under the leadership of Chief Big Soldier, a son of White Hair, had brought to St. Louis a large number of horses stolen from the whites, which they were restoring in compliance with the demand made upon them (*idem*).

[31] Kappler, *op. cit.,* II, 69.

[32] *American State Papers,* "Indian Affairs," I, 765.

treaty was the cession by the Osage to the United States of all that vast country lying north of the Arkansas River and east of a line running south from Fort Clark to that stream;[33] it included substantially all the land within the present state of Arkansas north of the Arkansas River and a large part of what is now the state of Missouri.

Exploring parties sent out by the Cherokee brought back favorable reports and soon bands of emigrants began moving toward the new open country, where game abounded. The leader in this movement was their chief, Tahlonteskee, who emigrated to the West in 1809 at the head of a party of three hundred Cherokee, including seventy warriors.[34] By 1813 the number of Cherokee in the new country had increased to such an extent that the Government considered it necessary to send them an agent; accordingly, William L. Lovely,[35] who had been assistant to Colonel Return J. Meigs, Cherokee agent in Tennessee,[36] was assigned to the Arkansas Cherokee. He arrived in July, 1813, and selected as his home a location in what

[33] This line is almost identical with that now marking the western boundaries of Missouri and Arkansas. It was first surveyed in 1816 by Joseph C. Brown (Sullivan to Clark, April 19, 1818, OIA, RCF).

[34] Joseph McMinn to Secretary of War, January 10, 1818, OIA, RCF.

[35] Before the Revolution, Lovely had lived for some time in the family of Madison's father. In 1815 from his lonely post on Arkansas River he wrote a long letter to the President: ".... When I took leave of you in the year 1774 you were sitting on your father's fence; little did I expect to write you after nearly half a century had elapsed; my situation in those days being precarious as I entered into the Shawanoe expedition as assistant to the commissary General & in January 1776 into the continental army in which I remained until its final end; from its beginning I never was absent a day. During nearly the whole I commanded one of the Virginia Company attached to the regiment commanded by Col. Mullenburg; from thence was transferred into Col. Morgan's Corp of light Infantry and from which after the capture of Burgoine was transferred to Gen Wayne with him at Stony Point and with him finished my military career by the capture of his Lordship Cornwallis, Shortly after which I again entered into the service of my country & have every since remained in it .... My situation is I can assure you disagreeable living at upwards of three hundred miles from a post office no ways of procuring information but those which are owing to chance and those seldom happen. So I may say with propriety

formerly had been an old Osage settlement, in the midst of a plum orchard of fifty acres, the fruit of which he said was the finest he ever ate. He found there a few Choctaw, Delaware, Miami, Pawnee, and Quapaw, the latter ".... an exception in the mildness of their manners, but very poor and wanting the fostering hand of the Government." Lovely marveled at the ".... quantities of the very best kind of furs—dressed deer skins, bear skins all neatly handled, but the poor fellows get little or nothing for them of which they complain very much."[37] Of the type of people making up the sparse white settlements adjacent to the new home of the Cherokee, Lovely gives a sad picture:

> I am here without a cent, and among the worst banditi; all the white folks, a few excepted, have made their escape to this Country guilty of the most horrid crimes and are now depredating on the Osages & other tribes, taking off 30 horses at a time, which will show the necessity of giving some protection to this place, the most valuable as to soil and valuable minerals that belongs to the Purchase in all the country.[38]

The white people slaughtered the buffaloes only for tallow and the bears for oil. One party, he wrote, headed by Scull and Louismore, half French and half Quapaw, were conspicuous offenders.

On Lovely's arrival at the Arkansas Cherokee village he found the Cherokee and Osage engaged in violent hostilities.

that I am entirely secluded from the land of the living surrounded on all sides by Indians together with the Worst of White Settlers living just below me betwix whom there are daily disturbances arising & against whom there are no possible means in my power of enforcing any laws ...." (Lovely to Madison, September, 1815, AGO, ORD, WDF).

[36]Return J. Meigs died January 28, 1823. The agency was then taken over temporarily by Joseph McMinn.

[37] Lovely to Meigs, "Cherokee Village up the Arkansas, 400 miles from the Post," July 16, 1813, OIA, RCF.

[38] Lovely to Meigs, August 6, 1813 (OIA, RCF), facetiously dated by Lovely at "Fort Meigs on the Arkansas." His station was within the present Pope County, Arkansas, where the Cherokee were then living.

The latter had recently killed a chief of the Cherokee; they retaliated by killing twenty-one Osage.[39] Lovely persuaded a Cherokee chief and eight men to go to Clermont's on the Verdigris and make a proffer of peace; this was followed by a return visit in the fall of 1813 by a band of Osage headed by Clermont, and Lovely prevailed on them to make peace. However, the visit of the Osage was due in a large measure to a desire to induce Lovely to use his influence with the Government to take some notice of them, to appoint an agent for them and make it possible to market their furs; then as well as on subsequent visits to Lovely, they stated that they were separated for all time from the village of White Hair,[40] and wanted to have nothing more to do with Pierre Chouteau, the Osage agent, and charged that White Hair and Chouteau were not friendly to the United States. The Osage also desired the friendship of the Cherokee with whom they hoped to find a market for their furs, since the Cherokee were in touch with the whites and able to furnish them ammunition and some of the other necessities of life they could not secure elsewhere. In order to give the assurance of peace some aspect of formality, Lovely later induced Cherokee and Osage representatives to agree to meet in full council at the mouth of the Verdigris in August, 1814.[41] He

[39] Lovely to Secretary of War, May 27, 1815 (*ibid.*). Lovely adds the following curious information: ".... the Osages have Taken satisfaction of the powanoe [Pawnee?] Indians for the stroke given them by the Cherokee .... The Powanoe Indians Live on the red River. They are very unfriendly Toward the Americans and the Causes are attributed to [explained by?] Dr. John Sibley of States having been Intirely annihilated at the Battle of Medina where Gl. friendly is that the idea which they had of the power and strength of the United Natchitoches Indian agent of the Broken Tribes. The reasons of their being un-Toledo, the Spanish Republican Commander was defeated by Arredondo has never been Removed. This is only from information." In this battle fought near San Antonio, in August, 1813, General Toledo, the head of the Republican Government, had under his command 850 Americans and twice that number of Mexicans (H. Yoakum, *History of Texas,* I, 174).

[40] White Hair had usurped the chieftancy from Clermont while the latter was too young to assert his rights.

[41] Lovely to Clark, August 9, 1814, OIA, RCF.

undertook to secure from Clermont's band the delivery of the men who had murdered two white hunters, Alexander McFarland, killed August 17, 1812, near the Tawehash villages,[42] and R. Geterlan, killed on the Arkansas. They agreed to give up the murderers, but a renewal of hostilities with the Cherokee in 1814 interfered with this arrangement.

While the Cherokee were authorized by President Jefferson to remove to Arkansas, they had no title to the land. The legislature of Missouri Territory, ignoring the presence of the Indians, passed an act on December 31, 1813, creating the county of Arkansas with an area embracing two-thirds of the present state and with the seat of government "at the Village of Arkansas," also known as Arkansas Post. The Cherokee were much disturbed by thus being brought under the civil jurisdiction of Missouri Territory, and Lovely's subsequent correspondence with Governor Clark contains accounts of his efforts to prevent disturbances between the Indians and white people, and requests for a solution of the difficulties presented by the new situation. There was also frequent mention of the necessity for sending troops and establishing a military post in the country, to prevent trouble between the Indians and whites, a suggestion that found much favor with Clark. Though there was no legal authority for it Lovely established a boundary line around the Cherokee country for the purpose of maintaining order.

The Cherokee chief, Tahlonteskee, was a man of much force of character.[43] In the early part of the year 1815 he and John D. Chisholm, a white member of the tribe, headed a delegation

---

[42] For an account of the cruel murder of this hunter by the Osage, see that of Nuttall (Thwaites [ed.], *op. cit.*, XIII, 251; and Foreman, *op. cit.*, p. 74; and Coues, *op. cit.*, p. 558, for mention of "McFarlane").

[43] Tahlonteskee wrote a quaint letter to Lovely before the latter went west: "Arkansas March 13, 1813. My Friend and Brother .... Tell my friend Rogers that I have commenced digging a salt well. I have dug a considerable depth and have swore off drinking whiskey until I find salt. I unfortunately fell in the well & was very near dieing in consequence of the fall. I have got a solid rock &

of chiefs who went to St. Louis to lay their grievances before Governor Clark.[44] They complained that the Government had not kept faith with them, that in compliance with the agreement with the President they had removed to the Arkansas five years before, but their country had been swallowed up by the Missouri legislature and some of their privileges had been taken from them.

> Here I am my land overwhelmed with strangers from all parts.[45] .... Under the faith of the President of the U.S. we have been industrious; we have cleared nine miles on each side of the river. We wish our boundaries run according to our agreement. We wish to be friendly with our brethren the whites, but at the same time we wish to know that we walk upon our ground.

Though he wanted to remain always friendly,

> .... it is impossible to do that in the present situation in which the whites and Cherokees are, to prevent depradation being committed by both parties. . . . . I am here settled, fond of my situation, loving my present house and field. . . . . When our father sent us here he told us there was plenty of game but to our sorrow the French and others do not destroy less than five thousand buffaloes every summer for no other profit but for the tallow. We are far from having any objection to any persons killing game, provided they take it away, but a thousand weight of meat is thrown away for no other profit than perhaps 20 pounds tallow. This is the thing which will render game shortly scarce and we must then see our children suffer.

By the early part of 1816 the Arkansas Cherokee numbered a little more than two thousand.[46] They were

would be glad if he would send me some augurs & powder for boring & blowing the rock. I am Your Kanalee Tahlonteskee."

[44] Lovely to Clark, "Cherokee Agency on the Arkansas 29th May, 1815," OIA, RCF.

[45] See also *American State Papers*, "Indian Affairs," II, 11.

[46] Return J. Meigs to Wm. H. Crawford, February 17, 1816, OIA, RCF, "Arkansas." Colonel Meigs wrote: "The Cherokee have during the Presidency

good hunters, and their women spin and weave cotton cloth while the men are hunting. But they cannot dispose of their furs and skins to any advantage—the traveling traders impose on them excessively in the sale of goods and ammunition, and blankets are charged at two or three prices,

and there was much complaint that the Government had not established a factory in their country, where they could trade their furs for supplies, as President Jefferson had promised them. The Arkansas Cherokee had another grievance arising from the fact they were not receiving any part of the annuities paid to the tribe in the East, where the majority of the nation held that the western members who had expatriated themselves were not entitled to share in the public funds.

The turbulent Osage soon broke the peace with the Cherokee; restless bands of Indians who defied the authority of their chiefs, robbed the Cherokee hunters of traps, arms, ammunition, and horses, and murdered some of them, though killings had occurred on both sides. In November, 1815, Major Lovely delivered a talk to a deputation of Osages from the Verdigris who had called on him, warning them against further outrages on the whites and other Indians;[47] Lovely told them he had learned that the Cherokee had just killed one of their people and that the Osage had killed two Cherokee and four white men. At the same time Major Lovely wrote the Secretary of

of Mr. Jefferson & the Presidency of Mr. Madison been emigrating to the River Arkansas in small parties, by permission of the Government—the first object was only for hunting; but the numbers increasing an exchange of lands with them has been in contemplation by the Government & by the Emigrants; but the numbers there not being large enough to induce an exchange of countries they remain insulated from the Nation; their numbers as they state amount to 2600 including men, women, and children—they may exagerate as to their numbers; but we may safely assume them 2000." Their exaggeration may have misled Governor Clark who reported 3,600 Cherokee on the Arkansas (Wm. H. Clark, November 4, 1816, "Indians in Missouri Territory [Tabulation]," OIA, RCF).

[47] "Speech to the Osages who live on the Head Waters of Arkansas River by Maj. Lovely, Novr. 1815," AGO, ORD, WDF.

War urging him to send troops to preserve order on the Arkansas.[48] Clermont and Tallai responded the following January with a melancholy message to the sympathetic Lovely:

.... We are the Chiefs & warriors the most miserable—after we had seen you we all went for the purpose of receiving our presents at the prereree du chien Which received. On our return we were attacked by a band of our Enemies lost ten of our brave men, since we have not dared to venture there again & we have received no present. We should be glad if you could appoint some person close to us that could see our conduct towards our brothers the Whites & that could see our presents brought to our village.[49]

They charged that White Hair's band were committing the robberies on the whites and Cherokee on Arkansas River for which the former were blamed.[50]

In April another delegation of Cherokee chiefs headed by John D. Chisholm went to St. Louis to protest to Governor Clark against the depredations of the Osage[51] and to convey a letter from Major Lovely requesting that a military post be established on the Arkansas to maintain peace among the Indians.[52] Governor Clark promised the delegation that he would request authority to call a general council of the Osage, Qua-

[48] Lovely to Secretary of War, November 15, 1815, AGO, ORD, WDF.

[49] Speech of Clermont and Tallai at "Mouth of the Verdigris 16 Jany. 1816," recorded in French and crudely translated for Lovely, AGO, ORD, WDF. The Osage doubtless received their presents at Prairie du Chien from the British. More than a year earlier a party of Sauk Indians carried a British flag to the Osage (*Missouri Gazette*, June 25, 1814). In 1817 the Osage stopped at the Sauk village at the site of the present Rock Island, Illinois, on their way to Malden and Detroit in response to an invitation from the British extended through the Sauk (Wisconsin Historical Society, Draper Manuscripts, "T" IV, 46).

[50] Lovely wrote that he believed Clermont to be a good man though he had many bad young men in his village (Lovely to Clark, January 20, 1816, OIA, RCF).

[51] Lovely to Secretary of War, April 16, 1816, AGO, ORD, WDF.

[52] Clark to Lovely, May 2, 1816, OIA, RCF, "Cherokee Agency—Arkansas," the delegation were absent from home on their mission from April 2 to May 22.

[53] Clark to Lovely, April 29, 1816, OIA, RCF, "Cherokee West, Saint Louis Council."

paw, and Cherokee;[53] and he informed Major Lovely that he had made application to the War Department to establish a military post on the Arkansas.[54]

Pierre Chouteau sent word to Lovely that he would meet him with the Osage and Cherokee representatives at Clermont's Town on June 1.[55] Chouteau did not keep the engagement, but Major Lovely met the Indians at the mouth of the Verdigris, where he presided at a conference between representatives of the tribes. He proposed to the Osage that the Government would pay all claims against them for depredations they had committed if they would relinquish to the United States all the land lying between the Verdigris and the home of the Arkansas Cherokee; such an adjustment apparently would vacate a large expanse of country held by the Osage and leave it free for the Cherokee to hunt over in peace. Clermont and the other Osage chiefs agreed to this July 9,[56] and this great tract of land became known as Lovely's Purchase. It was bounded on the south by the Arkansas River, on the west by the Verdigris up four miles to the falls, and on the north by a line running thence northeast to where Salina,[57] Oklahoma, now is, and thence east to the Cherokee settlement.[58] Such inveterate thieves were the Osage that one of them stole Lovely's horse while he was striving to establish order in their country.[59]

The eastern Cherokee were approached upon the subject of ceding more of their lands to the United States, in consideration

[54] Clark to Lovely, May 1, 1816, *ibid.*

[55] Chouteau to Lovely, May 1, 1816, *ibid.*

[56] *U. S. House Document No. 263,* Twentieth Congress, first session, "Letter from Secretary of War, concerning Lovely's Purchase," p. 38; Foreman, *op. cit.,* p. 29.

[57] Called in the grant "the Upper Saline on Six Bull."

[58] This unauthorized cession was ratified by formal treaty made by representatives of the remainder of the tribe at St. Louis, on September 25, 1818 (Kappler, *op. cit.,* II, 116).

[59] During this tour Major Lovely who was then an old man contracted a malady from which he never recovered; on his return to the Cherokee settlements he took to his bed where he lingered until his death February 24, 1817.

of the removal of many of their number to Arkansas; this they instantly rejected. They further refused to consider the division of their annuities with their western brothren, and said that the latter should be compelled to return and live with the old nation. Difficulties over the boundary lines of the Cherokee Nation in the East entailed frequent correspondence and conferences, finally resulting in a treaty entered into on March 22, 1816,[60] by which the disputed line was defined. Immediately other controversies arose over the treaty from the objections of whites to the Cherokee reservation of lands north of the Tennessee River.[61] Under the pressure of Governor McMinn and Andrew Jackson another treaty[62] was negotiated September 14, 1816, by which the Cherokee were induced to yield the land coveted by the whites and a new boundary was drawn.

The cessions so easily obtained in 1816 gave the white people an appetite for more, and from all sides the Cherokee were importuned to exchange their lands for other lands in Arkansas. In March, 1817, Andrew Jackson was directed by the Secretary of War to hold a council with the Cherokee in June and to press upon them the subject of an exchange of their land[63] pursuant to the power vested in the President by the last congress. Governor Joseph McMinn of Tennessee had been endeavoring to induce them to meet and consider another treaty. Chief Path Killer, who was much opposed to further cessions of their lands, was able to prevent the conference for some time; but at last McMinn succeeded in getting a number of Indians to meet two hundred miles from the home of the resolute old chief,

He was succeeded by Reuben Lewis, a brother of Meriwether Lewis, who was appointed by the Secretary of War "agent for Indian Affairs, at Arkansas, in Missouri Territory" July 11, 1817. Lewis was compelled by ill health to resign the post in April, 1820, and on May 1 of that year David Brearley was appointed "Indian Agent on the Arkansas" to look after the Cherokee and Quapaw.

60 Kappler, *op. cit.*, II, 87.

61 *American State Papers*, "Indian Affairs," II, 98 ff.

62 Kappler, *op. cit.*, II, 92.

63 *American State Papers*, "Indian Affairs," II, 141.

when he was too ill to attend. The result was a so-called treaty, dated July 8, 1817, entered into at the Cherokee Agency, Calhoun, Tennessee, near where Dayton is now. It was signed by John D. Chisholm[64] and James Rogers for the Arkansas Cherokee, and also by a few of the eastern Cherokee, notwithstanding the fact that a majority of their representatives present at the conference opposed it resolutely. However, Jackson, Meriwether, and McMinn, in their zeal to secure the removal of the Cherokee, which was the main feature of the treaty, forwarded it to the Secretary of War as the treaty of the tribe.[65]

The Cherokee soon made it clear that this treaty did not express the will of the majority of the tribe, and vigorously protested against its ratification and the means employed to secure its execution. These means, perhaps not known in all their details to the Indians, are indicated by the testimony of Jackson himself and the other commissioners, who used them to procure the betrayal of the tribe through the avarice of their representatives. The Andrew Jackson Papers, in the Manuscript Division of the Library of Congress, contains voluminous correspondence from the commissioners, reporting almost daily to the Secretary of War the progress of the negotiations with the Cherokee. The last letter in the series is a private and confidential one in which Jackson and his associates explain about a "private article" not embodied in the published treaty in which provision is made for paying money to some of the individual Indians:

.... We were compelled to promise to John D. Chisholm the sum of one thousand dollars to stop his mouth & obtain his consent, we have drew a bill in favor of Col. Meigs for this sum—

[64] Chisholm was living with the Cherokee in Arkansas as early as 1816. In September of that year he wrote Colonel Meigs: "Mr. Rogers and his son James has just this moment arrived here they are well" (Chisholm to Meigs, September 23, 1816, OIA, RCF, "Cherokee [West] Dardanelle"). Unlike most of his associates Chisholm could read and write.

[65] *American State Papers*, "Indian Affairs," II, 151 ff.; Kappler, *op. cit.*, II, 96.

without this we could not have got the national relinquishment. In
the course of this conference we were obliged to promise the cheifs
from the Arkansas, one hundred dollars each for their expenses in
coming here—and to three other influential chiefs, the sum of one
hundred dollars in presents—this sum amounting to six hundred
dollars we obtained from Col. Meigs.[66]

In his reply approving the action of the commissioners, the
Secretary expressed the opinion that the treaty would be ratified though it would meet with opposition for several reasons,
one

.... that the treaty has not received the unbiased sanction of a
majority of that portion of the nation residing on the east of the
Mississippi, as evidenced by the small number of chiefs who signed
it, in proportion to the number who appear to have been present
during the progress of the negotiation.[67]

The treaty was subsequently approved by the Senate and the
President.

[66] Jackson, McMinn, and Meriwether to Secretary of War, July 9, 1817,
Jackson Papers, 6559. Tahlonteskee, Black Fox, Sanawney, Waterminer, Kiame,
and Thomas Graves of the Arkansas Cherokee attended the treaty conference;
here they were induced to delegate by power of attorney to Chisholm and
Rogers such authority as they had to enter into a treaty. The document recited
that there were 3,700 Cherokee living on the Arkansas, but as the statement
was made in connection with their effort to secure their proportion of the
Cherokee annuity, it may have been exaggerated. The eastern Cherokee de-
nounced Chisholm as a white man "whose general character is too generally
known to admit of vindication," and protested against his participation in their
deliberations (Jackson Papers, 6421, 6422, 6596).

[67] Graham to Commissioners, August 1, 1817, Jackson Papers, 6708.

IV

WARFARE AND DISORDER ADVANCE
THE MILITARY FRONTIER, 1817

THE difficulties of the Arkansas Cherokee with the Osage, and their dissatisfaction with the encroachments of the whites and the government of Missouri Territory, were pressed upon the attention of the Government at Washington with increasing earnestness. Lovely had been urging that troops be sent to the Arkansas River to restrain the lawlessness in that country. He wrote to Governor Clark:

> It is my opinion absolutely necessary that there should be two companys of troops stationed here. I beg therefore that if they can possibly be spared that you will send two companys to the place, or one at least as there are some white of the worst character in this country whose influence with the Indians is dangerous to the peace of the same.[1]

When Clark responded favorably, Lovely wrote:

> It does me much pleasure to find in your letter the probability of troops being stationed in this quarter. I would recommend their being as high up the Arkansas at least as this place. It would have a tendency to keep the Osages at Bay.[2]

Return J. Meigs, the Cherokee agent in Tennessee, added his argument in support of Lovely's solicitations; and though Governor Clark promised that troops would be sent, nothing was accomplished until after the execution of the Cherokee treaty in 1817.

This was a period of considerable unrest and bloodshed in

---

[1] Lovely to Clark, October 11, 1814, OIA, RCF.

[2] *Ibid.*, May 17, 1815. Lovely is writing at his agency in the modern Pope County, Arkansas.

the future Oklahoma, and the need of a military establishment
was becoming more apparent; the Indian agent at Natchitoches
reported that ".... a large party of Americans who had been
trading with the northern tribe of Comanches were a few
weeks since attacked by a party of Omaha and Toweash Indians," at the Grand Saline (Alfalfa County, Oklahoma);
".... 20 Omahas were killed and seven wounded."[3] The next
winter the Indians issued a call for a grand council to convene
at this famous rendezvous in June to be attended by

> .... the Osages, Great & Little Pawnees, Arapahoos & a number
> of the Fox, Sieux & Kansas now in the Osage Nation. The Ietans,
> which are much the most numerous tribe west of this, will also
> attend. I am entirely at a loss to devine the cause of this large
> assemblage of the different tribes.[4]

The next September, Jamison sent a man named A. Woolf to
see

> .... the Towiach Indians (sometimes called Panis) who reside on
> Red River.[5] Traders & Others who fell in their power with but few
> exceptions were either murdered or robbed. I felt strong desires to
> bring them to an understanding and learn the cause of their hos-
> tilities. A. Woolf (the first individual who would consent to do this
> duty) set out about the 15th of September last for their village on
> Red River; when he reached that place he found these Indians had
> retired to the sources of the Brazos to save themselves from the
> ravages of the Osages; with great difficulty Mr. Woolf found them
> and after an absence of more than three months & ten days he

[3] Jamison to Secretary of War, August 17, 1817, AGO, ORD, WDF.

[4] Bradford to Calhoun, March 28, 1818, OIA, RCF. Bradford's letter associates the call for this great council with a recent visit of a body of Spaniards
from Santa Fe to the Canadian within the limits of the United States. In April,
1818, "a party of the Pawnees, consisting of four hundred, met a party of
Osages in the plains, within 50 or 60 miles of the Arkansas. The advance guard
of the Pawnees made a running fight, drawing after them the Osages into an
ambuscade formed by the main body of the Pawnees. The affair is said to have
resulted in the entire defeat and destruction of the Osages; only one escaped out
of 48 warriors. Our informant saw 47 guns taken from the Osages" (account in
the *Missouri Gazette* copied in *Niles' Weekly Register*, XIV, 388).

arrived at this Post with two chiefs & twelve others of the tribe. These have Frankly told me the cause of their being hostile was in consequence of Americans who had annually (& sometimes semi-annually) entered their country & robbed them of their horses & mules; on being informed that these men were scapes from justice in our own counties and that honest men nought to suffer for their conduct they have promised to protect all who have pass ports & those without who behave civil in their village.[6]

Bitterly resentful of the intrusion of white hunters on their ancestral hunting grounds and streams, bands of Osage continued their depredations on them.[7] The aggressions also of the immigrant Indians who hunted in the present Missouri, Oklahoma, Arkansas, and Texas provoked bloody retaliation from the enraged Osage, until in desperation the immigrants determined to combine forces against the overlords of this region. The Quapaw, Delaware, Choctaw, and Chickasaw living within the sphere of influence of the Cherokee who were looked to for leadership, readily consented to join in a war of extermination against the Osage.

At councils held in the Cherokee country on the Arkansas in January, 1817, talks were prepared and forwarded east of the Mississippi by express; that to the Eastern Cherokee contained an invitation to join in the proposed war on the Osage which it was planned to begin in May when the grass would

[5] These were the Wichita living in the present southwestern Oklahoma.

[6] Jamison to Calhoun, January 20, 1819, AGO, ORD, WDF.

[7] On the White River the hunting camps of John Wells were robbed in 1814, 1815, and 1818 by large bands of Osages who took their blankets, bear and beaver traps, and lead; Peter and August Friend, who were camped on the James River in 1818, were robbed of their beaver traps, powder, and bullet molds, by a band of one hundred Osage; Elijah and Abraham Eastwood, who were hunting on the "Osage Fork of the Gasconade" were robbed January 13, 1814, of their horses, traps, and other hunting equipment; William H. McMurtry and James McMurtry, who were encamped on the Arkansas, were robbed of their horses, guns, and blankets by Osage of "Clairmore's village on the Verdigris River," in April, 1821; and claims for their damages were lodged with the Government (OIA, RCF, "Special File," claim No. 191).

support their horses.[8] The talk to Colonel Meigs[9] informed him that after nine years of fruitless effort to make peace with the Osage, at last they had determined to make war. After several boatloads of Cherokee warriors had descended the Tennessee River to join their western brothers in their war, orders from the War Department were received by Meigs to prevent this participation, and he succeeded in stopping the departure of more recruits.

Either from the influence of Colonel Meigs or from the fear of finding the Osage warriors at home, the campaign was delayed, but it was not abandoned; for in July, Tahlonteskee and Takatoka sent word to the governor of Missouri Territory of their purpose to attack the Osage.[10] They detailed some of their grievances and related how the Osage had stolen all their best horses and reduced them to work the soil with their hands; they had recently killed two young Cherokee warriors and now the Cherokee were going in deadly earnest to seek revenge.

This latest threat of the Cherokee finally caused the War Department to act on the recommendations long urged by Major Lovely; and the Secretary directed General Jackson to establish a post to be garrisoned by one company at a point on the Arkansas River where it was intersected by the Osage line.[11] This action had become necessary he said, in order to check hostilities between the Osage and Cherokee and for further reasons arising from the recent Cherokee treaty. A

[8] Col. Return J. Meigs to George Graham, Secretary of War, March 12, 1817, AGO, ORD, WDF, and OIA, RCF, "Cherokee Agency"; William L. Lovely to Meigs, January 20, 1817, OIA, RCF. On his deathbed Major Lovely dictated this letter telling Colonel Meigs that the Cherokee were determined to go to war with the Osage; with the knowledge of his impending death, he asked Colonel Meigs to interest himself in the welfare of Mrs. Lovely; this letter was carried to Tennessee by the express who bore to the eastern Cherokee the invitation to join in the war on the Osage.

[9] Tahlonteskee and Takatoka to Meigs, January 25, 1817, AGO, ORD, WDF.

[10] Takatoka, Tahlonteskee, and others to the governor of Missouri, July 11, 1817, AGO, ORD, WDF.

[11] Graham to Jackson, July 30, 1817, Jackson Papers, 6696.

detachment of eighty-two recruits for the Rifle Regiment, who had reached Philadelphia, were to take boats at Pittsburgh to transport them to their regiment at St. Louis; and Jackson was authorized by the Secretary to divert them with their boats and equipment to the Arkansas.

These orders were received on August 19 by Jackson, who communicated them to General Thomas A. Smith in command at Belle Fontaine, near St. Louis.[12] On the fifteenth of the next month he ordered Major William Bradford in company with Major Stephen H. Long to descend the Mississippi to meet and assume command of the detachment of riflemen; with them to ascend the Arkansas River to the point where it was intersected by the Osage line; then with the advice of Major Long to select

> the best site to be found upon it near to that line and thereon erect as expeditiously as circumstance will permit, a Stockade most sufficient for the comfortable accommodation of one company, with necessary quarters, Barracks, Storehouses, Shops, Magazines and Hospital, conformable to the plan furnished by Major Long, which he will adapt to the nature of the position.
>
> The department of War, having ordered the establishment of a Post on the Arkansas with the men to prevent the Indian Tribes in that quarter continuing hostilities with each other, you are required to represent to the Chiefs and warriors of those tribes the wish of the President on this subject and use every legal means in your power to restore tranquility among them. Should the executive of this Territory call upon you to remove any portion or all of the Intruders from the public land in that Section of the country, you will take suitable measures for its accomplishment.[13]

Long and Bradford arrived on October 1 at the mouth of the Ohio where they met the company of recruits, of whom thirty were ill; they proceeded, however, and reached Arkansas Post

[12] Jackson to Secretary of War, August 19, 1818, AGO, ORD, WDF.

[13] Missouri State Historical Society, *Smith Collection,* Letter-book v, 42, O'Fallon to Bradford, September 15, 1817.

on the fifteenth. While Bradford was obliged by the sickness of his men to remain there, Long proceeded in a skiff with provisions for twenty-four days to ascend the Arkansas to the mouth of the Verdigris. After making astronomical observations there, he descended the Arkansas to the mouth of the Poteau, the proposed site of the new post, which had been called by the French, Belle Point. The garrison was named Cantonment Smith for General Thomas A. Smith, and was later known as Fort Smith. It was some time before Major Bradford was able to move his command, and they did not reach their new station at Cantonment Smith until December 25.[14]

Before Major Bradford's command could reach its station and prevent it, the little Indian army, which had been augmented by recruits from the Koasati, Tonkawa, and Comanche and eleven white men numbering six hundred warriors, in October, marched into the Osage country. The Eastern Cherokee had sent a company of warriors under a leader named John McLamore, who with rank of captain had headed a company of Cherokee in the Creek War under General Jackson.[15]

An account of the bloodshed that followed is furnished by Major Bradford in a letter he wrote January 1 to General Jackson reporting his arrival at his post. The Cherokee, he said, sought to make it appear that the attack was to avenge an incident of a year earlier: a party of Cherokee who were hunting on Osage land, stole some horses from the Osage; the latter pursued the thieves, and in retaking their horses killed

[14] *Ibid.*, Maj. Stephen H. Long to Gen. Thomas A. Smith, October 15, 1817; Bradford to Jackson, January 1, 1818, Jackson Papers, 7020. Bradford writes to his superior officer: "1st Jany 1818 Sir: I Have the Honor to report to you I arrived at this post on the 25th of last month with the detachment under my command.....I have them all comfortably situated together with a hospital for the sick, a store house for the Public, a provision house for the contractor, and am about a hut for myself."

[15] Joseph McMinn to Secretary of War, January 10, 1818, OIA, RCF, "Cherokee-Knoxville."

a Cherokee named The Choctaw, who was mounted on one of the stolen horses. But this killing only served as an excuse for the hostilities employed in effectuating their deliberate purpose to drive the Osage out of what is now eastern Oklahoma, and divide the country among themselves and their allies.

The strategy employed by the Cherokee, as reported by Major Bradford aroused his righteous indignation:

> The friendly letter they wrote to the Osage when they got near their town, inviting them to come to the lick[16] to make a treaty assuring them that there was only ten or fifteen of them that had come to make a treaty of peace. After getting an Osage chief to come down and smoke with them in friendship, to fall on him a lone man, and murder him is a species of barbarity and treachery unknown among Indians of the most uncivilized kind; this also under the eye of their cheifs Tulentuskey & Tuckatochee, the Black Fox and Bowls—the latter gave him the first stroke, immediately aided by several whites, Isaacs, the Chissoms and Williams. Isaacs and King, the whites among them, is more savage than the Cherokees themselves. The Choctaws and Chickasaws that is incorporated with the Cherokees together with the whites that live among them is a set of the most abandoned characters ever disgraced a gallows.

Clermont and the Osage warriors were away on a hunting trip; seizing this opportunity, the attacking force, numbering at the time 565 warriors, fell with typical savagery upon the Osage village occupied by a defenseless company of women, children, and old men who had been left at home.

> The Cherokees had several men wounded, the Deleways one killed. The Osage were persued and on their retreat lost 14 men killed, 69 Boys, women & children killed, several wounded in the retreat, and a hundred and 3 or four prisoners by the Cherokees, who also took a great quantity of Plunder. The town was Burnt and crops destroyed—was found in possession of the Osage 25

[16] The salt spring on the west side of Grand River where Union Mission was to be established soon afterward.

white scalps and a number of Indian scalps. This information is from young August Chouteau who has been down and seen several of the chiefs who were of the party.[17]

The casualties included several drowned in the Verdigris River where they were driven by their relentless pursuers in their desperate efforts to escape. The hapless prisoners were carried to the Cherokee Nation in the East, together with the horses and loot taken by the invaders. News of the great "victory" were carried in advance to the Eastern Cherokee Nation in November by a runner.[18] On receipt of the news the Eastern Cherokee indulged in war dances and other demonstrations of joy. Local tradition speaks of the massacre as the "battle of Claremore's Mound," referring to the hill near Clermont's Town; contemporary accounts say that the Osage fled from their "encampments, men, women, and children, to the mountains and vales where they were overwhelmed by their pursuers."

Out of that slaughter the Rev. Elias Cornelius preserved the tragic story of a little Osage girl whose parents had been killed by the Cherokee; touched by the account as told by her Cherokee captors on their return to Tennessee, Mr. Cornelius was instrumental in having her ransomed, and she was named Lydia Carter for the benefactress who paid one hundred dollars for her freedom. She remained for some years at Brainerd Mission where she was greatly loved, and the establishment was full of grief when the Government directed her return to her people in order to carry out the conditions of the treaty between the tribes.[19] She died on the way at the home of Mrs. Persis Lovely.

[17] William Clark to G. C. Sibley, November 11, 1817, Missouri Historical Society, Sibley Manuscripts, Vol. III. For further accounts of this massacre which occurred near the site of the present Claremore, Oklahoma, see *Niles' Weekly Register* (Baltimore), XIII, 80; Thwaites (ed), *op. cit.,* XIII, 192; XVII, 20; Foreman, *op. cit.,* p. 30.

[18] Houston to Secretary of War, November 24, 1817, AGO, ORD, WDF; McMinn to Secretary of War, November 25, 1817, *ibid.*

[19] Elias Cornelius, *The Little Osage Captive, an Authentic Narrative* (Boston,

Mr. Cornelius preserved the episode in a quaint little book.[20] Lydia was one of a number of children brought home as part of the loot promised the Eastern Cherokee for their assistance against the Osage. However the high-minded chief, Path Killer, sternly frowned on attempts to traffic in these children. Lydia's brother, also a captive, was redeemed by John Ross and placed in the mission at Brainerd where he was given the name of John Osage Ross. Evidently an attractive child, he was taken east by Governor Miller who introduced him to the President.[21]

About the time of the introduction of a military establishment and the Cherokee treaty of 1817, there were other signs of impending changes in this virgin wilderness. Frederick Bates, as secretary of Missouri Territory, on August 23, 1817, issued a license to "Chouteau and Rivar [Revoir]" to trade with the Osage Indians.[22] The year before, Colonel A. P. Chouteau with Julius De Mun returned from a disastrous trading expedition on which they had been imprisoned in Santa Fe by the Spaniards, who confiscated all their furs and merchandise. On his release from captivity, Chouteau determined to abandon the Indian trade in the Far West[23] and confine his activities among the Osage Indians.

Joseph Revoir, Chouteau's associate in this venture, was a member of the Osage tribe, the son of a French father;[24] his

1822); Rev. Elias Cornelius to Secretary of War, July 17, 1818, OIA, RCF; American Board of Commissioners for Foreign Missions, Congregational House, Boston, Manuscript Library, Vol. XVII, Journal of Brainerd Mission; *Missionary Herald*, XVII, 21.

[20] Cornelius, *op. cit.*

[21] This boy was reared by Governor Miller and taught the saddler's trade. In 1836, though he spoke only the English language, he was sent back to his tribe (American Board of Commissioners for Foreign Missions, *ibid.*, Vol. LXXIII, No. 213, Requa to Greene).

[22] Department of the Interior, General Land Office, "Missouri File," No. 18; Department of State 4760 B.R.L. A month later a license was issued by the same official to Hugh Glenn (*ibid.*); his trading house was at the mouth of the Verdigris.

[23] Foreman, *op. cit.*, pp. 77 ff.

mother was a captive member of the tribe called by the whites a Pawnee, but possibly a Kiowa or Wichita. The location of their trading post was where Salina, Oklahoma, is now. Chouteau did not remove to the site of their post, but Revoir was established there on the bank of Grand River. He continued to live there with his family until June 24, 1821, when a war party of Cherokee Indians under Walter Webber killed him.

In September, 1822, with the removal of White Hair's band from the Osage River to join the remainder of the tribe, Colonel Chouteau occupied the trading post and extensive improvements abandoned on Revoir's death, which he called "La Saline"; that year a trader's license was issued to A. P. Chouteau and P. L. Chouteau. The next year Chouteau enlarged his operations and purchased the trading house owned by Grand and Barbour just below the falls of the Verdigris,[25] and from that time operated both trading houses.[26] Licenses were subsequently issued to A. P. Chouteau to trade with the Osage at the "Big Saline[27] on the Neosho and at a place formerly occupied by a Mr. Barbour about half a mile below the Rapids of the Verdigrease."

More than two years before the establishment of the little garrison at Fort Smith, there was inaugurated on Grand River the first industrial enterprise in Oklahoma of which there is any record—the installation of kettles for the manufacture of salt at a spring on the west bank of the river. Major Amos Stoddard, who was commissioned in 1804 to take possession of Upper Louisiana under the treaty of cession, devoted several

[24] Revoir was "formerly a respectable inhabitant of Cote Sans Dessein on the Missouri" (Graham, "Graham Papers," 1821, Missouri Historical Society).

[25] This settlement, called the Three Forks of Mouth of the Verdigris, became a well-known trading post and was the location of a number of trading houses erected within four miles of the mouth; for a more extended account of this trading settlement see Foreman, *op. cit., passim.*

[26] Oklahoma State Historical Society. Union Mission Journal.

[27] So named because of the presence nearby of a large salt spring which in later years was operated for the manufacture of salt.

pages of his report[28] to description of salt springs and deposits in the recent purchase as bearing on its value; of this spring on Grand River he said:[29]

> One spring of this nature, remarkable for its size and the productive quality of its water, deserves to be noted in this place. It is situated on Grand River..... The Indians and Indian traders procure their salt from it..... About four hundred Osages living near the mouth of the Verdigris river, a short distance from the spring, obtain their supplies of salt from it, and it is situated on a navigable stream.

In the early part of 1815 Major William L. Lovely granted a license to Bernard R. Mouille for himself and on behalf of his company to operate these salt springs.[30] Lovely wrote the Secretary of War:

> .... You will also find a letter of some Gentlemen To whom I had given permission at the particular request of the Osages and Cherokee Indians to Work a Salt Springs near the Osage Village; an Establishment of that Kind is indispensably necessary To the convenience of the inhabitants of their part; I therefore command your patronage & hope that my having given them permission will meet with your approbation.

Mouille wrote Lovely of the difficulties of installing and operating his works:

> .... The necessary untensils must be brought from a Considerable Distance to the mouth of the Arkansas, thence up that River Seven Hundred & fifty miles Which has in that distance many Rappids, Ripples & falls which render the navigation of the River

[28] Maj. Amos Stoddard, *Sketches, Historical and Descriptive, of Louisiana* (Philadelphia, 1812).

[29] *Ibid.*, p. 400. On a map of a proposed survey of Missouri Territory attached to a letter of April 20, 1814, from William Russell to William Rector, at this approximate location is legended "Salt Springs" (Department of State, Territorial Records).

[30] OIA, RCF, Mouille to Lovely, May 12, 1815; Lovely to Secretary of War, May 27, 1815; Lovely to Meigs, May 29, 1815.

Extraordinary Difficult. Thence up the Six Bull[31] River fifty miles, a River but little better than the Arkansas, the Navigation of the River being a great Consideration & one which will put a great obstacle to the working of those works to advantage. Provisions will have to be brought from a distance of Three hundred & Fifty Miles up the Arkansas.

To procure men to live at a distance of 300 miles from any white Settlement Very high wages will have to be given them for no human will live that far in the wilderness without great encouragement. The danger which there is to be subject to the caprices &c of a nation of Indians living close at hand the Depredation which will of course be Committed By them must be Considered. The price of salt at present on this River is from $25 to $30 per Barrel. This shows what difficulty there must be where Salt bears that price & this place[32] is only half way up to the Works from the Mouth of this River.

Mouille's equipment was apparently installed at the spring still flowing copiously about five miles northeast of Mazie, Mayes County, Oklahoma, on the west bank of Grand River. Whether or not they were associated with Mouille, David Earheart and Johnson Campbell later appear to be the operators of the salt works there and the place was noted on old maps as "Campbell's Salt Works,"[33] though sometimes it was spoken of as Earheart's.[34]

[31] In the early days the Grand River was known by this singular name given by the French hunters and trappers. English-speaking whites called it the Grand River; Neosho is the Osage name for the same river. The original Osage pronunciation was "Ni-ozho"—"Ni," river; "ozho," the main (authority of Dr. Francis la Flesche, Bureau of American Ethnology). The missionaries at Union Mission said that "....Neosho, the name of our river signifies 'pure water'" (American Board of Commissioners for Foreign Missions, *ibid.*, Vol. LXXIII, Vaill to Greene, July 26, 1833). "Grand River, more prettily and distinctly called by its Indian name Neosho (water-white or clear)" (P. St. G. Cooke, *Scenes and Adventures in the Army* [Philadelphia, 1857], p. 236).

[32] Mouille was probably writing this letter at Lovely's Agency in the modern Pope County, Arkansas.

[33] "Map of Arkansas Territory," *American Atlas* (Carey and Lee: Philadelphia, 1822), p. 35; here "Campbell Salt Works" is shown on the west bank of

The perils of this wilderness were not alone from the Indians; Campbell was murdered about the first of May, 1819, and David Earheart and William G. Childers were charged with the crime;[35] they and a witness named John Bounyon were taken into custody by Samuel Lemmons who upon his own responsibility guarded them for three weeks and then delivered them to Hewes Scull, sheriff of the county of Arkansas, at Arkansas Post. This, probably the first criminal case arising within the present Oklahoma to be taken into an American court of law, found the authorities ill prepared; after Lemmons captured the murderers and conducted them to the seat of government of the newly formed territory, the governor and judges recommended that he be paid $132 "for his great trouble and expense in securing and guarding the prisoners aforesaid"; and on August 3, 1819, one of the first acts of the Arkansas Territorial General Assembly made the desired appropriation. On the same day the Assembly enacted a measure reciting that

WHEREAS it is represented to the Governor and Judges of the Territory of Arkansas John Bounyon, David Earheart, and William G. Childers stand charged with the murder of Johnson Campbell and that they are delivered to Hewes Scull,[36] Sheriff of Arkansas,

"Grand or Neosho River," and there is no mention of any works on the east bank; the town of Clermo's Band, Clermont's or Claremore's Town, is shown on the Verdigris northwest of Campbell's.

[34] It was known as Earheart's Salt Works in the summer of 1817, according to the *Missouri Gazette* of August 23, 1817; this paper said that the Osage had built a fort there as a defense against the contemplated attack by the Cherokee. This was an error, for the Cherokee attack that autumn took by surprise the Osage old men, women, and children at their town near the Verdigris.

[35] Nuttall met Childers at the Cadron thirty-eight miles above Little Rock, and attempted to hire him as a woodsman and hunter; but afterwards congratulated himself on his failure; this was on April 1, about a month before the "remorseless villain" Childers "shot and barbarously scalped Mr. Campbell for the purpose of obtaining his little property" (Thwaites [ed.], *op. cit.*, XIII, 242).

[36] Hughes (or Hewes) Scull was appointed sheriff of Arkansas County of Missouri Territory, November 20, 1817.

and that the jail of said county is unsafe and unfit for the confinement of said prisoners,

and directing the guards to convey them to the county of Lawrence and confine them in the jail there.[37]

Timothy Flint says[38] the prisoners

. . . . who were supposed to have murdered their partner on the Saline far up the Arkansas, under circumstances of atrocious barbarity, were brought up to the post[39] while I was there. Never were seen more diabolical countenances. I spoke seriously to them, but they held all council, reproof and fear in utter derision. They were imprisoned and would undoubtedly have been executed, but they contrived in a few days to escape.

In June, 1819, Nuttall visited the Campbell salt works,

. . . . now indeed lying idle, and nearly deserted in consequence of the murder of Mr. Campbell, by Earheart, his late partner, and two accomplices in their employ.[40] [He gives a good picture of the] saline, which appeared to be a gravely, alluvial basin, of about an acre in extent, and destitute of all vegetation. A small fresh water brook, now scarcely running, passed through this area, and the salt water, quite pellucid, issued copiously to the surface in various directions. At one place it boiled up out of a focus of near six inches diameter, emitting fetid bubbles of sulphuretted hydrogen, which deposited a slight scum of sulphur. All the springs are more or less hepatic, which circumstance is attributable to a bed of bituminous and sulphuretted slate-clay, visible on the margin of the stream, and, probably, underlaid by coal through which

[37] United States Department of State, *Early Territorial Records*; at the time these early acts of the Territory of Arkansas were examined by the Author, the State Department was engaged in assembling all such territorial records for publication and reference; *Arkansas Gazette*, February 5, 1820, p. 2, cols. 1 and 2. Davidsonville was then the county seat of Lawrence County; this town, no longer to be seen on the maps, was at the junction of Spring and Black rivers.

[38] Timothy Flint, *Recollections of the Last Ten Years in the Valley of the Mississippi* (Boston, 1826), p. 270.

[39] Arkansas Post; for an account of this, the first capital of Arkansas Territory, see Foreman, *op. cit.*, p. 15 n.

[40] Thwaites (ed.), *op. cit.*, p. 242.

the water rises to the surface. . . . . The only well dug upon the premises for salt water, was about five feet deep, and quarried through a bed of dark colored limestone, containing shell and nodules of black hornstone, similar to the chert of Derbyshire. . . . . When the works were in operation, 120 bushels of salt were manufactured in a week, and the water is said to be so strong, that after the second boiling, it became necessary to remove the lye. No mother water, or any thing almost but what is volatile, appears mixed with this salt, which is of the purest whiteness on the first boiling and only takes about 80 gallons of water to produce a bushel.[41]

Mark Bean of Tennessee came to Crawford County[42] in 1818 and acquired the salt kettles at the abandoned Campbell's salt works; these were transported down the Grand and Arkansas rivers, then up the Illinois and overland a mile or two and installed on a small stream, now called Salt Branch, on an old Indian trail over which the military road was later surveyed and constructed. The next year Bean and a man named Sanders secured from the governor of Arkansas Territory a license to operate these salt springs.[43] Captain Bell, who visited them in September, 1820, while traveling from the mouth of the Verdigris to Fort Smith, says of these works:

[41] *Ibid.* A map made in 1822 by R. Graham and forwarded by Governor Miller to the Secretary of War designated a place below Union Mission as "Priors Salt Works." This was near Nathaniel Pryor's home where he died in 1831 (Miller to Calhoun, May, 1822, AGO, ORD, WDF).

[42] This part of Oklahoma was soon after included in Crawford County, Arkansas.

[43] Arbuckle to Calhoun, October 27, 1823, AGO, Old Files Division (referred to hereafter as OFD), 64 A 23. The Cherokee Indians, assuming that Lovely's Purchase was intended for them, on January 14, 1820, authorized John W. Flowers who was intermarried in the tribe, James Rogers, and John L. McCarty to operate the springs for the manufacture of salt. The year before Flowers had erected some improvements at the springs; after expending considerable labor and money in their preparations they were dispossessed by Bean and Sanders whose license from the Government gave them a better claim to them; the Indians long cherished a grievance for depriving them of these springs (Jolly to Cherokee delegation—instructions, March 25, 1821, AGO, OFD, WDF).

They are situated on a small creek which flows into the Illinois creek about a mile below, and at the distance of about seven miles from the Arkansas. Mr. Bean commenced his operations in the spring, and has already a neat farmhouse on the Illinois, with a considerable stock of cattle, hogs, and poultry, and several acres of Indian corn. Near the springs he has erected a neat log-house, and a shed for the furnace; but his kettles, which were purchased of the proprietors of the Neosho establishment, were not yet fixed.[44]

Passing over the trail from Fort Smith to the mouth of the Verdigris, Jacob Fowler crossed Illinois River

.... and about one mile farther stoped for the night at Beens Salt Workes,—this is the Second night Since We left the fort—the Workes one small Well With a few kittles about 55 gallons of Watter make a bushil of Salt and the Well affords Watter to boil the kittles about three days in the Weake Been and Sanders Has permission of the govern [government] to Worke the Salt Spring —they Sell the Salt at one dollar per bushil.[45]

Under Bean's management these works produced a large output of salt which contributed much to the comfort of the white settlements along the Arkansas River. The *Arkansas Gazette* said: ".... we have salt of the first quality, and produced at the saline on the Illinois, about 50 miles from Fort Smith in great abundance."[46] In 1822 on the expiration of Bean's license, Governor Miller extended it for three years,[47] and in 1825, Governor Izard extended it for twelve months and said:

.... Your proposal of making over to the use of the United States all the Improvements executed by you at these works (with the exception of the Iron Pots and Boilers) in three years from

[44] Thwaites (ed.), *op. cit.* XVI, 286.

[45] Elliott Coues (ed.), *The Journal of Jacob Fowler,* p. 2. Mr. Chapman passed these salt works on November 10, 1820 (Morse, *op. cit.,* Appendix, p. 220).

[46] *Arkansas Gazette* (Little Rock), July 23, 1822, p. 3, col. 1.

[47] Arbuckle to Calhoun, October 26, 1823, AGO, OFD, 64 A 23.

this time, on condition of having the use of the Property rent-free during that Period, will be laid before the Department of War. It is however stipulated that you shall deliver at least two thousand Bushels of marketable salt at this place [Little Rock] for a price not to exceed $1 50/100 pr. bushel at any time within the first year after this Date should you be called upon by the executive to do so.[48]

Fifteen miles above Campbell's salt works and on the opposite side of Grand River is a salt spring that was visited by Washington Irving in 1832. It is difficult to fix the time when this spring, where Salina, Oklahoma, is now, began to be worked. After describing Campbell's salt works, Nuttall says in 1819:[49] ".... Mr. S. informed me, that on the opposite side of the river, and two miles from hence, another strong salt spring breaks out through the incumbent gravel; and that there are other productive springs 25 miles above," but he says nothing of their being operated. The next year Captain Bell, at the mouth of the Verdigris, says:[50]

.... We also learned, that at the distance of twenty-five miles was a copious salt spring, lately worked with the permission of the Indians, but at present it is abandoned, and the apparatus removed..... Mr. Nuttall—in his interesting *Journal of Travels in the Arkansas Territory,* has given an excellent account of this saline.

But Bell apparently had not heard of any other spring in that country being worked.

When this salt spring at Salina was seen by Lieutenant Hood in 1828 he reported:

.... About 1 mile S.E. of Mr. Chouteau's on the E. side of the Neosho, there is a salt spring, rising from a lime-stone rock covering from 1 to 2 acres; several openings are made in this rock by

---

[48] Izard to Bean, August 7, 1825, OIA, RCF.
[49] Thwaites (ed.), *op. cit.,* XIII, 242.
[50] *Ibid.,* XVI, 283.

the water, which has a strong saline taste. . . . . The quantity of salt which this water would yield is not known, as no experiment of that kind has been made but it is probable that it would produce abundantly.[51]

These salt springs were included in the reservations made by treaty in 1825 to some of the half-breed Osage members of the family of Colonel A. P. Chouteau who lived nearby. In 1830 Chouteau sold them to Samuel Houston who believed they would make him rich;[52] but finding that a white man would not be permitted to work them, he sold them to Thompson and Drennan.[53] The springs were soon after acquired by John Rogers, a Cherokee, who called his home at the salt works Grand Saline; there he made salt until the springs were taken from him by act of the Cherokee Council of October 30, 1843,[54] declaring all salines in the Cherokee Nation to be public property except the one granted to Sequoyah by the treaty of 1828.

[51] *U.S. House Report No. 87,* pp. 28, 29, Twentieth Congress, second session.
[52] Foreman, *op. cit.,* p. 188.
[53] *Ibid.,* p. 260.
[54] *Laws of the Cherokee Nation,* edition of 1868.

V

CHEROKEE IMMIGRANTS AT WAR WITH THE OSAGE, 1809-21

BY the treaty of 1817 the Government agreed to give the Cherokee in Arkansas as much land as they relinquished in the East, to provide boats for the emigration of those who were willing to move to Arkansas, and to supply the poorer members of the tribe with guns, kettles, beaver traps, and ammunition. It also provided for the removal of all white persons from the lands to be surveyed for them in Arkansas, except Mrs. Persis Lovely who, at the request of the Indians, was to be permitted to reside there during her life. She desired to remain in her wilderness home within the present Pope County, Arkansas, endeared to her by its association with her dead husband, Major William L. Lovely.

Immediately upon the execution of the treaty the commissioners hastened to contract for the construction of sixty flat-boats[1] for use in the removal of the Cherokee, to be delivered between the mouth of the Little Tennessee and Sequatchie rivers,[2] and for the delivery of four tons of lead, five hundred rifles, traps, kettles, blankets, and twenty-five hundred pounds of powder. The large majority of the tribe under the leadership of their chief, Path Killer, resolutely opposed the efforts of Governor McMinn to enrol for emigration but the removal of those who wished to go was expedited, so that they[3] were soon

[1] The contract was made with W. Rockhold; the boats were to be sixty feet long by twelve feet wide, and two-thirds of each boat was to be covered; two side oars and a steering oar were provided. The contractor was paid $2.00 per lineal foot for each boat (Rockhold to Graham, August 6, 1817, AGO, ORD, WDF).

[2] *American State Papers,* "Indian Affairs," II, 144.

[3] During the summer, before the treaty was ratified, some of the Indians requested means of transportation to Arkansas. Colonel Meigs furnished them

on the way to their new home.[4] Among these were John Rogers
and John Jolly,[5] a brother of Tahlonteskee upon whose death
Jolly became chief of the Arkansas Cherokee, soon after his
arrival in the West. In February, 1818, Jolly began his descent

some flat-bottom boats, provisions, blankets, powder, lead, flints, and brass
kettles of from two to four gallons regarded by the Indians as indispensable. In
1817 John Rogers ".... a white man of more than forty years residence in the
Cherokee Nation has removed to the Arkansas with a very numerous tribe of
connections" (OIA, RCF, "Cherokee Knoxville," Gov. Joseph McMinn to Secretary of War, November 11, 1817). Rogers departed October 18, 1817, with
thirty-one emigrants whom he delivered on April 18, 1818, to their new home
on the Arkansas (*ibid.*). A considerable number of Cherokee who had sold their
property and incurred expense in preparations to remove, abandoned their plans
whn ordered to do so by their chief, Path Killer (*U. S. House Executive Document No. 136,* Eighteenth Congress, first session).

[4] In February, 1818, McMinn started nineteen boats down the Tennessee
River, carrying four hundred Cherokee emigrants (McMinn to Calhoun, February 28, 1818, OIA, RCF, "Special File" No. 131). In the Journal of Brainerd
Mission was frequent mention during 1818 and 1819 of pupils taken from school
to join the emigration to Arkansas (American Board of Commissioners for Foreign Missions, *ibid.*, Vols. XIV and XV, *passim*). A prominent Cherokee named
The Glass with his family began the descent of the Tennessee in the autumn of
1818; but the boat furnished by the Government was so near worthless that it
had to be abandoned one hundred miles down stream. After some weeks The
Glass purchased another boat and on January 16, 1819, he hoisted the American
flag and at the head of a party of 167 again began the descent of the river. Warm
weather overtook them before they reached their destination as a result of
which there was much sickness in the party. The son and one of the wives of
The Glass died and soon after the end of the journey death overtook The Glass
also (OIA, RCF, "Cherokee West Agency," Meigs to Calhoun, November 15,
1819; *ibid.*, "Cherokee [West] Dardanelle," Rogers to Meigs, October 30, 1819).

[5] When Nuttall stopped among the Cherokee in Arkansas in 1819, he wrote
of Jolly: "In the evening, the brother of their late principal chief Tallantusky,
arrived here, accompanied by his wife and two or three other Indians. He last
year took leave of the old nation in the Mississippi territory, and embarked
with the emigrants, who are yet far from forming a majority of the nation.
Being a half Indian, and dressed as a white man, I should scarcely have distinguished him from an American, except by his language. He was very plain
and unassuming in his dress and manners; a Franklin amongst his countrymen,
and effectionately called the 'beloved' father..... Mr. D. who had in the Mississippi territory become acquainted with Jolly, the chief, tells me that his word
is inviolable, and that his generosity knew no bounds, but the limitation of his
means" (Thwaites [ed.], *op. cit.,* XIII, 181 ff.).

of the Tennessee River[6] in command of a flotilla of thirteen flatboats and four keel boats laden with Cherokee families and their property. He was armed with a passport over the signature and seal of their venerable agent, Return J. Meigs, bespeaking for the party friendly treatment by the civilians and military with whom they might come in contact. There were 331 persons in the party of whom 108 were warriors, each armed with a new rifle; they carried provisions for seventy days, as it was supposed they would require that much time to make the journey to their new home on the Arkansas.[7]

These migrations were hazardous undertakings; many whites regarded the Indians as having no rights and made a practice of stealing their horses when they were on their migrations; some Cherokee who came from as far as Georgia reported that they had "nothing to dread except the danger of being plundered and murdered in passing through a white settlement in Alabama Territory of about 70 miles in length," which was

[6] On the eve of his departure for the West, Jolly addressed Mr. Calhoun: "....Father you must not think that by removing we shall return to the savage life, you have learned us to be herdsmen & cultivators, and to spin and weave. Our women will raise the cotton & the Indigo & spin & weave cloth to cloath our children. By means of schools here, numbers of our young people can read and write, they can read what we call the Preachers Book sent from the great spirit to all people. It is the wish of our people that you will send us a branch of the Missionary schools, or some other teachers. We shall settle more compactly on our new lands than we were here, this will be of advantage in teaching our Children. We find that by intermarriages with our white brethren we are gradually becoming one people, these connections are already numerous & are increasing.

"We shall live in peace & friendship with all the Indian tribes west of the Mississippi river if in our power, & it is our wish that our difference with the Osage Nation may be amicably adjusted. John Jolly, a Cherokee Chief his Mark x Cherokee Nation 28th January 1818 Return J. Meigs present" (OIA, RCF).

[7] Meigs to Calhoun, February 19, 1818, OIA, RCF, "Cherokee Agency"; Colonel Meigs said that Jolly was "....a discrete man possessed of considerable personal property besides his plantation here." He had a precedent for the allowance of provisions for the journey "....having in 1811 sent a boat to the Cherokee settlement on that river where it arrived in 66 days."

also feared by the white travelers.[8] In November, 1818, twenty-two families of Cherokee emigrants who had been supplied with boats and provisions, began their descent of the Tennessee River, after starting their horses overland. The water was too low for them to pass Muscle Shoals; there they consumed their provisions and became destitute while waiting for the ripening of little crops they planted near the river to provide them the means of resuming their journey the next year.[9] The boats purchased of the contractor were delivered before a sufficient number of emigrants were ready for them, and they were permitted to ride at the river bank in the sun until they became all but worthless;[10] and the travelers at Muscle Shoals were compelled to wait for new boats before they could proceed.

At the time of the execution of the pretended treaty of 1817, there were a few more than two thousand Cherokee in the West. Royce estimates that by 1819 the number had increased to six thousand.[11] He bases his estimates on the figures reported by McMinn,[12] which are not dependable because McMinn, in his zeal to show results to his superiors at Washington, reported hundreds if not thousands who were persuaded to enrol but who afterward refused to depart; some were induced against their inclination to enrol, and many others who really wished to emigrate, were intimidated by the dominant faction of the tribe into refusing to leave. The Cherokee themselves said that by February, 1819, not more than 3,500 had removed.[13]

Governor McMinn of Tennessee spent the year 1818 in acrimonious contention with the Cherokee chief and other leaders

[8] McMinn to Calhoun, September 28, 1818, *ibid.*

[9] Lewis Ross and others, June 22, 1819, OIA, RCF.

[10] Meigs to Calhoun, November 15, 1819, OIA, RCF.

[11] Charles C. Royce, *The Cherokee Nation of Indians,* Smithsonian Institution, Bureau of American Ethnology, p. 218.

[12] McMinn reported that, prior to November 15, 1818, a total of 5,291 persons had removed or enrolled to go (*ibid.,* p. 218 n.).

[13] *Ibid.;* in 1830 Sam Houston wrote that the western Cherokee ".... in the census are rated at some seventeen or eighteen hundred, when in fact they exceed

of the tribe who bitterly assailed the Government for the means employed in procuring the pretended treaty and the policy and efforts used to carry it into effect. McMinn, who dealt extensively in trickery sanctioned by the Government in its relations with the Indians, frequently gave out figures of those enrolled for removal, compiled to persuade the Cherokee that they were waging a losing fight. By the third article of the treaty the Government agreed to take a census of the Cherokee on the Arkansas and those east of the Mississippi who enrolled for removal; this was to be done in June, 1818, but the next month McMinn wrote to the Secretary of War that he had postponed the census until November as ". . . . that period would keep back a comparison of numbers until next spring."[14]

A delegation of Western Cherokee headed by Tahlonteskee[15] proceeded to Washington in the winter of 1817 to convey a memorial to the Secretary of War, asking among other things that they be recognized as a separate and independent people with power to set up their own government after the manner of their brethren in the East. They also requested a more definite understanding about the boundaries of their country and an outlet through the Osage country to the hunting grounds to the west; or as Takatoka expressed it "we want a clear opening to the setting of the sun" and "no white people to be in front of us."[16] Under the direction of Governor McMinn of Tennes-

four thousand in number" (Houston to Cass, "Wigwam Neosho 13th June, 1830," AGO, OFD). Captain Vashon, Cherokee agent, reported in 1833 that there were only four thousand Cherokee in Indian territory not counting some who resided on the White and Red rivers.

[14] *American State Papers,* "Indian Affairs," II, 529.

[15] Nuttall spelled his name Tallantusky; to the missionaries he was To-lin-tis-kee; to Sam Houston's ear the name was Tah-lohn-tus-ky; and it was spelled in many other ways by his contemporaries. Takatoka was known to the missionaries as Ta-kau-to-caugh. This venerable chief was selected to accompany the delegation to Washington but his illness prevented.

[16] Takatoka and fifteen other chiefs to the President, August 3, 1819, OIA, RCF, "Cherokee (West) Nation." The Secretary of War wrote Governor Clark to comply with the wishes of the Cherokee as far as possible and to restore

see this delegation was joined at Knoxville by Touchaler and The Glass of the Eastern Cherokee,[17] and all under the guidance of Sam Houston left Knoxville on January 16 and proceeded to Washington.

On their return to Tennessee, Houston bore to McMinn a letter from Secretary Calhoun, of which the following is a part:

> . . . . By the direction of the President very considerable presents were distributed to the delegation. To Toulonteskee one thousand dollars, and to each of the others five hundred dollars. This will no doubt have important effects in aiding operations now going on; in fact I trust that your excellency will see in all that has been done, the zeal with which this department under the direction of the President, has entered into the execution of the late treaty which contains stipulations so important to Tennessee and the rest of the Union.

To this frank recital of double-dealing with the Indians, McMinn wrote to Mr. Calhoun felicitating him on the fact that they were of such uniform views on the subject of dealing with the Indians; and, he added:

> . . . . I am truly pleased to learn that the usual plans had been taken with the Chiefs in purchasing their friendship, for such has been the 'course pursued with the natives for time immemorial, and corrupt as it may appear, we are compelled to have to resort to the measure. They have disclosed the secret to me with much gratification.[18]

The President had authorized the payment of these sums to the Indians.[19]

---

peace between them and the Osage; for he said: ". . . . the President is anxious to hold out every inducement to the Cherokees and the other Southern nations of Indians to emigrate to the west of the Mississippi" (Calhoun to Clark, May 8, 1818, OIA, RCF).

17 Jackson to Secretary of War, July 9, 1817, OIA, RCF, "Cherokee Agency."

18 Joseph McMinn to J. C. Calhoun, Knoxville, April 12, 1818, OIA, RCF, "Special File" No. 131.

19 *American State Papers*, "Indian Affairs," II, 478.

The Cherokee, perhaps influenced by the white men among them, coveted the fine land in what is now eastern Oklahoma, then possessed by the Osage; the beautiful Illinois, Neosho, and Verdigris rivers and their tributaries were rich in beaver, the forests abounded with bear, and the country was a hunters' paradise. Some of the valuable saline springs in the country were being used for the manufacture of salt, and the Cherokee were operating lead mines there. The emigrant Indians pressed the war against the Osage to gain possession of their valuable and beautiful country.[20] The conflicts between them occurred on the Osage land; Cherokee hunters who were killed were usually trespassers on the land of the Osage; the home of the Cherokee down the Arkansas was never invaded in force by the Osage. In order to accomplish their purpose the Cherokee bargained craftily with the Quapaw, Shawnee, Delaware, Chickasaw, and Choctaw for their assistance, with the promise to give them some of the land they might secure by conquest.

They told Major Bradford that they desired peace, but this he knew was false; on the contrary, they were much dissatisfied with the location of the garrison, since it would interfere with their plans of aggression against the Osage. Having by their latest stroke, as they believed, dislodged the Osage from the region coveted by them, they set about consolidating their gains and making the division agreed upon with their allies living among them who were relied upon to help hold it against the Osage; to this end the delegation headed by Tahlonteskee had departed for Washington to take the matter up with the Secretary of War. In their conferences in Washington in February, 1818, the Cherokee displayed a shrewd knowledge of the custom of warring white nations of despoiling the loser to reward the victor. On that occasion Tahlonteskee delivered a

---

[20] Bradford to Jackson, January 1, 1818, Jackson Papers, 7020. The Cherokee told Colonel Meigs that they "intend to possess by conquest the country on the upper Arkansas" (Meigs to McMinn, August 7, 1818, OIA, RCF, "Cherokee Agency").

talk to Governor Clark, who had been directed to make peace
between the tribes; this talk disclosed the Cherokee chief as
an astute leader and advocate, and a man of parts:

> We .... submitted to many insults from the Osage who stole
> our property & killed my people—and when forced into a war with
> that Nation, I did not expect a return of property as they had
> none to give, but my object was to be remunerated by an accession
> of their country. I hope (if you make peace between us) that the
> Osage in satisfaction for our claims on them, give up country—
> we do not wish to be cramped by them. . . . . The Osage could not
> be restrained by the U. States nor persuaded into a compliance
> with justice. War was the necessary result which did not take place
> without reflection and a candid declaration on my part. . . . . . If we
> went to war it would be for country & honor—we expect country
> in payment for the various losses we have experienced, &c. If I
> had been unfortunate in war, our claims for an outlet would not
> have been as good against them, perhaps, as it is in our present
> relation with that Tribe.[21]

The campaign of the year before having resulted in such a
decisive "victory" over the Osage, albeit the vanquished were
old men, women, and children, the Cherokee insisted that they
were entitled to the fruits of victory and demanded the Osage
land in what is now eastern Oklahoma; mainly they desired
this land for its natural wealth, but they also wanted it as the
outlet to the buffalo grounds farther to the west, promised to
them by President Monroe. Secretary Calhoun took their view
of the subject and instructed Governor Clark that the Osage,
who had been beaten in the war, should be compelled to yield
part of their land as an outlet to the west or should grant the
Cherokee undisturbed passage to and from the western hunting grounds.[22]

During the spring and summer of 1818, the emigrating Indians, who came up the Arkansas, located on the south side of

[21] OIA, RCF, "Cherokee (West) Tolentiskee," February 21, 1818.
[22] Calhoun to Clark, May 8, 1818, OIA, RCF.

that stream instead of joining the earlier settlers living on the north side, which was considered by the Government as the only land belonging to the Cherokee. Soon after the arrival of John Jolly, he accompanied other leading men of the tribe and their agent, Reuben Lewis, to Fort Smith to enlist the assistance of Major Bradford in negotiations for peace with the Osage; but their venerable war chief, Takatoka, refused to join in these measures.[23] Governor Clark, who was instructed to aid in restoring peace between the tribes, wrote:

> . . . . As it was thought by both parties that no treaty they could make would be considered as reciprocally binding upon them unless it should be ratified and confirmed in my presence, I invited both tribes to send a deputation of eight or ten of their principal men to meet in council at this place. The Osage chiefs and considerable men (to the number of about sixty) arrived early last month and I have awaited the coming of the Cherokees which was not until last week.[24]

With the attendance of the chiefs and headmen of the Great and Little Osage at St. Louis, a treaty[25] was made September 25, 1818, by which the Osage ceded to the United States approximately the area known as Lovely's Purchase[26] for no other consideration than the satisfaction of claims amounting to $4,000, held by white people for alleged robberies committed by the Osage. Thus there passed to the United States the lovely country coveted by the Cherokee, which was actually held for their use as a hunting ground and western outlet for the next ten years, until in 1828 it was conveyed to them by a formal grant.

A few days later, on October 6, in the presence of Governor Clark, the Osage and the Cherokee and their allies, the Dela-

---

[23] Meigs to McMinn, August 7, 1818, OIA, RCF, "Cherokee Agency."

[24] Wm. H. Clark to John C. Calhoun, October, 1818, OIA, RCF, "Cherokees. —St. Louis."

[25] Kappler, *op. cit.*, II, 116.

[26] Ceded in 1816 by the Arkansas Osage.

wares and Shawnees, entered into a treaty by which they mutually agreed to a permanent peace; in this treaty the Cherokee further undertook to meet the Osage at Fort Smith as early as possible in the following spring and to give up to them all the prisoners they or their allies had taken from the Osage in the war. The Osage made a similar promise and also agreed that the Cherokee and their allies might have an undisturbed passage or outlet to the hunting grounds west of their home, with permission to hunt on the lands claimed by them south of Arkansas River. This treaty was accepted by forty-six Osage, twelve Cherokee, and one Shawnee chief.[27]

In order to gain greater security in their new home against the hostile Osage, the Cherokee, with the consent of the Government, made overtures to the Shawnee and Delaware then living in the vicinity of Cape Girardeau to relinquish their land and join the Western Cherokee on the Arkansas;[28] similar overtures were made to the Oneida of New York.[29]

Before the treaty conference was held in St. Louis, during the summer of 1818, a party of Cherokee attacked a larger party of Osage.[30] In the same season, Nuttall says, the Osage called a general conference at their village on the Verdigris which was attended by Shawnee, Delaware, Creeks, Quapaw, Kansa, and Foxes; on this occasion the Osage presented their guests with three hundred horses. To the overtures of the Osage the Foxes said they would join them against any nation at any time. But the hosts said the Creeks had insulted them by bringing spoons in their pockets, evidently to avoid the Osage custom of dipping their hands in the vessel containing food.[31]

[27] *American State Papers,* "Indian Affairs," II, 172; Governor Miller to Secretary of War, June 20, 1820, OIA, RCF.

[28] The delegation of Western Cherokee in the spring of 1818 requested of the President permission to do this; and the President directed Governor Clark to ascertain whether the Shawnee and Delaware were disposed to make the change of location (Calhoun to Clark, May 8, 1818, OIA, RCF).

[29] Royce, *op. cit.,* p. 221.

[30] Meigs to McMinn, August 7, 1818, OIA, RCF, "Cherokee Agency."

After the treaty at St. Louis had been concluded and the Cherokee were returning to their home, they encountered near the White River a party of Osage from whom they stole forty horses; the Osage in council then determined to renew the war unless the Cherokee at once gave up the Osage prisoners, whose return was promised the next spring. Information of their plans was carried to Fort Smith by Captain Pryor, who induced the Indians to wait until his return. Major Bradford then visited Clermont's Town, and by his intervention with both tribes averted a renewal of hostilities. He said there were "a number of Sacks, Ioways, Mohaws and Zotos among the Osages urging them to commence hostilities and offering their assistance." Besides the theft of the Osage horses, the Cherokee had killed four and wounded three of their animals, which was regarded by the Indians as an act of war. After the Cherokee had got possession of some of the horses of the Osage, their victims retaliated by stealing the furs cached by the Cherokee.[32]

Only in the summer of 1819 were the Osage informed that the Cherokee were prepared to redeem their promise to return the prisoners. On July 27 Clermont and some of the other Osage chiefs arrived at the settlement[33] at the mouth of the Verdigris, on their way to Fort Smith to receive the prisoners from the Cherokee. A week later they returned unsuccessful, with the report that under the pretext of attending to their harvest the Cherokee had postponed the meeting until September.

The Osage, eager to greet their relatives, arrived punctually

[31] Thwaites (ed.), *op. cit.,* XIII, 248; it is doubtful whether the Osage had so many horses to give away; the Quapaw, Kansa, and Foxes were in a measure allies of the Osage; the Shawnee and Delaware had fought against them, but doubtless desired to conciliate them so as to be allowed to hunt beaver on the Neosho.

[32] Bradford to Calhoun, February 4, 1819, AGO, ORD, WDF. The road from St. Louis crossed the White River at the site of the present Batesville, Arkansas. Schoolcraft says the Cherokee made off with twenty Osage horses on this occasion (Henry R. Schoolcraft, *Tour into the Interior of Missouri and Arkansaw* [London, 1821], p. 38).

[33] Thwaites, *op. cit.,* XIII, 247.

at Fort Smith in September but not the Cherokee, who sent
word that the prisoners who were mostly women were adopted
into the tribe and wished to remain with it. Tallai and Clermont
insisted on compliance with the treaty and the Cherokee were
ordered by the post commander to produce the prisoners in ten
days. The eleventh day arrived without the appearance of the
Cherokee or the prisoners and the disappointed Osage started
on their return home. Only Tallai and Clermont remained behind. The next day the Cherokee appeared and messengers
were sent to secure the return of the Osage.

The Osage were headed by Clermont, Tallai, and Mad Buffalo, accompanied by their friend Captain Nathaniel Pryor.
Takatoka, the venerable war chief[34] of the Cherokee, presided
at the meeting. The Cherokee continued reluctant to produce
the prisoners, some of whom had married their captors. Nuttall,
who had descended from the Verdigris to Fort Smith, describes
the parting of one of the Osage women from her Cherokee
husband.

> Their parting was a scene of sorrow; the Cherokee promised to
> go to the village, and ask her of her father, she also plead with the
> chiefs to stay, but Clermont, unmoved by her tears and entreaties,
> answered, "your father and mother lament you; it is your duty to
> go and see them. If the Cherokee loves you, he will not forget to
> come for you."[35]

But the Cherokee did not deliver all the Osage prisoners as
they had agreed, though they continued to hunt on the lands
on which freedom was granted by the Osage as a consideration
for the return of their people. In retaliation, in February, 1820,
a war party of Osage under Mad Buffalo, son of Clermont, who

---

[34] This interesting old Cherokee chief was also called "the beloved man." In
1828 the name of the post-office at Dardanelle where the Cherokee lived was
changed to "Te ka to ka" (*Arkansas Gazette,* May 28, 1828, p. 3, col. 1). The
council ground at or near what is now Tahlequah, Oklahoma, was at first
called Tickatoke.

[35] Thwaites, *op. cit.,* XIII, 278.

were hunting on Poteau River, intercepted a party of Cherokee hunters, of whom they killed three,[36] and robbed the party of their furs. The Cherokee met in council at Webber's on February 10 and prepared a memorial to the Indian superintendent, demanding that the Osage be required to pay for the furs stolen and surrender for atonement by death as many warriors as they killed of the Cherokee.[37] Afterward Mad Buffalo's party, on their return to Clermont's Town, called at the trading house of their friend Pryor on the Verdigris, one and a half miles above the mouth. There they were surprised by a larger war party of Cherokee under Dutch, in quest of the murderers. While the Cherokee were rejoicing in their capture, Pryor contrived a method of escape for his Osage friends. He directed a man working for him named David McGee, to call Dutch to a place on one side of his trading house out of sight of the Osage; there Dutch was entertained in some manner long enough for Mad Buffalo and his followers to make their escape; and though the Cherokees gave chase when they discovered the deception, they were unable to overtake the fugitives.[38]

The Cherokee, incensed at the ruse that deprived them of the satisfaction of carrying Mad Buffalo to their tribe, decided on revenge against Pryor. That night they broke open his trading house and stole one hundred and fifty pounds of his beaver fur. When charged with the theft, Dutch admitted it but claimed that as the Osage and Cherokee were in a state of war against each other, citizens of the United States should remain neutral and that Pryor interfered in their affairs at his peril. Pryor laid a claim for his losses before the War Department, based on the protection guaranteed by his trader's license but the Department took the view of the Cherokee and, although

[36] James Miller to Secretary of War, Arkansas Post, June 20, 1820, OIA, RCF, "Cherokee and Osage"; *idem,* March 24, 1820, AGO, ORD, WDF.

[37] Takatoka and nine other Cherokee to Indian superintendent, February 10, 1820, AGO, ORD, WDF.

[38] *The American Historical Review,* XXIV, 255. Documents in Office of Indian Affairs concerning Nathaniel Pryor, compiled by Stella M. Drumm.

Pryor's claim was pending for ten or fifteen years and even after his death, continued to hold him responsible.[39]

James Miller arrived at Arkansas Post[40] in December, 1819,[41] to assume his duties as governor of the territory. Soon afterward he visited the Cherokee whom he found in a restless state on account of the killing of their hunters by the Osage; some of the leaders were promoting a plan to exchange their lands for that in Lovely's Purchase as soon as they could gather sufficient force to overwhelm the Osage. The Caddo had agreed to aid them and they had also solicited the Quapaw chief, Saracen; he however took counsel of Governor Miller, who discouraged the idea.[42] The Cherokee were determined on launching another campaign against the Osage; but Reuben Lewis, their agent, prevailed on them to wait until Governor Miller was given an opportunity to adjust their differences.[43] After reporting the situation to Governor Miller, Lewis called the Cherokee chiefs to a council with the governor for April 20; at the suggestion of Miller, four Cherokee chiefs accompanied him in August[44] to Clermont's village in an effort to make peace

[39] *Idem;* OIA, RCF, "1832 Cherokee West, Agency, Geo. Vashon, claim of N. Pryor."

[40] Governor Miller left Pittsburgh on the seventh of October with arms and ammunition, "all which I have stored in this village until further provisions are made for the same" (Governor Miller's message to the Legislative Council, February 10, 1820, Territorial Records, *State Department*).

[41] By Act of Congress of March 2, 1819, Arkansas Territory was established July 4, embracing substantially all of what are now the states of Arkansas and Oklahoma. James Miller of New Hampshire was appointed the first governor (Foreman, *op. cit.,* p. 5).

[42] Miller to Calhoun, March 24, 1820, AGO, ORD, WDF.

[43] At the same time the Secretary of War wrote Maj. William Bradford commanding at Fort Smith, that the Cherokee must be prevented from renewing hostilities against the Osage (Secretary of War to Bradford, May 12, 1820, Territorial Records, Department of State).

[44] Governor Miller was accompanied by an escort from Fort Smith composed of a sergeant and seven privates (AGO, Post Returns for Fort Smith, August, 1820), and by John McElmurray, a trader and justice of the peace of Missouri Territory, who carried twenty pounds of tobacco to be used in the "talk" (receipt of John McElmurray to Barack Owens, April 25, 1820, OIA, RCF).

between the tribes, a mission on which he was engaged for two months. The governor reported[45]

> .... The settlement of the Cherokee is scattered for a long extent on the river [Arkansas], and appears not much different from those of white people. They are considerably advanced towards civilization, and were very decent in their deportment. They inhabit a lovely, rich part of the country.
>
> The Osage town consisted of one hundred and fifty dwellings, with ten to fifteen in each house. The average height of the men is more than six feet. They are entirely in a state of nature. Very few white people have ever been among them. They know nothing of the use of money, nor do they use any ardent spirits. I pitched my tent about half a mile from the town and remained five days. They made dances and plays every night to amuse me.[46]

Admitting to Governor Miller that some of their tribe had killed the Cherokee hunters, the Osage said they ought not to be compelled to give up the murderers until the Cherokee had returned a number of Osage prisoners, as they were bound to do by their treaty. The Cherokee admitted that they held four Osage prisoners; but sought to excuse themselves by saying that some of them were at school in Tennessee, that one child ran and hid when she heard she was to be returned to her tribe and they were unable to find her at the time the other prisoners were returned. The governor then told the Cherokee he could do nothing for them until they had performed their part of the agreement. After obtaining the promise of representatives of both tribes to meet at Fort Smith on October 1 and return all prisoners and stolen horses,[47] he descended the Arkansas to the Cherokee settlements. There he found a party of Caddo and Choctaw painted for war and ready to join a band of Cherokee

---

[45] *Louisiana Herald*, January 6, 1821, p. 4, col. 1; Morse, *op. cit.*, Appendix, p. 213.

[46] *Ibid.*

[47] Miller to Calhoun, June 20, 1820, OIA, RCF; *Missionary Herald*, XVII, 21.

under their war chief, Takatoka, in proceeding against the Osage; he ordered them to disperse.

Late in September, as Major Long's party was proceeding through their country, they arrived at Point Pleasant where the Cherokee were counseling with reference to the meeting with the Osage to be held at Fort Smith when the prisoners were to be exchanged for the Osage murderers. Four of the prisoners, a woman and three children were present, the woman weeping bitterly at the decision to return her to her tribe. She had long been among the Cherokee, whose customs she had adopted and to whom she was attached. Captain Bell stated in his journal[48] that

> On his way from the Arkansas to Cape Girardeau, September, 1821 [1820], he met Captain Rogers, a half-breed Cherokee, on his way to Belle Point [Fort Smith] with a number of Osage prisoners, who were to be delivered up. Among them was an Osage woman, who was unwilling to return to her own nation, having accustomed herself to the dress and manners of the white people, and to make her own clothes. To return to the savage manners and customs was painful to her. Her children were well dressed and appeared to have been well brought up; had been at school and spoke English.

The arrogant Osage, resentful of the growing intrusion of white hunters and Indians upon their hunting grounds, continued their hostilities with increasing violence. They were bitter at the means employed to oppress them, and complained that they had been deceived when they were induced to cede their land to the Government.[49] The Western Cherokee, wish-

---

[48] Morse, *op. cit.*, Appendix, p. 255; Thwaites (ed.), *op. cit.*, XVII, 23, Maj. Stephen H. Long was sent in 1819 in charge of an expedition to explore the headwaters of the Arkansas and Red rivers; a section of the party descended the Arkansas River under the command of Capt. John R. Bell who wrote some interesting descriptions of the country and Indians seen; the account of the expeditions was published in four volumes (Thwaites [ed.], *op. cit.*, Vols. XIV, XV, XVI, and XVII).

[49] "They say that they never would have sold that land [Lovely's Purchase]

Osage Group: Mun-ne-pus-kee, Ko-a-tunk-a, and Nah-com-ee-shee. Painted by George Catlin, 1834. Courtesy of Smithsonian Institution, Bureau of American Ethnology.

ing to strengthen their government in their new home, met on July 1, 1820, in full council, and enacted some wholesome laws; one provided for the organization of three companies of mounted police or light-horse, authorized to suppress thefts of all kinds and to collect and restore to their owners all stolen property within their knowledge in the Cherokee country. Some of the Cherokee had been stealing horses from the Osage and whites; these were sold to other whites who ran them off to the settlements and disposed of them. The Indians proposed to stop this traffic.[50] These light-horse were also empowered to enforce the payment of "debts from those who refuse to pay which they have contracted."[51] By the end of the year forty horses stolen by the Cherokee had been restored to their owners and five remained in possession of their chief, John Jolly, awaiting lawful claimants, of which notice was given in the press. Since the organization of the light-horse,"there has rarely been a theft committed in the nation. Their laws are very severe, and any one convicted of theft, even of the least consequence, is flogged without mercy."[52] The same year the Cherokee in the East divided their country into eight districts, appointed circuit judges, sheriffs, constables, and justices, and laid a tax on the people to build a courthouse in each district.[53]

to the United States had they supposed it would be given to any other tribe of Indians, particularly the Cherokees; but sold it with the express understanding that it should be settled with white people .... to learn them how to cultivate the soil & to live as the white people..... If the Cherokee get the above described land as far west as the Osage boundary, they will get with it much the most rich and desirable part of this Territory with all the salt springs and lead ore known in this part of the Territory" (Miller to Calhoun, June 20, 1820, OIA, RCF).

[50] Letter from John Jolly and Walter Webber to Governor Miller July 2, 1820, in *Arkansas Gazette,* July 29, 1820, p. 3, cols. 1 and 2.

[51] *Ibid.*

[52] *Ibid.,* January 20, 1821, p. 2, col. 4; p. 3, col. 1.

[53] *Ibid.,* May 26, 1821, p. 2, col. 4; *American State Papers,* "Indian Affairs," II, 280.

VI

ADVENTURES OF THE MISSIONARIES IN THE WILDERNESS, 1821

FROM this time there is no other source of information touching the warfare between the Osage and Cherokee, and contemporary events in Oklahoma and Arkansas in the early eighteen twenties, more extensive, detailed, and interesting than the chronicles left by the missionaries located among these two tribes at Union and Dwight missions, respectively. Indeed, the careers of these missions are an essential part of the history of this virgin country.

In the autumn of 1817 when Elias Cornelius, agent for the American Board of Commissioners for Foreign Missions, was making a tour of the Cherokee nation in Tennessee, he met Tahlonteskee with others returning from the massacre of the Osage. He proposed to the chief that the missionaries send teachers among his people in Arkansas and subsequently they accepted the proposal.[1] Afterward, in the spring of 1820, Alfred Finney of Vermont, and Cephas Washburn of Georgia, departed from Elliot Mission to locate their school, and in June reached Arkansas Post which they reported a very immoral place. Here they were joined by two other missionaries, J. Orr and Jacob Hitchcock, from Massachusetts.[2]

---

[1] American Board of Commissioners for Foreign Missions, Vol. XI, No. 25, Tahlonteskee to Evarts, June 10, 1818; *Missionary Herald,* August, 1818, p. 207. Captain Bell says in 1820 that Tahlonteskee died in 1817 (Thwaites [ed.], *op. cit.,* XVII, 24) but obviously he is in error. He was reported October 7, 1820, as having returned to the old nation to secure pay for his abandoned improvements (OIA, RCF, "Cherokee-Fortville," C. R. Hicks to Calhoun, October 7, 1820). Nuttall in 1819 speaks of "the late principal chief Tallantusky" (Thwaites [ed.], *op. cit.,* XIII, 181).

[2] American Board of Commissioners for Foreign Missions, Vol. XI, Journal of the Arkansas Mission.

The missionaries continued their journey, and by the time they reached the Cherokee settlements they became desperately ill; but their distress was relieved in the home of Mrs. Persis Lovely.[3] At first they encountered the hostility of Takatoka, who suspected the missionaries were agents of the Government attempting to make peace between the Cherokee and the Osage.[4] However, Chief John Jolly and Captain James Rogers made them welcome and gave them permission to select a site for a mission school.[5] On August 25 they decided to locate their establishment[6] on the west bank of the Illinois Bayou, and immediately began work on their first house.[7] Laboring there until October, they then returned to Georgia and brought their families to the Cherokee country where they held their first service on May 13, 1821; the sermon was preached by the Rev. Cephas Washburn.[8] The mission was named by them Dwight, after Timothy Dwight, the former president of Yale College and friend of the Indians.

In 1819 the United Foreign Missionary Society of New York sent Epaphras Chapman and Job P. Vinall to locate stations for missions in Missouri Territory. They ascended the Arkansas River to the settlements of the Western Cherokee, to whom

[3] *Ibid.*

[4] *Ibid.*

[5] *Ibid.* Congress had just authorized the expenditure of $10,000 annually to instruct the Indians in agriculture and to teach their children reading, writing, and arithmetic; the act (Act of March 3, 1819) empowered the President to select the agency to carry it into effect and he chose the missionary organizations for that purpose.

[6] In what is now Pope County, Arkansas, across the river from Dardanelle.

[7] Journal of Arkansas Mission, *ibid.* The first tree was felled on August 25 (Morse, *op. cit.,* Appendix, pp. 214, 215).

[8] Journal of Arkansas Mission, *ibid.* "The side selected for the Establishment, is on the west bank of the Illinois river, a northern branch of the Arkansas, about five miles from their junction, on a gentle eminence, covered with a growth of oak and pine. At the foot of the eminence issues a large spring of pure water..... The Illinois, three fourths of the year, is navigable for keel boats, as far as the Establishment" (Morse, *op. cit.,* p. 214). This Illinois River in Arkansas is not to be confused with the river of the same name in Oklahoma.

they proposed the plan on July 13. As these Indians were already negotiating with the American Board of Commissioners for Foreign Missions, Chapman and Vinall continued to Fort Smith; there they interviewed the Osage who were holding a council[9] with the Cherokee, and on September 27 received a favorable reply. At Fort Smith they were both seized with fever, from which Vinall died. Chapman, however, continued to the Osage country where the chiefs gave him permission to establish a mission on the west bank of the Neosho River. He then returned to New York and reported to his board, who relinquished the Cherokee country to the American Board of Commissioners for Foreign Missions, and prepared to establish their first mission among the Osage.[10]

The organization[11] was then completed, named Union Mission,[12] and the members departed from New York in April, 1820. They embarked in two keel boats at Pittsburgh and descended the Ohio River; stops were made at points along the river, where sermons were preached and donations of money, food, and clothing were made for use in the western wilderness. They continued down the Mississippi and up to Arkansas Post

[9] Described by Nuttall (Thwaites [ed.], *op. cit.*, XIII, 278). At the request of the Osage living on the Osage River the United Foreign Missionary Society in 1821 sent to them a mission that was called Harmony.

[10] *Missionary Herald*, VII, 25; in 1826, Union Mission was transferred to the American Board of Commissioners for Foreign Missions. The mission was located on the west side of the Grand River near a good fresh-water spring, and about a mile from a salt spring that had been used by the Osage and others for making salt. The site of the mission is in Mayes County, Oklahoma, five miles northeast of Mazie. For a further account of Union Mission, see Foreman, *op. cit.*, pp. 42 ff.

[11] For the names of the members and other details touching this mission family, see Foreman, *op. cit.*, p. 43 n.

[12] "The principal support of the Missionary Family .... is to be derived from the United Foreign Missionary Society, an institution constituted by the united exertions of the general assembly of the synods of the Associate Reformed and Reformed Dutch churches in the United States. In honor of this union, the site of the mission is to be called Union" (Account from *New York Advertiser*, in *Arkansas Gazette*, July 8, 1820, p. 2, col. 4).

where they presented to Governor Miller their credentials[13] authorizing them to pass into the Indian country. After they left the Post, passengers and crew alike rapidly succumbed to deadly fevers on the Arkansas; and before reaching Little Rock two of the missionary sisters died,[14] and later a member of the crew. Sickness, heat, and low water compelled the party to remain there until autumn.

On October 3 William C. Requa, Mr. Redfield, and Mr. Ransom, of the missionary party, and a number of hired men left Little Rock in a pirogue for the site of the mission, to erect log houses for the occupancy of the family on their arrival. After ascending the river 150 miles farther to the Cherokee country, they found the water so low that they could proceed no farther with their boat, and from there they traveled on horseback.[15] Mr. Chapman and Mr. Woodruff left Little Rock by horse on October 16 to join the other contingent bound for Union Mission.[16]

Soon after the arrival of the vanguard of the Union missionaries at the site of their station on November 15, 1820,

. . . . some of the Indians[17] came, as they said, to shake hands with us. We found them equal to our expectations in every respect, a noble race of people. In this introduction we agreed, at their request, to hold a council with them at their town, within ten days.

[13] These letters from the Secretary of War and McKenny to the Indians and officials in the West appear in full in *Niles' Weekly Register,* October 21, 1820, pp. 122, 123.

[14] Miss Dolly Hoyt on July 21, and Miss Susan Lines four days later. A boat laden with provisions for Fort Smith had been detained by low water at Arkansas Post all fall and nearly all summer, and did not reach Little Rock until December, 1820 (*Missionary Herald,* Vol. XVII, letter from William F. Vaill).

[15] *Missionary Herald,* XVII, 89.

[16] From Fort Smith they followed an early trail on the north side of the Arkansas River that passed Bean's Salt Works, about seven miles north of what is now Gore, Oklahoma. On November 10 they "examined the celebrated saline on Illinois river, and the apparatus just erected for making salt" (Morse, *op. cit.,* p. 220). This trail was afterward employed in part of the construction of the military road from Fort Gibson to Fort Smith, the first in Oklahoma.

[17] Osage.

At the appointed time, I was one of the four, who went over to the council. In passing that distance, about twenty-five miles, we found the land a continued level, and rich prairie. When we came in sight of the town, we had one of the grandest prospects I ever beheld. . . . . At two or three miles to the north of the town, there are several natural mounds, rising directly from a perfect plain, to the height of about two hundred feet. All the mounds appear to rise just to the same height, and as level as the top of the adjacent plains. The one nearest the town has about three acres on the top, and is accessible only in one or two places.

As we approached the town, the head Chief came out to meet us, and bid us welcome. In a short time we were surrounded by hundreds, apparently happy to see us. The Chief took us to his lodge. In walking through the town we were continually annoyed by a host of surly, snarling dogs, who were not accustomed to the dress and appearance of the whites. The dress of the Indians consists of buckskins dressed, made into leggins, reaching to the hips; on their feet mockasins and a buffalo robe or blanket about their shoulders. The females have short skirts and covering for the breasts. They shave off their hair close to their heads, except a line, about half an inch wide, running round the head. The hair thus left, is cut about an inch long; within this line of hair they fasten an ornament. Their ears are slit in several places, and filled with strings of beads. In addition to these, they have many other kinds of ornaments about their arms and legs.

Their houses are made of poles, arched from fifteen to twenty feet, covered by matting made of flaggs. At the sides they set up rived planks, lining the inside with neatly made flagg matting. They build several fires in the lodge, according to its size, or the number of wives the owner has. For a fireplace, they dig a hole about as big as a bushel-basket, leaving the smoke to ascend through a hole in the roof. Around the fire they spread their mats to sit or eat.

Having entered the lodge, and had our horses turned out, we took a humble seat around the fire. Presently there was brought to us a wooden bowl, filled with food made of corn. In a short time we were invited to eat at another lodge, and before we had finished, at another, and another. In the same manner we were treated, during all the time we remained in the village. It is impossible to give you any idea of their cooking. It was so strange, as well as new, and withal they were so filthy, that I believe, if I were to live with them, I should have a dangerous seasoning.[18]

The remainder of the mission family continued at Little Rock until December. On November 6 Governor Miller called on them on his way from Arkansas Post to Fort Smith, where he was going to make a second attempt to bring about a treaty of peace between the Cherokee and Osage. On December 12, the members of the mission family having recovered sufficiently, they all embarked in their two keel boats manned by a captain and six hands to each boat; but their progress was arrested January 1 by impassable shoals at Billingsley's Settlement, thirty miles below Fort Smith. During their enforced stay there Dr. Palmer, one of the members of the party, who was handling a gun, unfortunately shot and killed a boat hand named John Muncey. On the fifth "John Billingsley, Esq.[19] one of the judges of the court of this county [Crawford County] at the particular request of Brother Palmer and of the members of the Mission came to our boats, to receive the testimony of those who were present, and witnessed the event of Muncy's death."

Mr. Chapman descended from Union to be present and Governor Miller had recently arrived at Fort Smith to officiate at the council of the Osage. But they found the situation more discouraging than ever; a party of seventy Osage had recently

---

[18] Account of Dr. Marcus Palmer in Morse, *op. cit.*, p. 288. This extract, copied in Morse, is erroneously dated 1820; it was written in March, 1821.

[19] John Billingsley was appointed justice of peace on June 23, 1814, when this was Arkansas County of Missouri Territory (T. M. Marshall [ed.], *Life and Letters of Frederick Bates*, II, 281, Executive Journal). "In 1814, three families named Billingsley, Adams and Williams, eighteen persons in all, left middle Tennessee in a flatboat and after a year at Cadron reached the Mulberry in 1816. After the signing of the treaty [of 1817] which gave the north side of the river to the Cherokee these settlers scattered along the south side" (Thwaites [ed.], *op. cit.*, Vol. XIII, 195 n.).

attacked a Cherokee hunting camp on the Poteau, and besides killing two and wounding one, had stolen all the horses, peltry, and other property of the Cherokee.[20] Governor Miller addressed the President from Fort Smith:[21]

> .... I am here now with a view of making another attempt to complete a settlement between the Cherokee and Osage Indians. I had believed I could do so, but on my arrival at this place I was informed that the Osages had a few days before robbed a party of the Cherokees, killed two and wounded one. I have sent for both nations to come in agreable to their mutual agreement when with them last spring. I have not yet heard from either, but expect to soon.

A war party of Osage commanded by the Chief Big Soldier of White Hair's village had set out on a mission to Red River; it was made up of warriors from White Hair's village on Osage River, from the Gross Côte[22] on the Verdigris and from Clermont's Town. Hugh Glenn, who had a trading house at the mouth of the Verdigris, was at the latter village in company with Governor Miller when they returned; and he wrote an interesting letter describing the five scalps of white men they brought home with them after attacking a hunting camp on Red River. That of the leader had short, curly, black hair, one black and gray, and two coarse black hair similar to that of their French laborers; the fifth was that of a boy twelve or fourteen years old who was kept as a prisoner for five days of the journey toward the village before they killed him. The Indians said the white hunters were all dressed in deerskins, that of the leader neatly worked and resembling the clothing worn by Glenn.[23]

[20] *Arkansas Gazette*, December 30, 1820, p. 3, col. 1; *Missouri Intelligencer*, February 19, 1821, p. 3, col. 3.

[21] Miller to the President, December 10, 1820, OIA, RCF; Miller to Secretary of War, December 11, 1820, AGO, ORD, WDF.

[22] Grosse Côte or Big Hill Town was on the Verdigris in the present Nowata County, Oklahoma.

[23] Hugh Glenn to Wm. Bradford, February 2, 1821, AGO, ORD, WDF.

During the cold weeks of January the mission family remained in their boats, tied up to the south bank of the river under the bleak shadow of high bluffs, lamenting ".... how unpleasant to be detained in this loanly wilderness, on expenses & without employment. The men occasionally bring in fresh provisions though game in this place is scarce."[24] But the delay gave them opportunity to receive news of the war raging in the country where they were going, and to consider whether it was advisable to proceed.

The sick are slowly regaining their strength in these cheerless boat cabins; religious services are held, and some of the brethren go to the Billingsley Settlement to preach to the Tennesseeans and Kentuckians who make up the community.[25] On the seventeenth a fall of nine inches of snow is followed by extremely cold weather. And

.... Brother Woodruff came to us this evening. He left the brethren at Union on friday morning of last week, at their particular request, to bring them shoes and stockens and other clothing together with medicine. He states that Brother Redfield had been sick of a fever for several days before he left there. Brother Woodruff has been in iminent danger from a panther and preserved by the aid of his gun, and the kindness of Providence.[26]

Two days later Mr. Spaulding set off with Mr. Woodruff for the new mission station. They were accompanied as far as Fort Smith by Mr. Chapman[27] who went to the garrison hoping

[24] Union Mission Journal, Oklahoma Historical Society.

[25] Billingsley's Settlement for a time succeeded Fort Smith as the county seat of Crawford County, when the former was known as Crawford Courthouse. In 1836 the seat of justice of Crawford County was removed eighteen miles up the Arkansas to Van Buren. Crawford Courthouse was a small settlement opposite the mouth of Frog Bayou.

[26] Union Mission Journal, *ibid.*

[27] Chapman had returned to the boats after his descent from the mission to Fort Smith. On the twelfth he again went to Fort Smith and learned that Governor Miller had gone up the river to confer with the Osage who had failed to keep their engagement with him (*ibid*).

to find the Osage chiefs in conference with Governor Miller; however, he returned three days later with a report from the governor that the Osage had refused to attend a council there. The missionaries were disappointed, as they had hoped for the opportunity of explaining to the Indians their purpose in coming among them.

On the twenty-ninth, after a delay of four weeks, the water having risen and the river being cleared of ice, the mission family embarked and reached Fort Smith in two days. They had been favored by wind and by using their tents as sails, as they occasionally did, they made more rapid progress. At the garrison they saw Major Bradford and Governor Miller. The latter the same day set out

> .... for the Post of Arkansas. He expects to hold a council with the Cherokees; designs if possible to induce them to comply to the terms of peace which the Osage purpose, which are these: That the Osages do not deliver up the murderers, and that the Cherokees retain their captives. These terms will appear reasonable when we consider the fact that most if not all the Cherokees who have been killed, were killed in consequence of their encroaching on the Osage hunting ground, contrary to the former treaty.[28]

After delivering a few words of reassurance and advice to the young missionaries who were about to plunge into the sinister environment created by the warring Osage, Governor Miller took his departure from Fort Smith and descended the Arkansas to the home of the Cherokee; he then returned to the capital at Arkansas Post[29] after an absence of three months[30] spent in vain councils with the Osage and Cherokee, endeavoring to prevent a renewal of hostilities between them.[31] Before his return, there came the report:

[28] Union Mission Journal, Oklahoma Historical Society.

[29] On February 27, 1821.

[30] *Louisiana Herald* (Natchitoches), January 6, 1821, p. 4, col. 1.

[31] *Arkansas Gazette,* March 3, 1821, p. 3, col. 1.

The long-expected war between the Osage and Cherokee Nations has at length broken out. . . . .[32]

Both parties have been equally eager for bloody combat . . . . as both are powerful nations a long and sanguinary conflict may be expected. The Osage are said to be the strongest in point of number, but the Cherokee are much the best supplied with arms and ammunition.[33]

The Osage were bold but poorly armed, their principal weapons bows and arrows; they had a few muskets and shotguns, but made very little use of the rifle. The Cherokee were said to be well supplied with everything necessary for a vigorous prosecution of the war.[34] They were encouraged further by the fact that bands of Delaware and Shawnee were on the way from Indiana, intending to locate near and join them as allies against their enemies.[35]

[32] *Ibid.,* December 30, 1820, p. 3, col. 1; *Louisiana Herald,* February 3, 1821, p. 2, col. 3; *Missouri Intelligencer,* February 19, 1821, p. 3, col. 3. Governor Miller advised the Cherokee to protect themselves (*Louisiana Herald,* May 19, 1821, p. 3, col. 2).

[33] *Arkansas Gazette,* March 3, 1821, p. 3, col. 1.

[34] *Ibid.,* December 30, 1820, p. 3, col. 1; *Missouri Intelligencer,* February 19, 1821, p. 3, col. 3.

[35] *Louisiana Herald,* May 19, 1821, p. 3, col. 2, letter from Arkansas Post dated January 29, 1821; *Arkansas Gazette,* December 30, 1820, p. 3, col. 1; about eight hundred Delaware passed through Kaskaskia, Illinois, in October, 1820, on their way west (*Arkansas Gazette,* December 2, 1820, p. 2, col. 4). Nuttall found two or three families living with them in 1819 (Thwaites [ed.], *op. cit.,* XIII, 192). In 1816, 840 Delaware were living in three towns on the White River and one near Cape Girardeau (Wm. Clark, November 16, Tabulation of Indians in Missouri, OIA, RCF). "The Delawares in the spring will cross the Mississippi as soon as the grass can support their horses" (Missouri Historical Society, "Frost Collection," Clark to Graham, February 24, 1824).

VII

THE OSAGE AND THEIR WARFARE
1821-22

THE missionaries departed from Fort Smith on the flood waters of the Arkansas, which was bank-full, and did not reach the mouth of Grand River until the tenth of February; this stream they found so rapid and deep that the boatmen could not employ the poles and were forced to the primitive method of "bush-whacking"—pulling the boat by grasping the bushes along the bank. The first day on Grand River a wind storm carried away the sail and mast of one of the boats, and the current which swept the craft across the stream came near sinking it. At another stage the boatmen lost control of one of the boats, which was carried two miles down the river before they could check it. After eight days of great toil and danger the party finally reached the site of the mission at ten o'clock on the morning of February 18. Directly afterward they sold one of their boats and removed to cabins erected on the bank of the river by the first arrivals. Two days after the mission family landed at their post,

> .... they were visited by *Tally* the second Osage chief, and several councillors and warriors of the tribe. The chief expressed the warmest satisfaction at the arrival of the family..... After a friendly interview it was mutually agreed that the missionaries should visit the principal village in the course of a few days for the purpose of attending a council of the Chiefs, and of being formally introduced to the tribe. On the 5th of March, the Superintendent, Assistant, Physician and one of the other members proceeded, according to agreement, to the Indian village. On their approach they were met by *Clamore*, the principal Chief, who bad them welcome, and conducted them to his own residence.

At the general council next day, Clermont (or Clamore) expressed the highest satisfaction:

.... and in an animated and eloquent strain, recommended the Mission, and its object, to the attention and confidence of his people. He concluded with the assurance that, should war not prevent, he would send his own children to the Missionary school as soon as it should be opened for their reception. The Osages of the Arkansas occupy several villages. The principal village contains about three hundred lodges or huts, and about three thousand souls. . . . .

This village is situated about twenty-eight miles west of Union, near the Vermillion [Verdigris] on an extensive plain skirted with trees and natural mounds. . . . . Their lodges are generally from fifty to one hundred feet in length, irregularly situated within a half-mile square. They are constructed of poles, mattings, barks and skins. The poles are set in the ground with a crotch at the top and cross poles to support the roof. The side poles are about 5 feet in height, the middle or ridge posts about 20 feet. Some have barks set against the cross poles, most however have plank which they have split out, fastened in the ground one by the side of the other as people in some parts of the country make fence. The roofs are covered with skins or mattings. These lodges being of very light materials, can be taken down and removed or rebuilt in a short time. When a lodge needs to be rebuilt their wives meet in the morning, remove the covering in an hours time, take up the posts, and each woman digs a hole in the ground with a knife, and removes the dirt with her hands.

Thus 20 or 30 holes are dug at once, and the post set over again, and the covering replaced with the intended improvements in a few hours. In the middle of their lodges they make their fires on the ground without any chimney—leaving the smoke to pass out through a hole in the top of the roof. In some lodges they have two, others three fireplaces. They have neither floors nor seats, but spread their skins or mattings for strangers to lie upon. They sit in circles round their fires, part of the family round one fire and part round another.

They are remarkable for hospitality. No sooner does a stranger who comes on friendly designs, arrive among them, than he is welcome to their lodges. His horse is immediately taken care of by their wives. The house where he enters is thronged with spectators. Presently he is invited from lodge to lodge to partake of their simple fare. Their numerous invitations cannot be dispensed with without giving offense, the consequence is that you are often called to eat as many as 15 or 20 times the same morning or evening. They are irregular in their meals. They have a number of cooks whose business it is to wait on visitors and conduct them from one lodge to another. When you enter a lodge after you have spoken to the men you sit down; if you attempt to shake hands with the women or children, they think strange of it, for they are not used to compliments. When their food is ready it is presented in a wooden dish with as many ladles as visitors. The more freely you eat the more you please them. The cook if he chooses takes the residue and then leads you to another lodge. Their females perform the labor. The men do the hunting, go to war, and much of the time having nothing to do, while the laborious wife or daughter packing wood across the plain or bringing water or planting corn and the like. In their hunting parties the women take care of the horses, prepare their encampments, in short do all the drudgery, while the men spend their leisure time in smoking and diversion. The men are generally of a lofty stature, of a fine form, and of a frank and open countenance. In council they are dignified, and, in their speeches, eloquent.[1]

The women, though strong and active, were not proportionately tall; but they excelled in industry and ingenuity, and made every article of dress worn by the tribe, as well as every utensil in their huts. Before their town was burned by the Cherokee, their houses were chiefly covered with handwoven mats of bulrushes. Many of the women were married to French hunters and trappers who lived with the tribe. A man who married an Osage woman possessed the control of her sisters, either for himself or any person to whom he wished to give them.

Dr. George Sibley, who had been the agent for that part of

[1] Morse, *op. cit.*, p. 218; Union Mission Journal.

the tribe on Osage River, in describing them in 1820, said[2] that an Osage family, if extremely lucky, could save ten or fifteen bushels of corn and beans, besides a quantity of dried pumpkin. On this they feasted, with meat saved in the summer till September, when what remained was cached,[3] and they set out on the fall hunt from which they returned about Christmas. On these hunts they traveled in a body, men, women, and children. From the first of the year until sometime in February or March, as the season happened to be mild or severe, they stayed in their villages, making short hunting excursions occasionally, and during that time they consumed the greater part of the contents of their caches. In February or March the Indians went upon their bear hunts and afterward they hunted the beaver. This business they pursued until planting time, when they again returned to their villages, planted crops, and in May set out again for the summer hunt, taking with them the remainder, if any, of their corn and beans.

This was the circle of Osage life, here and there varied by war and trading expeditions. They eked out their wretched existence from the bounty of nature; and walnuts, pecans, acorns, grapes, plums, and persimmons were often their reliance. They were frequently reduced to a diet of acorns prepared with buffalo grease, as described by the first arrivals at Union.

Union Mission was the most remote venture of civilization in the American Southwest; its story as developed from the letters and journals written there is an absorbing one, without parallel in the region. These young missionaries, who resolutely traveled for months to reach their wilderness home, give us a stimulating picture of fortitude and courage. Upon arrival at their station they learned that the expected difficulty of inter-

---

[2] Morse, *op. cit.*, p. 205.

[3] *Cache* (from the French *cacher*) was a hole sometimes shaped like a cistern which the Indians dug in the ground in which to store and conceal their grain and other valuables when they departed from their villages to hunt.

esting a savage tribe of Indians in religious instruction was greatly increased by the deadly warfare raging between them and the Cherokee tribe. Filled as they were with enthusiasm for the endeavor of securing and educating Osage youth and winning them to the Christian religion, there were many material affairs to be attended to before these things could be accomplished. Logs were to be cut, clapboards rived, puncheons split out of the timber, and cabins constructed. Land was to be cleared of trees and underbrush, fences built, ground plowed and planted to grain and gardens.

During the first week of March the mission family removed from the river bank to the new cabins provided for them. "This evening[4] Brother Redfield and Sister Beach, having been engaged to each other before they left home, were united in the solemn bonds of matrimony. The ceremony was performed immediately after our usual prayer meeting." This was probably the first marriage within the state of Oklahoma under the auspices of a Protestant church.

On the thirteenth, the mission

> . . . . had a visit from nine Osages warriors, who by their statement had set out for the Garrison [Fort Smith] to learn whether the Cherokees meant to go to war with them; but some new fears being excited in their minds lest they should meet the enemy they tarried today and returned to the village. The nation has been some time waiting to hear from Gov. Miller who promised to inform them if the Cherokees were determined upon fighting. As they have had no letter, they are yet in doubt whether the war is declared.

However, two weeks later they

> . . . . received information from Maj. Bradford of the war being declared between the Cherokees and the Osages. He states that the Cherokees had requested that the white people might be removed lest their young men should molest them. We conclude it is our duty to trust God and continue here.[5]

[4] Saturday, March 10. [5] Union Mission Journal.

Clermont (Claremore) Osage Chief, with his war club and his leggings fringed with scalp locks taken from his enemies' heads. Painted by George Catlin, 1834. Courtesy of Smithsonian Institution, Bureau of American Ethnology.

Governor Miller told the Cherokee that in view of the depredations by the Osage he would interfere no longer with their war measures, provided they continued no offenses against the whites. The Cherokee then wrote Major Bradford on March 12, 1821, asking him to remove the whites from the danger zone.

> . . . . We expect to have to go to war with our neighbors in a very short time and there is a good many of you people in our way we do not wish to injure the persons or property of any Citizen of the United States and for that reason we wish them out of the way; you know very well that it is very hard to govern an army, there is wild young men among our people that is hard to govern which it is the case in all other armies. . . . .[6]

Imminence of the renewal of the war between the tribes increased.[7] The Cherokee were planning an attack on the Osage under the permission of Governor Miller; but he left for his home in New Hampshire, and the factor, Matthew Lyon, and Major Bradford induced the Cherokee reluctantly to postpone their measures of revenge against their enemies which threatened to involve the white settlements in savage rapine. The Cherokee then sent a delegation[8] to Washington to submit their grievances against the Osage, and other difficulties, to the President.[9]

While these matters were pending, the young Osage warriors broke from the restraints of their chiefs. Clermont hastened to Union Mission with some of his warriors to warn the missionaries.

[6] Cherokee Council, March 12, 1821, letter to Major Bradford—Matthew Lyon to Secretary of War, April 18, 1821, AGO, ORD, WDF.

[7] Bradford to Calhoun, February 10, 1821, AGO, ORD, WDF.

[8] The delegation was composed of James Rogers, Walter Webber, and Thomas Maw. They were particularly instructed to press their claim for compensation for horses stolen by white people from them while on the way from Tennessee to the Arkansas.

[9] Jolly and others to President Monroe, March 17, 1821, OIA, RCF.

. . . . He told us that four hundred of his warriors were going against the Cherokee; that after a short encampment for hunting on this side of the river they intended to cross, and march down to the Cherokee Nation and attack them on their own ground; that he himself had come so far here to warn us not to let cattle or horses be out of sight, lest some of his young men should take them. He stated in particular his fear of misconduct from those of the other villages over whom he had no control. Clarmore appeared to be much attached to us, and we doubt neither his friendship for this Family, nor his loyalty to the Government.[10]

This war party of Osage, under the leadership of Mad Buffalo, or Skitok, after their hunt along the Grand River had provided them with meat, descended the Arkansas River along the trail on the north side of that stream until they arrived opposite Fort Smith. Their leaders crossed to the post and requested permission for the whole body to come over; they pretended that they wished to hunt on that side of the river though their real object was to secure ammunition to use against the Cherokee. While there they refused to eat or drink, or to shake hands, but took the opportunity to examine the fort minutely and ascertain how many men defended it. On being refused by the commander at the post the desired permission to cross, the chiefs returned to their band. Soon they were discovered conveying timber to the river, with which they made forty or fifty rafts; some of them embarked, crossed above the post, and secreted themselves in the cane on the opposite side of Poteau River. The chiefs, disregarding the warning of the officers, persisted in their attempt to land at the foot of the post, and the commanding officer, Lieutenant Martin Scott, ordered two six-pounders loaded with canister brought into position to fire on the Indians. At sight of the guns with lighted matches in the hands of the soldiers standing by to discharge them, the Osage abandoned their effort to land at the fort, but remained on the west bank of the Poteau. There they killed

10 Union Mission Journal.

and mangled three Quapaw Indians in the employ of a hunter named Etienne Vaugine; a fourth escaped by swimming the Poteau. When Mr. Vaugine sought to escape to the fort the Indians on their rafts attempted to intercept him, but the artillery was brought up to cover his landing and he safely reached shelter. Several white families fled to Fort Smith for protection, while the Osage plundered the homes of the settlers on the Poteau and Lee's Creek, and of some soldiers living within a mile of the post, taking horses, guns, and any other movable property they fancied. They also killed three Delaware Indians on Lee's Creek.[11]

This foray of the Osage caused great excitement among the Cherokee and whites along the Arkansas River above and below Fort Smith. News of their coming was brought by messengers who said that the Osage were out to ravage the Cherokee settlements and that every warrior carried a halter as he expected to ride home on a Cherokee horse. The Cherokee at Spadra Bluff started under the command of Captain James Rogers for Mulberry Creek, where they joined a party of warriors under Major Maw; another party from Piney Creek joined one from Illinois Bayou and went to Spadra Bluff "where they stopped awhile & after conjuring a while returned, saying it was a false alarm." Later, at news of the demonstration at Fort Smith, the excitement flamed up again. The women and children were collected at one of the groups of houses for defense, and the men came to the factory to secure ammunition; but as this was the prize for which the Osage were coming, Mr. Lyon had loaded his 113 kegs of powder and 50 rifles in a boat and sent them down the river.

---

[11] *Niles' Weekly Register*, June 30, 1821; *Arkansas Gazette*, May 12, 1821, p. 3, cols. 2 and 3, letter from Fort Smith, dated April 23, 1821. The attempt of the Osage on the post occurred the afternoon of April 9. A number of claims against the Indians were afterward filed with the Government by whites who had been robbed by the Osage on this raid; William Murphy lost horses, merchandise, and tools; Reuben Landers was robbed of corn, bacon, and horses; Mark Bean, who had just inaugurated his salt works on the old trail near

A number of white movers running from the neighborhood of the garrison, as they passed on down the river told a man on the bank that there were 800 Osages out divided into 3 gangs one of which had crossed the Arkansas and were coming down the south side of the River, another were coming down on the Mountains back of the Settlements on the North side, and the third were killing and driving all before them in the settled country. They said that the Osages had broke into the Garrison and plundered it. This news caused fresh alarm.[12]

Houses were picketed or surrounded with palisades and the people were concentrated for defense. While most of the reports proved exaggerated, Acting-Governor Crittenden requested the Secretary of War to furnish ". . . . swords and pistols for two hundred troopers, who might be raised at any moment to repel invasion and outrage."[13]

On the twenty-fifth of April Mr. Ransom returned to Union from a journey which took him as far as the Sallisaw in a quest for laborers; he was able in that distance to secure only three men who were willing to return into the Osage country. According to the reports he brought back from below

.... we fear that the war between the Osages and Cherokees will be carried on to the great distress of the Osage people. Their conduct in their last incursion was very bad. It appears evident today by people who are going to the Village[14] to recover their horses, that they killed some of the Delaware Tribe who fell in their way, supposing them to be Cherokees; that they also robbed some families of the white people; and that they killed the Quappaws who

Illinois River also suffered, as did William McMurtry and Samuel Guthery; from the latter were taken horses, four bee stands, pewter plates, and other household possessions (OIA, "Special File" No. 191; Foreman, *op. cit.* p. 74).

[12] Lyon to Secretary of War, April 7, 1821, AGO, ORD, WDF; Matthew Lyon, government factor at Spadra Bluff, kept a journal of these exciting events on the Arkansas River, which he transmitted to the Secretary of War, *ibid.*

[13] Crittenden to Calhoun, May 17, 1821, AGO, ORD, WDF.

[14] Clermont's Town, about twenty-five miles northwest of the mission.

are at peace with them at the instigation of a young Chief[15] to revenge the death of some of his relations in a former quarrel. It is expected that the Cherokees are about to make a general attack upon this unhappy nation. Brother Chapman went this morning to the Village to ascertain as near as possible what were their intentions and to gain what information he could to direct us on our measures the ensuing summer.

Two days later

Brother Chapman returned. . . . . He found the Chiefs more united than usual; sick of the war and sorry for the conduct of their people in killing the Quappaws and Delawares, and robbing the whites. Clamore said "he did not send his men down to conduct so." It is said that the conduct of the young Chief is wholly disapproved and he has escaped from the Village.

By the middle of May the mission family had planted and fenced a field of corn in addition to a garden of four acres. Realizing the necessity of learning the Osage language, Chapman departed for the Osage village to join them on their hunt and during this association to acquire as much of their language as possible. On the fifteenth he returned and reported that the whole village had been vacated, and though he pursued them across the Verdigris River he was compelled by lack of food to abandon the chase.

On the seventeenth they received a visit from a white man who had just left the Osage encampment twenty miles beyond their village, where he had gone to recover some horses stolen by the Osage. He bore from Clermont a message to Walter Webber, the Cherokee chief, that Clermont desired peace, that he did not wish to injure the white people whose homes lay between the two tribes, that he proposed an armistice of three months during which time the Cherokee could determine

[15] The wife and child of Moi-neh-per-sha had been killed some years before by the Cherokee, and he caused the death of the Quapaw as a vicarious atonement.

whether they wished to make peace or continue the war, that
if they would send an agent or other properly authorized person with a chief he would conclude a peace which would stand,
that if afterward any of the people of his village committed
depredations he would assist the Cherokee in gaining satisfaction, but as he could not control the other villages he did not
want to be held answerable for the damages which they might
commit. He said that he did not beg a peace because he could
send an army of fifteen hundred warriors, and if they saw fit
to carry on the war he should on his part carry it on with vigor.

On Saturday, May 26, 1821, the mission family organized a
church, undoubtedly the first Protestant church in Oklahoma.
Three days later there arrived a large keel boat from the mouth
of the White River, carrying thirty-three barrels of flour, a
large pair of millstones and bolting cloths, besides a large box
of clothing for Indian children from a missionary society in
Philadelphia.

Finding little timber suitable for building in the vicinity of
the mission, they located a pine forest about twenty miles up
the river. There they cut 140 pine logs, of which they constructed a raft to float down the river. On the descent the raft
struck the rocks and was broken to pieces. This misfortune,
followed by a rise in the river, caused a loss of fifty of the logs.
Those that were saved were cut into boards by a ripsaw. The
members of the mission had searched diligently for a mill site,
but not finding one had been compelled to abandon the idea of
a water mill and substitute a treadmill worked by oxen.

The Osage had been obliged to abandon their invasion of the
Cherokee country by lack of ammunition which at all times
prevented their meeting the enemy on equal terms; they were
poor and miserable and sick of war, and would have been
happy if Clermont's proposal of an armistice had been accepted
by Webber. But instead of that, following the failure of the
Osage, the Cherokee made preparations for pushing the war

with renewed vigor; and the recorder at Union Mission, on June 24, noted the arrival of the members of Joseph Revoir's family

.... who have been alarmed by the Cherokees. They state that the Cherokees had taken their horses and that they had not seen their father since early in the morning. Mr. Revoir is a half breed French and Osage, a decent citizen, and lived 15 miles up this river. He had just formed a settlement in that place,[16] and is making good improvements.

Two days later the body of the murdered Revoir was found.

He was an innocent victim and fell a prey to the jealousy of the enemy. The family intend soon to leave this for Missoury and have requested us to milk their cows amounting to ten until they should be disposed of. For our kindness in giving them a temporary residence they have presented us with 50 fowls and two younk elk.....

Mr. Revoir had no interest in the war, and probably when he met his pursuers he hailed them as friends, not knowing that they had searched two hundred miles on purpose to take his life.[17]

Webber and his war party returned to the Cherokee settlement with Revoir's scalp and his fourteen horses, and there was great exultation over their achievement.[18] In July a rumor that the Osage were on their way to retaliate caused the Chero-

[16] The modern Salina, Oklahoma. From Revoir's son Charles the missionaries bought four hundred bushels of corn in Revoir's field which they carried down the river in a boat.

[17] ".... Joseph Revoir, a man of civilized life and industrious habits. This man tho' he pursued his business peacably at home, because he lived on Osage ground and had Osage blood in his veins, is marked out as a victim and destroyed..... The enemy is everywhere. He thirsts for indiscriminate slaughter. He spares none. It is a war of extermination" (Vaill to Calhoun, October 30, 1821, OIA, RCF; *Arkansas Gazette*, July 14, 1821, p. 3, col. 1).

[18] American Board of Commissioners for Foreign Missions, Vol. XI, Journal of Dwight Mission.

kee to prepare to defend the settlements. Though this report proved unfounded, the Cherokee made further preparations for prosecuting the war.

> A small company of Delaware Indians, about twenty-five or thirty, came in as allies to the Cherokees in their war. They have taken their stand for the present, within two miles of Dwight. Three or four blacksmiths are employed in shoeing horses for the purpose of an expedition against the Osages.[19]

Meanwhile Captain Douglass arrived at the mouth of Grand River with supplies for the mission from Cincinnati, but on account of the high water he was unable to ascend the river. Some of the men of the mission with horses rode down to the boat to pack home potatoes and bacon; they could not wait for the arrival of the boat to bring them the salt meat, for they had tired of the game[20] the prairie and forest afforded. They justified their return on the Sabbath by the fact that the mission family was in need of the bacon, and the trading settlement at the mouth of the Verdigris,[21] where the boat was tied up, was not a proper place for them to spend that day. On the sixteenth of July their keel boat was washed away by the swollen waters and was later discovered upside down on a bar in the Arkansas River, about fifteen miles below the mouth of the Grand River. Captain Douglass was able to bring his boat to the mission on the twentieth; he delivered there flour and biscuit, twenty barrels of pork and bacon, beans, vinegar, shoes, mill irons, and a wagon.

In August it was exceedingly hot, and there was much sickness in the mission family. On the fourth of the month:

19 Morse, *op. cit.*, Appendix, p. 232; Journal of Dwight Mission.

20 They became surfeited with fish, turkeys, prairie chickens, deer, and buffaloes taken near the mission; early in September six deer were killed, one of which yielded quarters weighing 155 pounds.

21 The mouths of the Verdigris and Grand rivers are within a half mile of each other; boats brought merchandise up the Verdigris to the trading houses where there were good landing places.

Col. Glenn passed here with a hunting party from Missouri.[22] He told us that the other Mission Family to the Osages had probably reached their station[23] by this time as they were about half way up the Osage river on the 12th July. He also stated to our great joy that an agent from the Gov. of United States is passing thro' the tribes in Missouri to dissuade them from becoming allies to either party in this war. Such a measure will have a direct tendency to stop the war.

The weather continued so warm that their hands deserted them, including the men who were cutting the logs into lumber to build their houses. On the tenth of August they reported that they had cut from one and a half to two tons of hay to an acre.

[August 27] Four children were brought this morning half breeds, three of whom belong to a Frenchman who serves as an interpreter in the village. We gladly received them. Took off their tattered dirty garments, and clothed them with some of the new and clean clothes which we have had in readiness. These children are between the age of 4 and twelve.

[September 1, 1821] .... moved into our new school house[24] this week. Mr. Spaulding has the charge of the school when able, but is visited with attacks of the intermittent.

[September 28] .... Col. Glenn sets out with a large hunting

[22] Col. Hugh Glenn passed the mission over the Osage trail on the way to his trading house on the Verdigris about a mile above the mouth; here he was joined early in September by Jacob Fowler and other hunters who had come up the Arkansas River by way of Arkansas Post and Fort Smith, for the purpose of securing from Governor Miller a license to hunt, trap, and trade in the Indian country.

[23] The other mission family had proceeded up the Missouri and Osage rivers to establish themselves among the Osage who remained on the latter stream; this mission was to be called Harmony.

[24] This was probably the first schoolhouse within the state of Oklahoma. The three native children first instructed there were Joseph, Abigail, and Charles Donne (American Board of Commissioners for Foreign Missions, *ibid.*, Vol. XXXIV, No. 129).

party for the Rocky Mountains.²⁵ It is his intention to learn the
state of the Indian tribes through which he has to pass.

By the sixth the missionaries had constructed a canoe thirty
feet long for use in crossing the river and to secure building
material for their mill.

²⁵ The party of twenty men headed by Glenn and Fowler are setting out on
their hunting, trapping, and trading expedition to the Rocky Mountains (Coues
[ed.], *The Journal of Jacob Fowler* [New York, 1898]): "Conl. Hugh glann
Haveing Left us and gon by the mishenerys" rejoined the party before they
reached the Osage village; Fowler was interested in the hills and country around
Clermont's Town: "Heare is one of the most delight full peace of Cuntry I
Have Ever Seen.....Heare we find not one sole in or about the vilege the
Indians are all gon a buffelow Hunting and are not Exspected to return till in
the Winter" (*ibid.,* p. 8).

VIII

ALLIED INDIANS MASSACRE THE OSAGE
1821

THROUGH the summer of 1821 the Cherokee were counseling and planning for another attack on the Osage. Major Bradford, whose views differed from those of Governor
Miller, attempted to dissuade them, and through other agencies
induced some of their allies not to join in the attack. He and
Captain Pryor visited Clermont's Town, and urged the Osage
to cease their warfare against the Cherokee and their depredations against the white settlers whose homes between the tribes
had been raided on their foray in April. The Osage told Bradford that the Cherokee should not see their tracks on Cherokee
soil if they would keep off the land of the Osage

> .... and out of our town—we dont want the Cherokees to steal
> what game there is on our land, we want it for ourselves, our
> women and our children .... we cannot farm like the Cherokees,
> we have not yet learned how to raise Hogs, Cattle and other things
> like the Cherokees—when we want meat for our women and chil-
> dren and clothing, our dependence is in the woods—if we do not
> get it there we must go hungry and naked.....
>
> [When the President] .... sent the Cherokees on this side of
> the Great River and gave them land we had sold him he certainly
> did not give to the Cherokees all the Beavers, Bears, Buffaloes and
> Deer on our lands. We sold him land but not game on our land
> when the Cherokees hunt on our land and kill our game we will
> always have trouble, they will steal our horses and our young men
> will kill them—this has always been a principal cause of all our
> difficulties..... We made a peace with the Cherokees at St. Louis,
> that peace has been broken—I am willing that the President our
> great Father at Washington shall settle all the difficulties that have
> happened since the Treaty of St. Louis and make another Peace

between us and the Cherokees. . . . . we will not disturb the Cherokees between now and the time peace may be made if they will not
disturb us. . . . .[1]

With the understanding that their controversies were to be submitted to their "great Father" for adjustment during the armistice, and in the meantime relying on Bradford's assurance that
he would prevent the Cherokee from passing up the Arkansas
River to attack them, they turned their attention to securing
their fall and winter supply of food.

On the twentieth of September Captain Pryor called at
Union Mission and reported that the Osage were just leaving
for their fall hunt. Their trail lay in a westerly course and
crossed the Arkansas River near the mouth of the Cimarron.
The tribe divided, most of the warriors proceeding to fight the
"Pawnee"[2] who frequently drove them from the buffalo hunting grounds. This was the opportunity for which the Cherokee
were waiting;[3] they had continued their preparations for an
attack on the Osage, disregarding the advice of Major Bradford. He asked for an opportunity to counsel with them on the
subject, but they replied on September 28 that their plans had
been completed and it would be impossible for them to tarry
longer to meet him. However, they said that when they passed
Fort Smith he could see them;[4] accordingly in the early part
of October Bradford visited the Cherokee at their camp about
fourteen miles from Fort Smith, and urged them to turn back
and accept the armistice proffered by the Osage. They said that
they had started for war and were determined to have satisfaction in their own way. There were three hundred of them, in-

[1] Speech delivered by Clermont at Council, September 15, 1821; Bradford to
Calhoun, October 1, 1821, AGO, ORD, WDF.

[2] The object of this chastisement may have been the Kiowa or Wichita.

[3] "The Osages are gone from their towns where it is likely the women and
children will be massacred" (Lyons to Calhoun, October 20, 1821, AGO, ORD,
WDF).

[4] Brearley to Bradford, September 28, 1821, *ibid.;* Jolly to Bradford, September 28, 1821, *ibid.*

cluding ten Delaware, twelve Creeks, twelve Choctaw, fifteen Shawnee, and a number of white men;[5] these Major Bradford ordered back, while the Indians continued. When Major Bradford found he could not induce the Cherokee to turn back, from some inexplicable motive he gave them a barrel of gun powder to use on their expedition.[6]

Richard Graham, the Indian superintendent at St. Louis, under instructions of the Secretary of War, was endeavoring to secure the attendance of deputations of the two tribes in his presence for the purpose of making peace between them. The refusal of the Cherokee to return the prisoners, as promised by them in the treaty of 1818, had kept alive the bitterness between the tribes which manifested itself by killings and theft of each other's horses until the score stood some forty or fifty horses in favor of the Osage; they had also exacted a greater toll of Cherokee lives than they had lost. The Cherokee refused to attend at St. Louis, but a delegation of Osage responded to Graham's invitation. Government officials had assured them that their proposal of an armistice would be imposed on the Cherokee, who would not be allowed to pass Fort Smith, and that the Osage would be permitted to hunt in security if they would send a peace delegation to confer with the superintendent. But the Cherokee seized upon this occasion to proceed against their enemies; they pursued the trail of the Osage bound for their hunting grounds, and dispatched parties on all diverging trails to fall upon isolated camps.[7]

A month after the Cherokee passed Fort Smith one hundred of them returned bringing with them thirty prisoners, and stated that they had killed forty Osage and had captured sev-

[5] Bradford to Calhoun, October 21, 1821, *ibid.*

[6] Missouri Historical Society, "Graham Papers," R. Graham to Calhoun, December 28, 1821.

[7] *Ibid.* Graham was much mortified and embarrassed in his dealings with the Osage by the failure of the troops at Fort Smith to prevent the massacre of the Osage.

enty horses. Soon afterward the remainder of the Cherokee
army reached the post. Accounts of the engagement with the
Osage differed so much that it was some time before Major
Bradford could arrive at the truth; but it appeared that while
the former party had succeeded brilliantly against a company
of women and children, the main body of Cherokee had engaged a band of Osage warriors, been badly worsted, and compelled to retreat. The Cherokee were surprised in the evening
as they were unsaddling their horses; the Osage charged so
savagely and at such close quarters that some of the Cherokee
were powder-burned, and two of their warriors were killed.
They claimed however that they killed five of their enemies;
they exhibited a number of scalps, including two of their own
warriors, which the Cherokee themselves took from their dead
to prevent the Osage from bearing home these emblems of
victory to be displayed at triumphal dances in their towns.[8]

Captain Pryor, who brought the news of the massacre of
the Osage, reported to Union Mission on the tenth of December:

.... It was about the 1st of Nov. that the Cherokees came on
them very unexpectedly. The Osage warriors relying on Maj.
Bradford to keep the enemy from coming against them, had gone
almost to a man to fight the Pawnees. The very few who were at
the Osage camp when it was attacked, kept the enemy at bay till
the women and children could get off, but the resistance of 10 or
12 warriors against a large body of Cherokees was small, and 100
of the Osage people are supposed to have been killed and taken
prisoners. Several of the prisoners have returned, some have been
killed, since they were taken. It may be a greater number are miss-
ing than they have yet known. How distressed their situation at
present. They have returned with no provisions and are very poor.
Their situation calls for our prayers and for the prayers of all
good people. Charles Donne (the frenchman whose children are
with us) came in with a trembling heart lest his children had been

[8] Bradford to Calhoun, November 18, 1821, AGO, ORD, WDF.

destroyed like many poor little ones among the hunters. Finding them well he rejoiced greatly and said he would not take them away, because they would not be in so good a place as this. He loves his children and seems to regret that the Osages do not see that their children would be in a better situation here than roving through the forest.[9]

The Cherokee reported this massacre as a great victory over the enemy. In the middle of November, 1821, the Dwight journal contains their version:

> The warriors of this nation with a few allies have for about six weeks been in pursuit of the Osages. Today a party of the Cherokees returned from the campaign. When they separated from the main body of the Cherokees they were within one day's march of the main body of the Osages. This party consisting of about eighty fell in with a party of Osages about 75 in number all of whom were killed and taken prisoners without the loss of a single man on the part of the Cherokees.[10]

Instead of the proud achievement boasted by the Cherokee, it was a wanton slaughter of a party of old men, women, and children, while their warriors were absent.[11] With the captives, sixty-three scalps, and peltries taken from the Osage, the triumphant Cherokee returned to their settlements where there was great rejoicing; to such excess was the celebration carried that the Cherokee barbarously butchered a number of their defenseless prisoners.[12] The leader of this atrocity was a man named Tom Graves, who ".... killed one of the women and her infant child. The circumstances are too horrid to be re-

[9] Union Mission Journal.

[10] American Board of Commissioners for Foreign Missions, Vol. XI, Dwight Mission Journal.

[11] *Niles' Weekly Register,* March 30, 1822; *Louisiana Herald,* January 19, 1822, p. 3, cols. 1 and 2; *Arkansas Gazette,* March 19, 1822, p. 3, col. 1; here it is stated that the Cherokee claimed to have killed or taken prisoners 102 Osage.

[12] *Louisiana Herald,* January 19, 1822, p. 3, cols. 1 and 2; Missouri Historical Society, "Graham Papers," Menard to Graham, January 3, 1822.

lated."[13] Graves, who was a leading man among the Cherokee, cherished an implacable hatred for the Osage. He was indicted for these murders and the murder of several other Osage children, and brought to trial at Little Rock in April of the next year; on a plea in abatement, the court held that as the murders were committed on Indian land, in accordance with tribal custom, it had no jurisdiction, and the prisoner was discharged.[14]

The summer and autumn of 1821 was a busy period for the members of Dwight Mission. They had been compelled to send to Union Mission two hundred miles away for nails; Mr. Orr was obliged to ascend to Fort Smith to get a letter that had been carried there by mistake; as nearly everybody was ill the erection of the buildings had been much delayed, and it was October 24 before the main body of the dining hall and

[13] Dwight Mission Journal, ".... killed 29 women and children and took ninety odd prisoners chiefly old men women and children, three of whom a woman and her child and a young girl they most barbarously murdered after their arrival at their village—& threw their bodies to be devoured by the hogs which was seen by Mr. Scott on his way to this place—this murder was perpettrated by one Graves a white, who was taken when very young by the Cherokees & brought up by them & is now a Captain and commanded 100 of the Party & is a farther evidence to me that there is more savage verocity [sic] in the whites brought in Indian life & the half-breeds than in the genuine Indian" (Graham to Calhoun, *ibid.*).

[14] *Niles' Weekly Register*, May 31, 1823; *Arkansas Gazette*, April 29, 1823, p. 3, col. 1. Graves was taken into custody on February 25, 1823, and tried at the April term; the jury disagreed and on April 23 he was discharged by the court (Certified Copy of Records, OIA, RCF, "1828 Cherokees West"). Graves was prosecuted by Roane and Oden and defended by Locas, Sevier, and Walker. The *Arkansas Gazette* account of the trial says of "....the notorious Tom Graves .... he is said to be a full-blooded white man, but had been raised among the Indians from his earliest infancy, and is totally ignorant of his parentage or the place of his nativity. Although he is a white man by birth, he is said to possess, to their fullest extent, all the habits and principles of an Indian or savage." The missionaries said he was a half-breed (Dwight Mission Journal). When Major Long was descending the Arkansas River in 1820, his party had dinner on September 23 at Graves's home on Rocky Bayou in the Cherokee settlements. They called Graves a metif chief, and said he looked like a white man but could speak no English (Thwaites [ed.], *op. cit.*, XVII, 17).

kitchen was raised; the Indians had to be cultivated and their friendship won so they would send their children to school.

On November 23: "cold weather and snow, and we are unprepared as our dining hall and kitchen not completed. Have to eat our meals in a passage way between two cabins where we are exposed to the severities of the season;" and in juxtaposition to this state of unpreparedness, the next item, "Sister W[ashburn] gave birth to a daughter." Orr and Finney have traveled 170 miles to meet and guide to the mission, a party of four teachers and missionaries who have been on the road from Massachusetts for thirteen weeks, and for whom there was much anxiety; but on December 22, ".... made glad today by arrival of sisters E. Stetson and N. Brown & Bro. A. Hitchcock. One of the number, Br. Daniel Hitchcock,[15] died on the way." Chief John Jolly, full of the importance of their first school, makes frequent calls and wants to know when it will begin. He ".... hopes this part of the tribe would become as advanced as those in the Old Nation." On Christmas day, ".... Br. Jacob Hitchcock and Sr. Nancy Brown married."[16]

The first day of the year 1822 was celebrated by the opening of the school with three Cherokee children. On the next day ".... another little girl brought by her mother with request that we would keep her until she herself is satisfied that she has learned enough." On the eleventh, ".... two ragged dirty orphans brought for us to care for." But by the twelfth they had eighteen, which was a larger number than they were equipped to accommodate.

On February 6, ".... Party of Osage hunters came to Cherokee frontier—did some damage but no lives lost." And on the nineteenth ".... Sister Finney gave birth to a daughter." The war between the Osage and Cherokee had a singular effect on

[15] Daniel Hitchcock, 26 years of age, died of bilious fever; buried 33 miles from Gettysburg and 12 miles from Hargerstown.

[16] Dwight Mission Journal. Mrs. Asa Hitchcock died at Dwight Mission, March 3, 1827.

the missions at Union and Dwight. The Osage feared for the safety of their children at school and the Cherokee believed theirs safest away from home; on the twenty-third,

> . . . . six were brought to us today, in addition to five on the 14th, from the settlements above, that they might be out of danger from the Osages. One man who brought two children said that he expected to have to run soon and in that case he could run with his wife only, better than if he had his children with him.
>
> George Requa from Union Mission called upon us on his way down the river on business. When it is known that the journey of this Br. 200 miles through the wilderness was to obtain some files necessary in order to saw planks by hand and a small number of axes, the friends of missions living in civilized society and in lands abounding in everything needful may learn something of the smaller difficulties with which missionaries have to contend when far removed in the forest.

One is not surprised to read on March 18 of the death of Brother Finney's month-old baby.

Captain Morris of the steamboat "Eagle" brought goods for the missionaries from New Orleans and unloaded them on the bank of the Arkansas.[17] To get them, Orr and seven men had to go down the Illinois in their keel boat. Epaphras Chapman of Union Mission, on his way to New Orleans on business, stopped to call bringing a report of new Cherokee expeditions against the Osage.[18]

[17] It is the eighteenth of March; the "Eagle," the first steamboat to ascend so far up the Arkansas, reached Little Rock on the sixteenth. Governor Miller was aboard on his way to Fort Smith (*Arkansas Gazette,* March 19, 1822, p. 3, col. 1; *Missouri Intelligencer,* April 16, 1822, p. 2, col. 1).

[18] Mr. Chapman, who came by Fort Smith, brought word to Little Rock of two Cherokee war parties that had just taken the field against the Osage; one of these had stolen several horses from a white man living on the Poteau (*Arkansas Gazette,* April 2, 1822, p. 3, col. 1).

IX

THE PEACE CONFERENCE AND SURRENDER OF OSAGE CAPTIVES, 1822

IN order to suppress hostilities, General Gaines, in July, 1821, ordered Colonel Arbuckle at New Orleans to hold the Seventh Infantry in readiness to occupy the southwest frontier. Six companies were to go to the Red River near Natchitoches, and four to Fort Smith.[1] Colonel Arbuckle and four companies began their ascent of the Mississippi in November on the steamboat "Tennessee," but they were detained a long time at the mouth of the Arkansas by low water; with the aid of keel boats they reached Arkansas Post by the first of the year, and arrived at Fort Smith on February 26. A large number of Colonel Arbuckle's command died on this long passage. On his arrival, Colonel Arbuckle found a farm of eighty acres attached to the post, with one thousand bushels of corn, one hundred head of cattle, and four hundred hogs. But it continued a sickly station, due in large measure, he said to white settlers nearby who sold whiskey to the soldiers.[2]

With this increase of 250 men, Fort Smith assumed a station of considerable importance on this remote frontier.[3] Upon the

[1] Gaines to Arbuckle, July 14, 1821, AGO, ORD, Headquarters Western Department "Letter Book 1." Four of the companies on the steamboat "Courier" from New Orleans arrived at Natchitoches on November 14, 1821; the other two were "on the steam boat *Arkansas* which burst her boiler at the Grand Point" (*Louisiana Herald*, November 17, 1821, p. 2, col. 3).

[2] Arbuckle to Gadsden, January 3, 1822, AGO, OFD, 2 A 22; *ibid.*, March 4, 1822, 10 A 22; *ibid.*, March 26, 1822; Foreman, *op. cit.*, p. 59; *Arkansas Gazette*, November 24, 1821; Arbuckle to Adjutant General, August 2, 1823, AGO, OFD, 54 A 23.

[3] "The position of Fort Smith is commanding .... and if, as John Randolph (in his circular to his constituents, on his late departure for Europe) says our future enemy is to approach by way of the Arkansas River, the Anglo-Spaniards

arrival of Colonel Arbuckle, Major Bradford was relieved of his command and transferred to Natchitoches.[4]

Upon the movement of additional troops to Fort Smith, renewed efforts were made to establish peace between the tribes and prevent their depredations on the whites. Soon after the arrival of Colonel Arbuckle, Governor Miller again came to Fort Smith in the latter part of March. On his way up he

may one day find Fort Smith a little Gibralter in his way" (*Arkansas Gazette,* July 23, 1822, p. 3, col. 1). In fact, in 1818 ".... a party of Spaniards from Santa Fe have lately been up the waters of the Canadian within the limits of the territory of the United States .... but what were there intentions, whether for trade or to sound the feelings of the Indians in respect to their disposition for hostilities, I have not yet learned" (Bradford to Calhoun, March 28, 1818, AGO, ORD, WDF). However, Bradford sent "a spy in that section of the country to find out their object."

Less than two months after Major Bradford reported the presence of the Spaniards, they made a permanent record of their visit to the future Oklahoma. There has recently been discovered by Mr. William E. Baker an inscription on the rocks along Cimarron River, too weatherworn to be entirely deciphered, but yielding the following: "E my Terio Jueb ena Maio 1818." Fortunately the date, May, 1818, is quite clear (Alfred B. Thomas, "Spanish Reaction to American Intrusion into Spanish Dominions, 1818-1819," in *West Texas Historical Year Book, 1928*).

[4] In the autumn Bradford was a candidate for delegate to Congress from Arkansas, but was defeated by Henry W. Conway (*Missouri Intelligencer,* September 16, 1823, p. 3, col. 2). On April 7, 1824, he was appointed sutler at Fort Towson (AGO, "Post Returns for Fort Towson"). Gen. E. P. Gaines said of him: "He fought gallantly at the head of a company near ten years ago at Fort Meigs, where he received a severe wound. I afterwards frequently saw him before his wounds had healed sufficiently to enable him to walk without a crutch, hobbling along at the head of his company, upon more than one occasion, directing the fire of his musquetry against the warriors of Tecumseh" (Gaines to Adjutant General, January 24, 1823, AGO, ORD, "Letter Book 1," p. 137). Major Bradford never recovered from this wound; he died October 20, 1826, at Fort Towson, at the age of fifty-five (Foreman, *op. cit.*, p. 51 n.).

"William Bradford late a major in the Fourth Regiment of United States Infantry, being engaged in battle on the 5th day of May in the year 1813, at or near Fort Meigs in the Territory of Michigan, received a gun shot wound in his left thigh; & he is thusly not only incapacitated for any active business in his life, but in the opinion of undersigned is three fourths disabled from obtaining his subsistence by manual labor" (Th. Lauson Surgeon U. S. Army, Cantonment Jesup, 9th March, 1825: *U. S. Pension files*).

stopped at the Cherokee settlement, where he learned of the two large war parties that had gone against the Osage. He called a conference of Takatoka, Jolly, Black Fox, Tom Graves, and other chiefs and endeavored to get them to stop the war; they, however, would not commit themselves except to say that if their warriors returned successful, thus evening up the score of killings, they might agree to meet the Osage.[5] Straggling parties of Osage were killing cattle and harassing the Cherokee war parties by stealing their horses.[6]

Governor Miller was preceded by Nathaniel Philbrook, subagent to the Osage.[7] Philbrook went to the Osage town[8] on January 14, 1882, and on the twenty-fifth he returned to Union Mission where he reported that the Osage were much concerned with his proposal to make peace. Clermont, he said, was indifferent, having been influenced by one of the traders; but Tallai was much in favor of ending the war, saying: "I do not want to live always with my thumb on the cock of the gun."

On the first day of April the Dwight missionaries reported:

.... Governor Miller[9] called on us in the evening on his return from his tour up the river. He had a council with the Cherokees and proceeded no further than Fort Smith. He thinks there is little

[5] Miller to Calhoun, May, 1822, AGO, ORD, WDF.

[6] Lyon to Calhoun, February 24, 1822, *ibid.*

[7] In the fall and winter of 1822 most of the remainder of the Osage tribe removed from the Osage River to the Grand, and Colonel Arbuckle urged that an agent be appointed "who should reside with or near them, from whom they could receive advice, and who would have it in his power to check them from stealing from our Frontier Inhabitants" (Arbuckle to Nourse, November 2, 1822, AGO, ORD, 11 A 23). Philbrook who had been acting subagent since November 1, 1820, was formally appointed by the Secretary of War, May 18, 1821 (OIA, RCF, "Letter Book E," p. 100; *American State Papers,* "Indian Affairs," II, 365).

[8] In the winters Clermont's Town removed from the prairie, divided into several bands, and located in huts built along the Verdigris River so as to be near wood, water, and winter range (Union Mission Journal).

[9] Dwight Mission Journal; Governor Miller was engaged on his tour to the Osage for two months and returned to Arkansas Post on Apirl 27 (Miller to Calhoun, May, 1822, AGO, ORD, WDF).

prospect of restoring peace between the Cherokees and Osages. [On the twenty-third] .... last evening information was brought that the Osages, Kickapoos, Sacks, and Foxes were on their way to the Cherokees, and orders were given by the chiefs and head men for every Cherokee able to bare arms to be ready in two days to meet the Invaders. This information has produced considerable alarm and the whites in the nation are removing their effects to a place of safety as far as possible. The Department of U. S. Factory on the Illinois is thought to be unsafe and the sub-factor brought the goods to us, as it is thought the Osages will not molest us.[10]

This alarm was unfounded; the Osage had agreed to observe an armistice while Philbrook negotiated with the Cherokee. This they did, and for several weeks they frequently called at Union Mission to learn whether news had come of Philbrook's success with their enemies. The agent, diligent to prevent a renewal of hostilities, again ascended to the Osage village, stopping on the way at Union Mission from April fifth to eighth. He carried messages of friendship from Governor Miller to the Osage, telling them how it grieved him to see their women and children hewing wood and fetching water for the Cherokee. "When one of them, an old man, was told that his wife and children, who had been taken prisoners last fall, were alive, he wept aloud. Affecting was this interview."[11]

After a few days spent at the Osage town, Philbrook returned to Union Mission and reported that the Osage people were eager for peace; they had continued to observe the armistice proposed by them, and from fear of their enemies had waited in suspense in their villages, neglecting their hunting until they were nearly destitute of food. They were poor and wretched, having no meat and no ammunition with which to kill any game; with nothing to eat besides a little corn,[12] they were much distressed by the continuance of the war. They im-

10 Dwight Mission Journal.
11 Union Mission Journal.
12 Miller to Calhoun, May, 1822, AGO, ORD, WDF.

pressed everyone with their loyalty to the United States and were keenly disappointed that the Cherokee had not agreed to peace. Mr. Philbrook proposed on his return

> to urge the Commanding officer at the Garrison, if it be any way consistent for him to do so, to stop the Cherokees from distressing these people any further and he thinks their proposed terms are reasonable, and ought to be acceded to and nothing can be gained on either side by the continuance of the war. The Cherokees are better prepared for a war than the Osages, for though the latter are far more numerous, they have not the same advantages with their enemies to purchase powder.[13]

Philbrook descended to the Cherokee and with the assistance of their chief, Jolly, induced them to meet on April 26 in a council in their country, where he explained to them his plans for peace.

After considering the matter for eight days, the Cherokee finally agreed to the armistice. Philbrook then ascended to the Verdigris[14] and it was signed by mark by eighteen Osage chiefs May 16, 1822. This armistice, which was to be binding until the assembly of a peace conference at Fort Smith was a formal written instrument containing six sections. By its terms the Cherokee agreed not to send any more war parties[15] to the Osage country for twenty days[16] after the breaking up of the council to be held, and the Osage were similarly bound. The latter agreed that as soon as they were informed that the Cherokee had accepted the terms of the armistice, they would send runners out to recall all war parties against the Cherokee, and the latter were to send no more hostile expeditions. The "Great

---

[13] *Ibid.*

[14] *Arkansas Gazette,* May 28, 1822, p. 3, col. 1; Union Mission Journal.

[15] A Cherokee war party during the previous March had passed Fort Smith on an excursion against the Osage (*Arkansas Gazette,* April 2, 1822, p. 3, col. 1). Major Bradford reported at Baton Rouge on April 16, that a party of eighty Cherokee had been on a scout for twenty days looking for Osage (*Louisiana Herald,* April 27, 1822, p. 2, col. 4).

[16] Union Mission Journal says three months.

Talk" was to be held at Fort Smith on July 30;[17] in the event
that either party violated the armistice, they agreed that the
United States should punish the offender.[18]

Relieved and heartened by the prospect of peace, the Cherokee are bringing their plows and other tools to the Dwight
Mission shop to be repaired so that they can put in their crops.
A steamboat from the Ohio River had arrived with a load of
supplies for the Mission. The crew come to the Mission; some
of them are pious, but others—abandoned characters—bring a
boatload of lumber up the Illinois on Sunday. The missionaries
refuse to receive it; but instead hold another meeting in the
dining hall, where a sermon is preached to these men by Mr.
Washburn intended to impress them with a realization of their
transgression.

It is July 13, 1822; the Cherokee are in council to consider
measures of peace; delegates are named to go to Fort Smith on
the thirtieth to meet the Osage and the army officers. Takatoka,
the war chief of the Cherokee, has called at the mission to have
translated a letter sent by General Gaines to the Cherokee and
Osage commanding them to bury the hatchet and make peace;[19]

[17] Miller to Calhoun, July 15, 1822, AGO, ORD, WDF.

[18] *Arkansas Gazette,* June 4, 1822, p. 3, col. 1; Union Mission Journal. The
difficulty of dealing with the Indians is indicated by the statement of Colonel
Arbuckle that "the Osage Indians are extremely ignorant and faithless; their
chiefs are without useful authority, and their warriors are encouraged in dishonesty from their infancy." Major Bradford said the Cherokee were liars and
Governor Miller said they were engaged in a "marauding, thieving, cowardly
kind of warfare"; and that both tribes used their war to cloak depredations on
the property of the whites.

[19] From his post at Louisville, Gen. Edmond P. Gaines, commanding the
Western Military Department, notified the Indian chiefs to refrain from further
hostilities and said that he was going to meet them at their conference at Fort
Smith (Gaines to chiefs, June 24, 1822, AGO, ORD, WDF; Gaines to Calhoun,
June 24, 1822, *ibid.*). General Gaines on a tour of inspection earlier in the year
had come by way of the Red River and "Kyamesha . . . . then across the Hills
& Valleys upon the last mentioned river, and the Poto, to Fort Smith where I
arrived on the morning" of April 22, 1822. He had intended to call the chiefs
of the Cherokee and Osage together to admonish them against further hostilities,

he says the United States will not permit them to spill each other's blood any longer.[20]

The conference at Fort Smith which was attended by 150 Osage and a large number of Cherokee[21] resulted in a written treaty executed on August 9;[22] besides the declaration of peace between the tribes, the principal feature of the treaty provided for the return by the Cherokee of seventeen Osage prisoners. Eight prisoners were delivered at the time the treaty was made, with the agreement to produce the others on the twenty-first of September.[23]

Twenty-one more prisoners were taken by the Cherokee to Fort Smith in the autumn to be delivered to their people, exceeding the number stipulated in the treaty. The Osage who were to receive them had set out some time previously on a hunting expedition, and in due time bent their course toward Fort Smith. On September 12, while on the south side of the

but learning that Governor Miller, who had recently been there, had failed in similar attempts, abandoned the idea (Gaines to Secretary of War, May 16, 1822, AGO, ORD, Headquarters Western Department, "Letter Book 1," p. 242). General Atkinson also visited this region during the disorders of 1822, coming from Council Bluffs and stopping at Union Mission on his way (Vaill to Calhoun, October 1, 1822, OIA, RCF).

[20] When the letter was interpreted and returned to the implacable Takatoka he spat upon it, ground it into the dirt, and stalked away in silence (C. Washburn, *Reminiscences of the Indians* [Richmond, 1869], p. 117).

[21] The Osage were accompanied to Fort Smith by Clermont, Tallai, and other chiefs who, on their way, called at Union Mission on July 30; with them also was Tallai's son, a pupil at the mission who had been named by the missionaries Philip Milledoler. His father called at the school to request that his boy might be allowed to accompany him (*American Missionary Register*, Vol. VII, n. 36).

[22] Foreman, *op. cit.*, p. 62; *Missouri Intelligencer*, December 24, 1822, p. 2, col. 3; OIA, RCF, Folio Drawer, manuscript copy of treaty. Besides Miller and Arbuckle, the treaty was witnessed by Capt. G. Leftwich, D. Brearley, Cherokee agent, Nathaniel Philbrook, sub-agent for the Arkansas Osage, and Epaphras Chapman. For the Cherokee it was signed by Waterminnow, Wat [Walter] Webber, Thomas Maw, Young Glass, J. Martin, and James Rogers. Clermont, Tallai, and Skitok or Mad Buffalo, and thirteen others signed for the Osage.

[23] American Board of Commissioners for Foreign Missions, Manuscript Library, Vol. VII, No. 26.

Arkansas near the mouth of the Canadian River, they were surprised and attacked by a party of Indians whose identity they did not discover, and suffered the loss of two men killed and two children taken prisoners.[24] After this outrage the Osage recrossed the Arkansas and retreated to their village on the Verdigris. Captain Pryor carried the news to Fort Smith; and the Cherokee, on hearing of the attack, sent two of their chiefs, Rogers and Webber, with their agent, Colonel Brearley, and Captain Davenport, in command at the post, to the Osage to convince them that they had no agency in the affair. The Osage accompanied the messengers to Fort Smith, where they received the prisoners and other proofs of friendship of the Cherokee, and parted on good terms.[25] When these prisoners were returned, the missionaries at Union observed that the Cherokee had taught the Osage women to spin and weave, and by developing their aptitude for industry and improvement had made their enforced stay with their captors a distinct contribution to the welfare of the Osage people.[26]

Governor Miller had spent most of his time for nearly two years up and down the Arkansas and Verdigris rivers counseling with the Indians and endeavoring to restore peace; but much praise was given Philbrook for his good offices in bringing about the treaty between the warring tribes.

[24] *Missouri Intelligencer*, December 24, 1822, p. 2, col. 3. It later was ascertained that this attack was made by a party of nine Choctaw under a leader named Capt. Red Bag [Red Dog?] and the two children were in possession of another member of the party named Tab-a-natch-a-hab-ba. Captain Pryor picked up a pair of suspenders from the hiding place of the attackers from which it was deduced that there were white men among them. The Choctaw continued to the Osage towns where they stole a number of horses on the sixteenth (Lieut. R. Wash to Colonel Arbuckle, October 31, 1823, AGO, OFD, 10 S 24). Lieutenant Wash said that sixty Choctaw living on the Red River were responsible for the outrages committed by the Osage on that settlement (*ibid*). The feud between the Choctaw and Osage was of long standing (Foreman, *op. cit.*, p. 73). Two of the wounded Osage were treated for their injuries by Doctor Palmer of Union Mission (Union Mission Journal).

[25] *Missouri Intelligencer*, December 24, 1822, p. 2, col. 3.

[26] Vaill to Calhoun, October 1, 1823, OIA, RCF.

The execution of the treaty presaged benefits to both tribes. During the first year of Union Mission but three pupils were brought to the school.

> .... Besides these, no family in all the village could be found willing to trust their children so far from home, while the war between them and the Cherokee continued. They have repeatedly told us as soon as the war is over we will send as many children as you can take..... The enemy is everywhere. He thirsts for indiscriminate slaughter. He spares none. It is a war of extermination. No one who is tainted with the blood of the nation whose destruction is sought is left to breathe the air of heaven.[27]

Probably no more strange mixture of blood has been seen in any institute of learning in Oklahoma than that in the little school on the banks of Grand River at Union Mission. Of the three who attended during the year 1821, the children of their interpreter, Joseph Donne was Spanish and Osage; Abigail and Charles Donne were French and Osage. The majority who later attended were of pure Osage blood; and the missionaries enrolled them under English names, frequently naming them for supporters of the Mission living in the East. During the first five years of the school, children of mixed French and Osage blood were numerous there. Beside these were a number of mixed Dutch, Kickapoo, and Osage blood; some French and Sioux; French, Sioux, and Osage; and Missouri and Osage; a number of foundlings had been picked up about the country, babies that had been abandoned to die of exposure and be devoured by the wolves. Two white children who lived at Fort Gibson were in attendance.

It is the twenty-sixth day of August, 1822, at Union:

> This morning Brother Vaill, Brother and Sister Fuller and Dr. Palmer set off for the village [Clermont's]. On their arrival, they found that they were too late to attend the marriage of the chief's daughter. As this was an instance in which the man was to have

[27] Vaill to Calhoun, October 30, 1821, OIA, RCF.

but one wife, they had determined to perform the ceremony according to Clermont's request, had they arrived in season. They witnessed, however, the novel parade of an Indian wedding—guns fired, the U. S. Colors displayed, great feasting on buffalo meat, etc. etc.

Thursday, Sept. 1. Our supplies have not yet reached us. We have been reduced to corn for six weeks. Our hand mill is not sufficient to supply our family with meal, and boiled corn serves us for food. This with milk and with beef which we cure at this season of the year by barbecuing, constitutes our chief subsistence at this time. We feel thankful that our hired men are not dissatisfied with such food. None of the family complain; but those who are indisposed suffer considerably for want of a change of diet. Fearing that the boat with our supplies is delayed in consequence of not having a sufficient number of hands on board, we sent two men down the river this morning for the purpose of hastening it forward.

The wagon, having met the boat somewhere down the Arkansas, returned six days later with the much desired salt meat.[28]

The missionaries give us some primitive sketches of the country and events along Grand River. An Indian calls to have an ax mended; he brings a deerskin to pay for the work which he watches with great interest. Another Osage and his wife stop at the mission on their way to the trading house with a number of skins to purchase a blanket. This Indian is a "Wah-kun-duk-ka"[29] or medicine man, who wishes to display his prowess. White men from the Arkansas River stop on their way to Shingah Moineh's town to recover stolen horses. This Osage town, Grosse Côte, is above Clermont's and on the east side of the Verdigris. Instead of a recovery of the lost horses,

[28] American Board of Commissioners for Foreign Missions, Manuscript Library, Vol. XXXIV, No. 129; Union Mission Journal; *Religious Intelligencer*, Vol. VII, No. 36.

[29] Wakonda: A term applied by the Omaha, Ponca, Osage, Quapaw, Kansa, Oto, Missouri, and Iowa tribes of the Siouan family when the power believed to animate all natural forms is spoken to or spoken of in supplication or rituals (*Handbook of American Indians*, II, 897).

those ridden by the white men are added by the Osage of that town to their loot.

By the treaty of 1808 the Government had agreed to maintain at all seasons of the year a trading post or factory on the Missouri River at Fort Clark where the Osage could barter their furs and peltries. By an act of May 6, 1822, Congress determined to discontinue the factories; the Osage were induced on August 31, 1822, at the United States Factory on the Marais des Cygnes, to enter into a new treaty by which, for the sum of $2,329.40 in merchandise paid them, they relinquished all claims on the Government to continue the factory promised in the former treaty. This treaty was negotiated by Richard Graham for the Government and was signed by Pahuska, Big Soldier, and twenty other Osage.[30]

In view of the abandonment of their trading house on the Missouri, the pressure of the Shawnee, Delaware, and other emigrant tribes in western Missouri, and the consequent scarcity of game, it was an easy matter for Colonel A. P. Chouteau to interest the Osage in removing south to the country tributary to the Neosho, near the remainder of the tribe and their superior hunting ground. In September Chouteau arrived at Union Mission with a party of Pahuska's band of Indians whom he was assisting to find a location; the next month another party of the northern Osage arrived at the mission, engaged in the same quest of a location for a new home. A month later a boat belonging to Chouteau passed up the river, loaded with merchandise from St. Louis which the trader had purchased to traffic with the Indians. He had located at the trading post near the saline where he and Revoir were engaged in business before the latter was killed by the Cherokee. With the great influence he possessed over the Osage, he induced them to locate in the neighborhood convenient to his trading house. In December the missionaries went up to preach to the Indians in the new settlement. This community continued to grow, and

[30] Missouri Historical Society, "Graham Papers."

included a number of families of white men married to Osage women, who were engaged in agriculture as well as hunting. The missionaries continued to preach in this settlement and received in their school children from there as well as those from Hopefield four miles higher up the river and a similar settlement called Sommerfield on the river about halfway between Union and the saline; two or three years later they preached at a white settlement on the river ten miles below the mission composed of emigrants who had been compelled to remove from the Choctaw country. General Atkinson, on his way from Council Bluffs to Fort Smith to attend the treaty conference between the Osage and Cherokee, stopped at the mission; he arrived at Fort Smith after the treaty had been agreed upon.

It is December 1, 1822, and the temperature is "6 below cypher"; the place is thronged with Indians; but "surprising to see the little ones entirely naked without seeming to feel the cold." The next March two men stop at the mission and seek employment. They are deserters from a hunting and trading party to the Spanish country, who lost many of their horses and with others became discouraged; wandering down the Arkansas they struck the trading settlement at the Three Forks, and then ascended the Grand to the mission. One is a blacksmith from New York, and the other a farmer from Massachusetts; both promise to be useful to the establishment. In July two more men, who went to the Rocky Mountains with Glenn and Fowler, arrive at the mission almost famished and exhausted, having been four days without food. In this, the only white settlement for hundreds of miles, they are assured of sympathy and assistance. From time to time the mission employs other unsuccessful adventurers from the East.

In the summer of 1823 the missionaries are teaching the Osage girls to card, spin, sew, and wash: "We have two spinning wheels in motion." A messenger arrives with a letter from the Quapaw to the Osage asking for a conference on the subject of permitting the former to remove and settle with their relatives. Osage warriors are going on a war expedition against the Shawnee; Tallai is still intent on killing some Pawnee to avenge the death of his daughter, who has died recently. In November, 1824, Lilburn W. Boggs,[31] a trader formerly located near Harmony Mission, arrives at Union with a stock of goods to trade with the Indians; he decides to build his trading house on the Grand River opposite Hopefield, four miles above the mission. Travelers from the north, desiring to reach the old trail at Bean's Salt Works on the Illinois, are crossing the Grand River at the mission, having found it a "days journey nearer than the old trace" down the west side of the stream. A party of Osage on their way to hunt on the east side of the Grand River, call at the mission. In December a party of Delaware Indians arrive at Chouteau's trading house and hold a conference with the Osage on the subject of permitting the former to hunt beaver on the Verdigris and "the Grand of the Neosho as the Indians call it." The next year a party of Kickapoo are encamped fifteen miles from the mission where they are engaged in hunting and trading; they are superior hunters and a menace to the game of the Osage. The Delaware are also hunting nearby. Both tribes know themselves to be unwelcome trespassers and are circumspect in their movements.

During 1822 the missionaries at Union were able to enroll only seven children in all, yet they continued to enlarge their establishment until in 1823 they reported a large amount of property, including 9 yoke of oxen, and more than 150 head of cattle, 100 hogs, wagons, grain, 109 acres of cultivated land, a saw and grist mill, 20 log houses, shops, and much equipment of a total value of more than $23,000; this included also 500 bushels of lime and 60,000 brick that they had just burned to

[31] Governor of Missouri from 1836 to 1840. During part of 1822 Boggs was assistant to Dr. George C. Sibley, factor at Fort Osage (*American State Papers,* "Indian Affairs," I, 516). "He crossed the Plains in 1846 and Gen. S. W. Kearny appointed him alcalde of the District of Sonoma 'Territory of California.' "

carry out their ambitious building program.[32] They had raised cotton, flax, oats, corn, and wheat on their farm.

At Dwight Mission report was made of the death of Colonel Matthew Lyon, the United States Factor at Spadra Bluff, on August 1, 1822;[33] General Gaines called on the twelfth; and on September 2 Governor Miller stopped at Walter Webber's nearby, on his way home from Fort Smith. The Governor was ill and very feeble. A missionary meeting was held in November which was attended by Mr. Pixley from the far-off mission of Harmony, Washburn and Orr from Dwight, and Vaill and Chapman from Union; the next year a similar representation was in attendance. On August 14, 1823, word was received that a post office had been established at Dwight with Mr. Washburn as postmaster. The mission at this time occupied seven log cabins with piazzas on two sides; they had also a library, dining hall, meat house, lumber house, carpenter shop, saw mill and grist mill, and barn, all built of logs.

The mission had between fifty and sixty pupils. But the Cherokee did not understand that it was necessary to keep pupils in school continuously to benefit by their attendance; after a child attended for a time, the parents would decide to take him home. The missionaries tried to induce the Cherokee Council to pass laws on the subject; but its members were too busy with politics, or war, or ball games, or dances, to give the subject their serious consideration.

[32] Vaill to Calhoun, October 1, 1823, OIA, RCF.

[33] Matthew Lyon was born in Ireland in 1746 and emigrated to the United States in 1759; he served in the Revolutionary Army and later represented Vermont for two terms in Congress; he then moved to Kentucky where he was elected to Congress for four terms. After an interesting public life he was appointed government factor among the Cherokee Indians in Arkansas and took up his residence at Spadra Bluff on the Arkansas River; here he ran for delegate to Congress in the election of 1821, but he was counted out in the face of apparent victory; he died at Spadra Bluff on August 1, 1822. The Hon. William P. Hepburn, representative in Congress from Iowa was a grandson of Lyon (Josiah H. Shinn, *Pioneers and Makers of Arkansas* [Little Rock, 1908], p. 138; J. Fairfax McLaughlin, *Matthew Lyon, the Hampden of Congress* [New York, 1900]).

X

THE INDIANS REGRET PEACE AND RESUME WAR, 1823

THE treaty of 1822 did not fully restore peace between the tribes; the northern Osage declared that they were not parties to it, and were not bound to cease their warfare. The Osage of Clermont's Town were not content with the result of the treaty conference; they still had an unsatisfied account against Tom Graves for the murder of the Osage prisoners the year before, and their demand for his surrender was not complied with when the treaty was made. About January 1, 1823, some of the relatives of the murdered prisoners discovered a hunting camp of fifteen Cherokee headed by Graves on the North Fork of the Canadian; finding Graves's nephew, Red Hawk,[1] away from camp, they shot him, cut off his head, and chased the hunting party away from their camp.[2] As Graves was an influential man, the killing of his relative was destined to keep alive for many years the bitterness between the tribes and prevent the establishment of peace. Hunting was particularly good that season, and large quantities of skins descended the Arkansas past Fort Smith; herds of buffaloes ranged within fifteen miles of the post all the winter, which was of unusual severity.[3]

Not all the Cherokee, on their part, were satisfied with the treaty; many of them regretted having been induced by Governor Miller to enter into it when victory against their enemies seemed within their reach. Takatoka, the aged war chief who

[1] Arbuckle to Calhoun, January 12, 1823, AGO, ORD, WDF. The Cherokee claimed that the treacherous Osage enticed Red Hawk away from his band so they could kill him.

[2] Lieut. W. S. Colquhoun, February 1, 1823, AGO, ORD, WDF.

[3] *Ibid.*

was particularly incensed at the treaty, collected about fifty or sixty warriors, all of whom shared his views, and in the winter left the Cherokee tribe for a home on the south side of the Red River with other Cherokee already living there; but when they reached a point within Miller County they halted and put in a crop of corn in the fertile Kiamichi Valley. From there they made an incursion as far as the Osage village on the Verdigris, and stole nearly one hundred horses. Retiring, they awaited in ambush the expected pursuit by the Osage; when the latter came up, a battle ensued in which one Osage was killed and several Cherokee were wounded.[4] Report of this battle reached the Arkansas Cherokee in August, 1823; they had avoided doing anything that would involve them in responsibility for the conduct of Takatoka, but in these circumstances they dispatched a body of warriors to his relief.[5] It appeared that war would again break out.

In Colonel Arbuckle's account of this affair, he says that in the preceding autumn the Osage killed a Cherokee hunter, and in March a member of Takatoka's band who was on a visit to the settlement at the Three Forks. Mr. Philbrook, the sub-agent, went to the Osage village in July to secure the murderer, but he had gone on a buffalo hunt; the Osage agreed in full council to give him up on his return, in compliance with the treaty at Fort Smith. While awaiting this gesture of peace, a band of Osage, about July 1, stole ten horses from Takatoka's party. Eleven Cherokee pursued them to their town, stole more than forty horses of the Osage, and drove them to the Cherokee village on the Kiamichi, except a few that gave out on the way. Seven Cherokee went to secure the "tired horses" and to observe whether the Osage were pursuing; they were discovered by the latter, who opened fire; the Cherokee returned the fire,

[4] *Arkansas Gazette,* September 16, 1823, p. 3, col. 1; *Louisiana Herald,* September 24, 1823, p. 3, col. 2; *Missouri Intelligencer* (from *Arkansas Gazette*), October 14, 1823, p. 3, col. 2; Union Mission Journal, August 14, 1823.

[5] *Louisiana Herald,* September 24, 1823, p. 3, col. 2.

killed one Osage and wounded two or three others.[6] The Cherokee returned to their settlement on the Kiamichi with four of
their party wounded and the loss of five horses; they subsequently abandoned this settlement and returned to their nation
on the Arkansas.[7]

To demonstrate their desire to keep the peace and comply
with the terms of the treaty agreed upon the year before, two
hundred Osage took the murderer in custody when he returned
to their town, and started with him for Fort Smith to deliver
him to the authorities as a violator of the treaty. This great
cavalcade arrived at Union Mission on August 17 and departed
the next day; but when they reached Greenleaf Creek in the
present Muskogee County, the prisoner made his escape while
the party was in camp.[8] Excitement and threats of renewed
hostilities followed; to prevent this Colonel Arbuckle sent word
through the mission to the Osage that he would arrive there
soon. On September 14 he reached the mission in company
with the Cherokee chiefs, Walter Webber, Black Fox, and James
Rogers; the next day they proceeded to Clermont's Town, but
returned on the eighteenth, having accomplished nothing. "As
the Osage people complain of injuries from the Cherokee since
the treaty was made," Colonel Arbuckle agreed to investigate
their complaints, but warned both tribes to keep the peace.[9]

[6] One of these men who was shot through the body was carried to his home
about twenty miles from Union Mission where he was treated by Doctor Palmer
of the mission; however he died of his injuries.

[7] Arbuckle to Adjutant General, September 3, 1823, AGO, OFD, 58 A 23;
ibid., January 16, 1824, 10 S 24.

[8] Union Mission Journal.

[9] Union Mission Journal; Arbuckle to Adjutant General, September 3, 1823,
AGO, OFD, 58 A 23. "It has been reported to me that the Osage who stole the
Horses from the Cherokees did at the same time steal four Horses from our
Inhabitants on Red River, and rob a citizen of the whole of his household
property. This report I have no doubt is correct, and until our Inhabitants on
Red River are prevented from Searching for Wild Horses in the Osage Country
and the Choctaws residing within our Settlements on that River are restrained
from going to War against the Osages, similar and more unpleasant occurrences
may be expected to take place frequently in that quarter. I am informed that

Union Mission was established on an old trail, referred to by some early chroniclers as the "Osage Trail,"[10] probably followed by the Osage on hunting expeditions when they all lived on the Osage River. A few months after their arrival, the missionaries noted in their journal the passage over this road of travelers from Missouri who were seeking a new home on the Arkansas River between the Verdigris and Fort Smith; these emigrants increased in number until, in 1823, at times they were seen almost daily. Some of them stopped at the mission for food and others came for medical attention at the hands of the physician. In April, 1823, "Several travelers call upon us in distress for the want of bread but could not afford them a comfortable supply." A little later: "4 men called on their way to Missouri. They are about to remove their families to the Spanish country."[11] Again,

> three men very sick with bilious fever arrived last evening on their way to Missouri. They have taken much pains to reach this place in order to obtain the benefits of a physician and needed attention. We cannot refuse their request although it will greatly increase the labors of the Sisters who are feeble.[12]

Parties of traders[13] were passing and returning months later

many of the Horses brought into Red River by our people are the tired Horses left by the Osages at their camps. Horses so left by the Osages they expect to recover when they are in condition for service" (*ibid.*).

[10] Nuttall says: "From the Verdigris to St. Louis, there is an Osage trace" (Thwaites [ed.], *op. cit.*, XIII, 236).

[11] Numbers of emigrants are now on the move to join Colonel Austin's colony in Texas; while many of them descend the Mississippi River, others from western Missouri are passing Union Mission.

[12] July 7, 1823.

[13] An interesting entry was made in the Union Mission Journal, under date of November 22, 1823: "Mr. McKnight arrived at this station on a trading expedition among the Indians near Rocky Mountains. In his first tour which was made to the Spanish country in 1812, he and all his party were taken prisoners and put in irons as spies. He continued a prisoner till the late Spanish treaty. His second tour was among the Comanche Indians during the last year in which he lost a brother (who was supposed to be murdered) and nearly all of his property and yet he is not discouraged. But hopes still to get gain by

with great droves of horses they had bought of the Comanche Indians.[14]

On September 2, 1822, the mission was visited by General E. P. Gaines, with his aides de camp, and General Atkinson and Major Bradford, who remained overnight. General Gaines was on a tour of inspection of military posts and passed the mission going from Fort Smith to Council Bluffs. Gaines and Atkinson had become ill on the road and sought the hospitality of the missionaries.[15] This remote settlement, three hundred miles from the nearest post-office, was a place of outstanding importance in this vast wilderness, where all passers-by stopped to visit.

The missionaries were harassed by many trials and problems. When they succeeded in getting a few Osage children into the school, the parents would come after a short time and take them away upon various pretexts: the ridicule of their friends;

trading..... This gentleman gives us much valuable information respecting the Spaniards and Indians." The tour on which John McKnight was killed was described in Gen. Thomas James's *Three Years Among the Indians and Mexicans,* edited with notes by Walter B. Douglas (Missouri Historical Society, 1916). James says (p. 191) that his party started in the fall of 1822, and the inference is that after John McKnight had been killed by the Indians, his brother Robert, with General James and other members of the party, did not return home until 1824; the entry by the chronicler at Union Mission would indicate that they must have returned to St. Louis in 1823, so that Robert McKnight could pass there on November 22 on another expedition. In fact, on their homeward journey their "two pirogues ladened with Buffalo hides and peltries" arrived at Little Rock in July, 1823 (*Arkansas Gazette,* July 22, 1823, p. 2, col. 2).

[14] Union Mission Journal.

[15] Gen. E. P. Gaines reported: ".... From the extreme heat of the weather and badness of the water upon the route from Fort Smith I was attacked soon after my arrival on the 15 August last with a billious fever, which obliged me to delay my movement between the Fort and Saltworks, Lovelys Purchase, until the first of September. General Atkinson who I met at Fort Smith with Doctor Nicoll and Lt. Lowndes together with our servants were confined with the fever at the same time; but by the skill and attention of Doctor Nicoll who had fortunately accompanied General Atkinson, we were rendered able to travel at a moderate pace by the 1st September" (Gaines to Calhoun, December 11, 1822, AGO, ORD, WDF).

the missionaries were "going to make a white man out of the boy"; the father needed him to help on the next buffalo hunt; it was essential to the boy's health that he eat buffalo meat for a month. When he came back, as he usually did after a few weeks or months, for the food to be had at the mission, he had thrown away the clothes given him by the missionaries or carried them in a roll on his back to escape the derision of his friends as he returned naked to the mission. The journal of the mission is filled with accounts of irregular attendance which made it impossible to record any progress.

The domestic problems of the missionaries were novel and perplexing. Panthers destroyed a number of their large hogs within a few days, but the hunters soon killed three of these animals near the mission; the wolves killed only the pigs. They planted wheat on the prairie near the mission; but the multitude of prairie chickens, attracted by a new grain, devoured most of the seed before it came up, and they threshed but forty bushels in July. As soon as warm weather came on they were attacked by little flies that were a serious menace to live stock. The assaults were so fierce that a horse would die from the effect of an attack if he were exposed a few hours where he could not protect himself. For this reason the live stock was turned loose in the brush along the Grand River, where the animals could find immunity from the flies. To avoid them, necessary trips over the prairies through the summer were usually made at night.

The greatest trial of these pioneers, however, was that of continued sickness; nearly every white person in the country was ill at times from what they called bilious fever, or ague, or "intermittent." Some of them died and others became helpless invalids; one of the sisters broke under her hardships and became insane. The mission physician, Dr. Marcus Palmer of Greenwich, Connecticut, was the only medical man within hundreds of miles, and his services were in constant demand not only at the mission but among the Indians on the Verdigris and the white people on the Arkansas. A man had his arm badly lacerated by a bear on the east side of Grand River; an Osage Indian was shot through the hand; another through the body; an Indian woman and child were burned by the explosion of gun powder; a young woman was desperately ill at Bean's Salt Works near the mouth of the Illinois River. Dr. Palmer was constantly called for and rode many long miles to relieve the stricken ones. Colonel Arbuckle, commanding at Fort Smith, sent an express messenger to the mission to secure a small quantity of "Jesuite Bark"; thirty men at his garrison had died recently from the fever. The mission had none of the bark; they had lately sent to Fort Smith for some.

While the missionaries came to their country to minister to the Osage, the Indians did not understand the limits of their bounty; on occasions they came in great numbers and camped around the mission expecting to be fed, sometimes stealing movable objects within their reach. In March, 1823, the missionaries noted: "Multitudes of Indians surround us on their way to bear hunt east of Grand River." The next day,

> the Indians moved off early this morning, passing the station in single file, first the hunters then the women and children and pack horses. The procession was two miles in length. In their great buffalo hunts we are told they march in two parallel columns of six, eight, and ten miles each.

The Osage made some complaint against the mission for pasturing so much stock on their land and even killed some of the cattle belonging to the mission; the superintendent rode ten miles up the river to an Osage camp to find the man who had killed a cow;

> the party however had just decamped on a bear hunt. The sign which they left behind was a stick with a bark tier in the end bent in the direction they had gone with the number of families or lodges marked under it by five rings on the ground. When they go on a war party they leave a stick bending in the direction of their expedition, one half painted red, the other half black with the

number of warriors notched on the stick. [In April] we have many Osages round us today. They have resorted to the saline[16] to make salt. While the women are cutting and fetching wood and boiling off the salt, the men according to their custom are entirely at leisure. [Four days later] the Indians are scattering off homeward today. They are very particular to bring in the pots and kettles which we have lent them.[17]

Though there was a fine salt spring near the mission the large kettles had been removed to Bean's Salt Works near the mouth of the Illinois River, sixty miles away; there they were obliged to go for their salt, which they brought up on a pack horse, or by keel boat. For their funds they were directed to draw on their credit in New York; when money was needed to pay workers or buy supplies, one of the brethren went to Fort Smith to negotiate a draft with the traders. On one such errand there was no money at Fort Smith. The missionary then traveled north three hundred miles to Franklin on the Missouri River, with no better success; and Mr. Chapman was obliged to make the long river journey to New Orleans before he could secure the much-needed currency. Money was scarce in this country, and such as circulated was largely of Spanish mintage. Spanish coins are occasionally plowed up in the fields near the mouth of the Verdigris, the site of the once important trading settlement which was in touch with Santa Fe and Chihuahua. Trading expeditions from Mexico returned or broke their journeys here carrying "hard money"—Spanish or Mexican silver dollars—on mule back. Skins, merchandise, horses, and mules constituted the principal medium of exchange, and money was not much used. For many years the prairie Indians had no use for it and would receive only merchandise for skins and horses. During the extraordinary drought of 1934 when Grand River was lower than it had been known for many years, in the crevices of rocks thus revealed near the site of the original stockade

16 About a mile north of the mission.
17 Union Mission Journal.

at Fort Gibson a handful of Spanish coins were collected that were minted from 100 to 150 years ago.

Clermont, the Osage chief, was a staunch friend of the Americans and a man of great force of character who made a distinct impression on the white men who knew him. In 1825 he told Captain Pryor that soon after the Cherokee war chief, Takatoka, arrived in the West he

> . . . . came to my town with some of the Shawnees and Delawares. He wished my people to be called in council which was done. He said "your people have no sense. I have come to give you understanding and tell you how the Red People in the east have suffered by the whites who have purchased their land piece by piece and shoved them to the west. This together with the wars has reduced them to poverty. Before Americans came among us, we lived happy and comfortable and had everything we wished;" then, he said, "My brother Clamore, I know you have given your hand to the great American people; I have also, but now I wish to forsake that hand, and I wish you to do so too. We have nothing to gain from the whites, but everything to lose;" presenting a tomahawk —"if you accept this tomahawk, you shall be let into the secret."

Clermont told his visitors, however, that he could not entertain their proposal for "we have taken the President of the United States by the hand, and I intend to hold it fast. Nevertheless he was apprehensive for the future, and he said, ". . . . the Americans came in like a flock of pigeons and took possession," and he feared the Osage would lose all their land. He warned Pryor to beware, for Takatoka was likely to organize the disaffected Indians who had much reason to be hostile; ". . . . when the war whoop is once given, they will rush to arms. The first push would be to sweep the Arkansas, White and Missouri rivers."[18]

Dr. Palmer of Union Mission chanced to be in Chouteau's trading house one evening when Clermont came in and entered into a long conversation about his troubles. The substance

[18] Congressional House (Boston), Manuscript Library, Vol. XXXIV, No. 112.

was that in old times he enjoyed good hunting ground and was afraid of no enemies; but now he had trouble on every hand. He was poor, his hunting ground was occupied by his enemies who were strong and threatened to destroy him, and he knew not what to do or which way to turn.[19] About two years later the valiant old chief gave up the fight, and his friends of Union Mission give us a graphic contemporary appreciation of him:

.... Clarmore the principal chief of the Ark. Osages died last May—yes sir, Clamore that man of manly countenance, stately figure, robust constitution, and great intellectual powers is gone; that subtle, sensible, respectable chief, who could boast that he was never at war with the whites, and with almost equal truth could say that he was never at peace with the Indians, who had always respected the missionaries among his people and yet never favored the cause in which they were engaged; that jealous, thoughtful, fox-eyed observer, of all that was going on around him, that most eloquent speaker, and managing intrigueing politician; and I can truly say, that notwithstanding his failings, such was the greatness of his mind and friendship for the whites that all who were immediately acquainted with him respected him when living, and lament his death.[20]

Clermont was also called "The Builder of Towns." The reason may be found in the conception of himself given to the United States agent who was trying to induce him to remove with his band to a reservation on the Neosho:

Governor Clark took me with him to Washington. I saw my great father at Washington. He said, "If you wish to build a town, build on a good stream. There you will have a good fire—many children—many braves." I have built my town. I have done all I could.[21]

19 *Ibid.,* No. 54, "M. Palmer to Rev. Jas. C. Crane, Dom. Sec. Union, Ark. Ter." March 31, 1826.
20 *Ibid.,* No. 103, Vaill to Evarts, August 6, 1828.
21 *Missionary Herald,* September, 1826, p. 267. Clermont was said to possess four wives and thirty-seven children.

XI

MOVEMENT OF WHITE EMIGRANTS TO THE SOUTHWEST AFTER THE BATTLE OF NEW ORLEANS, 1815-20

AN interesting but little known phase of early southwestern history was the beginning of white settlements in what is now the eastern part of the state of Oklahoma, a substantial effort at white pioneering that was halted when the country was appropriated for the emigrant Indians and the usual formula reversed by driving out the whites. As far back as the days of the French traders, hardy white adventurers from the United States crossed Oklahoma with commodities for the Comanche and other prairie Indians of Oklahoma and Texas in exchange for herds of horses that they drove back to the States. The prairies teemed with deer and buffalo, the forests with bear, and the streams with beaver; and white traders established profitable relations with the Indian hunters who brought their peltries many miles to rude marts.

After the Battle of New Orleans had closed the war with Great Britain in 1815, there was considerable movement of white settlers, traders, and trappers up the Arkansas and Red rivers; traders from New Orleans located at Arkansas Post and as high up as the mouth of the Verdigris and at points on the Red River as high as the Kiamichi. Sutlers and camp followers of the army, and merchants of New Orleans who had stocks of goods left on their hands by the termination of the war, swarmed into the Indian country on the Arkansas and Red rivers to dispose of them and for a time by the competition improved the Indian trade which Major Lovely said had been "plunder in the first degree."[1] Discharged soldiers suddenly

---

[1] Lovely to Secretary of War, February 17, 1816, OIA, RCF.

thrown out of employment, in quest of adventure, homes, and
bounty lands, thronged this new country. Traders were continually passing through Natchitoches to the Indian country
above in defiance of laws of the United States. A number of
them stopped and made a settlement on the lands of the Caddo
Indians at Nanatscho or Pecan Point;[2] Caddo Chief complained to their agent at Natchitoches ". . . . It is the only
crossing place for Buffalo for many miles, and the only crossing
from which his people derive any advantages from their crossing."[3] In April of the next year, supported by a military detachment, the Caddo agent, Jamison, removed a dozen families
from their settlement to the north side of the Red River, beside arresting several unlicensed traders there and seizing their
merchandise. Another settlement was made at the mouth of the
Kiamichi.

At an early day the most important trading settlement in
the Southwest developed at the head of navigation made by the
junction of the Arkansas, Verdigris, and Neosho rivers, known
as Three Forks.[4] Here peltries taken on those streams were
brought down by canoe or overland from more remote hunting
grounds. There is occasional mention of traders located between the Three Forks and Fort Smith. The country tributary
to the Three Forks was dominated by the imperious Osage,
who countenanced no intrusion by whites or other red men.
Farther to the south, the Poteau, Kiamichi, Boggy, Blue, and
Washita had long been famous hunting grounds where bear
and beaver were found in great numbers; but the Blue was
particularly noted for its yield of beaver. And to these streams
and forests the white men came with bear[5] and beaver traps
loaded on their pack horses. Here they could hunt and trap in

2 Pecan Point was on the south bank of the Red River, south of the present
Kullituklo in McCurtain County, Oklahoma.

3 John Jamison, Indian agent, to Secretary of War, July 10, 1816, AGO,
ORD, WDF; *ibid.*, May 10, 1817.

4 For an extended account of Three Forks, see Foreman, *op. cit.*

5 Invariably called by them "bar" traps.

comparative security, the menace of the Osage to the north and other Indians to the west too remote to deter them; and for further protection they came in considerable companies. Some of these early parties were organized and financed at Arkansas Post, the earliest and for some years the most important settlement in Arkansas.[6] Here Antoine Baraque and Frederick Notrebe[7] outfitted trapping parties[8] which came to this far-western country for beaver skins, bearskins, and bear oil that they shipped to markets on the Mississippi and its tributaries.

Fort Smith was established in 1817, and the next year was negotiated the treaty with the Quapaw Indians by which this

[6] ".... the first white establishment made on the Arkansas river was about 30 or 40 miles by water below the present post or village of Arkansas .... between 35 and 40 years ago the established white settlements mostly overflowed by high waters, which was then represented by the commandant of the place to the Government in answer to which the commandant was requested to make an establishment either at point Chicho on the Mississippi about 50 or 60 miles by water below the mouth of Arkansas or at such place as he might think most fit on the Arkansas river. In consequence of which request the present post or village of Arkansas was selected as the most proper and suitable place for the white settlement;" the Quapaw Indians were then directed to remove to the south side of the Arkansas above Arkansas Post so they should have no claim to any land east of the white settlements ("Information given by the late Spanish Commandant of Arkansas" to Governor Clark, June 5, 1816, AGO, ORD, WDF). The post ".... of the Arcs or Arcansas, situated in the neighborhood of two hundred leagues from New Orleans, in following the course of the river, and a little above the thirty-fourth degree of latitude, a post almost altogether military, frequented by hunters and traders, and from where descend, in the spring, boats loaded with pelts, and bear oil the best of which is used in that colony, for the needs of the kitchen, like lard, and it is almost as good, and the common is used for the lamps and other purposes" (*View of the Spanish Colony of the Mississippi, 1802, by a Resident Observer on the Premises,* p. 60).

[7] "Frederick Notrebe took part in the French Revolution and was an army officer during the consulate, but left France when Napoleon became Emperor. Coming to Arkansas about 1815, to 1818, he became a wealthy planter, being considered in the forties the most prominent man in the county. He died of Cholera at New Orleans" (Nuttall in Thwaites [ed.], *op. cit.,* XIII, 106).

[8] Pryor and Richards, Joseph Bogy, and other traders at Arkansas Post sent their keel boats up the Arkansas River to trade with the Osage.

tribe ceded to the United States the great domain lying between the Arkansas and Red rivers, and the Mississippi and the Rocky Mountains, except a small tract in the middle of Arkansas Territory. The treaty of 1819 with Spain fixed upon the Red River as the boundary line between the Spanish possessions and the United States, and by its terms the Spaniards abandoned their pretentions to ownership of the contiguous country lying between the Red and Arkansas rivers. With these conditions to encourage them, the whites began adventuring in greater numbers to this hunters' elysium in eastern Oklahoma;[9] and finding the lands along the streams rich and productive many remained. They lived in a happy state. Squatters[10] upon the best public land, they had few cares; they built rude log

[9] Oklahoma and Arkansas abounded with game. General Arbuckle estimated in 1824 that there were two thousand French, American, Cherokee, and Delaware hunting between the Red and Arkansas rivers, destroying the game belonging to the Osage (Union Mission Journal). Game was so plentiful on the Arkansas that early French writers placed almost no limit to its extent or the credulity of their readers: "Game of all kind is plentiful there; wild oxen (Bison) stags, roebucks, bears, tygers, leopards, foxes, wild cats, rabbets, turkies, grous, pheasants, partridges, quails, turtles, wood-pigeons, swans, geese, bustards, ducks of all kinds, teels, divers, snipes, water-hens, golden pluvers, stares, throushes and other birds not known in Europe" (Bossu, *op. cit.*, p. 92). Bossu related many strange tales to entertain the people in Europe. He told of observing some green branches ascending a stream against the current much to his astonishment; when his negro told him that the branches were growing on the back of an alligator, he embarked in his pirogue to investigate; on his approach the alligator plunged in the stream, and with it the branches. He explained that hunters frequently shot them, the bullets only making holes in their backs without killing them. "These amphibians pass several months of the winter immobile and torpid in the oozy mud; it is at this time that there fall in the holes made by the bullets, the seeds of willows, elms or other trees with which the rivers of Louisiana are bordered; these seeds take root in the moss which covers the body of the animal, and favored by the moisture, form the branches that the animals carry with them when they recover, in the spring warmth and movement" (Bossu, *New Travels* [Amsterdam, 1777], p. 133).

[10] "It is practically impossible to trace the history of the squatters mentioned by Nuttall" (Thwaites [ed.], *op. cit.*, p. 213). Since this was written, fortunately, the author discovered material which gives considerable light on the subject.

cabins, and the industrious raised some corn and cotton. Their horses and cattle ranged over rich pasture; the hogs fattened on mast; mild winters, heavy forests, and protected valleys minimized the demand for feed. The settlers made hunting trips within convenient distances and returned with furs and peltries which they exchanged for the necessities of life; some engaged in salting buffalo meat which they shipped to New Orleans, and others maintained crude tanneries where they prepared skins for market. The more adventurous went to the great prairies to the west, now western Oklahoma, and traded merchandise to the Indians for horses or for mules stolen from the Mexicans. If their buffalo hunts were not succesful, skins could be purchased cheaply from the Indians. Accounts of the inducements to live in this section traveled far, and fugitives from justice and other desperate characters came to abide where there was no law. They installed in their houses stills with which they made whisky for consumption and sale to the whites and to barter with the Indians, and for some years there was no one to prevent. Nuttall said of them in 1819:

.... These people, as well as the generality of those who, till lately, inhabited the banks of the Arkansa, bear the worst moral character imaginable, being many of them renegades from justice; when a further flight from justice became necessary, they passed over into the Spanish territory, towards St. Antonio.[11]

A member of this settlement at the mouth of the Kiamichi, writing from "Jonesborough, Ark.," has left an account of the community along the Red River in 1820:

.... We are a motley crew, emigrants from all parts of the world, and of course have all kinds of people, good and bad! But the bad seems to predominate. We had a kind of camp meeting a few days since about six miles below Jonesborough, on the opposite side of the river, and just below the mouth of Clear Creek.[12] I had not been at church since I left Kentucky and thought I

[11] Thwaites [ed.], *op. cit.*, p. 222.   [12] Near Valliant, Oklahoma.

would go down for I was always fond of going to church. There were at the camp ground three ministers and a considerable congregation for a new country like this.[13]

Two hundred yards away was gathered a crowd of drunken rowdies; they attacked the camp meeting, drove away the preachers and congregation, and with axes destroyed the crude platform and pulpit.[14]

The Frenchman, De Mézières, lieutenant-governor at Natchitoches under the Spanish régime, gives a graphic picture of the people who lived on the Arkansas River fifty years earlier, most of whom he says ".... have either deserted from the troops and ships of the Most Christian King or have committed robberies, rape or homicide, that river thus being the asylum of the most wicked persons, without doubt, in all the Indies." Their principal activities, he says, were corrupting the Osage Indians, whom they induced to commit robberies on the Spaniards, and capture women from the Red River Indians to barter to the Arkansas River white men; so that the "greed and license of a depraved and wholly abominable people" had made the Red River district a "theatre of outrageous robberies and bloody encounters."[15] In 1719 and 1720 the French Government published lists of several hundred criminals and dangerous vagabonds who had been confined at Bicêtre and later concentrated at a seaport for deportation "to Louisiana and the islands of the Mississippi."[16]

The population on the Red River became so numerous[17] that

[13] W. B. Dewees, *Letters from an Early Settler of Texas,* compiled by Cara Cardelle (Louisiana, 1852).

[14] Dewees was accompanied by Gabriel Martin who was killed by the Indians in 1834; see Foreman, *op. cit.,* p. 121.

[15] Letter from Athanese de Mézières at Natchitoches, May 20, 1770 (Bolton, *op. cit.,* I, 166).

[16] Paris, Bibliotheque de l'Arsenal, Manuscripts 12708, 1719, 1720. Library of Congress, Manuscripts Division.

[17] In 1818 there was ".... a settlement of twelve families at Nanatscho, or Pecan Point; and one of twenty families at the mouth of Kiamisha. At the

Mushalatubbe (Mo-sho-la-tub-bee) Choctaw Chief. Painted by George Catlin, 1836. Courtesy of Smithsonian Institution, Bureau of American Ethnology.

it was deemed necessary to extend the jurisdiction of the Territory over the country and establish local government so that the rights and remedies of citizens could be enforced and order maintained. Under the direction of William Rector, surveyor-general for the district composed of Illinois and Missouri territories, in 1818 or early in 1819, a tract of densely populated land, lying between the Little River[18] and the Red River and extending east from near the mouth of the Kiamichi, was surveyed into nine townships subdivided into sections.[19] This land was advertised to be sold in August and October, 1820, at

lower settlement there are five, and at the upper settlement [Kiamichi] three, traders, who in consequence of this contiguity to the fine hunting grounds, have taken the Indian trade of that country from Natchitoches" (Report of W. A. Trimble, August 7, 1818, Morse, *op. cit.,* p. 259). A government factory or trading post had been established at Natchitoches in 1805 (*American State Papers,* "Indian Affairs," I, 768). Stephen F. Austin proposed to build a fort on the south bank of the Red River near the mouth of the Kiamichi; he said: ".... opposite to this place within the limits of the United States there is a settlement of about two hundred families, who are included within the limits of a district of country which has lately been ceded by the United States to the Choctaw Indians; those settlers would willingly remove and settle round the Fort at Pecon Point, and in a short time would supply the Garrison with Provisions" (American Historical Association, *Annual Report for 1919* [Washington, 1824], Vol. II, part 1, "The Austin Papers," edited by Prof. Eugene C. Barker, p. 508, Austin to [Bustamante?] May 10, 1822).

[18] The lower part of this stream in McCurtain County, was then called Little Red River; it was formed by the junction of Mountain Fork and Gloves Fork, now called Little River and Glover's Fork.

[19] Memorial of citizens of Miller County (1825, OIA, RCF); Brown and Barcroft's Map of Arkansas Territory, Congressional Library, Map Division; *Arkansas Gazette,* January 6, 1821, p. 3, col. 2; William Rector, surveyor-general to commissioner of the General Land Office (April 14, 1819, GLO, p. 276). On a map showing the survey, attached by Rector to his letter, is legended just east of Clear Creek "thickly settled." These surveyed townships were numbered from 35 to 39 west and 9 to 10 south. To give an idea of their location, township 10 south and 38 west coursed by Clear Creek, was almost identical with the present 7 south and 22 east. The surveyed territory was substantially the present townships 6 south 21, 22, and 23 east and 7 south 21, 22, 23, 24, and 25 east. This survey was part of that made in compliance with the order of the commissioner of the General Land Office of July 20, 1818, to survey sixty townships in Missouri Territory for soldiers' bounties.

Arkansas Post; but the sales were postponed by the non-arrival of the necessary forms and instructions,[20] and for other more compelling reasons to be related, were never held.

The General Assembly of Missouri, on December 31, 1813, created the County of Arkansas, embracing a large part of the present state of that name. By another act of that body, approved on December 17, 1818, the southwestern part of that county was divided into Pulaski, Clark, and Hempstead counties.[21] By limits that are now almost unintelligible, Hempstead County was so bounded as to include the Red River, and extended west vaguely to "the Indian boundary line," which was understood to be somewhere within the present state of Oklahoma. North of Hempstead, Pulaski County also extended west to the Indian boundary line.[22]

Soon after Arkansas Territory was established, the General Assembly, by an act approved on April 1, 1820, by Governor James Miller, created Miller County out of the western part of Hempstead;[23] it included all of what is now McCurtain County, Oklahoma, and the eastern parts of Pushmataha and Choctaw counties, the northern boundary being substantially identical with the present boundary of McCurtain County. It extended a short distance into the present state of Arkansas. By a later act, approved October 18, 1820, Crawford County was carved out of Pulaski, and extended from Miller County north to the present north boundary of Oklahoma. It embraced

---

[20] *Arkansas Gazette,* May 3, 1825, p. 3, col. 1.

[21] *Acts of the Territory of Missouri,* 1813-18.

[22] This same act apparently placed Clark County between Hempstead and Pulaski, also extending west to the Indian boundary line; but a map of Arkansas made by Robert T. Browne of Missouri, in 1825, now in the Congressional Library, does not so locate it; and contemporary accounts seem to exclude the location.

[23] U. S. Department of State, *Territorial Records, Acts of Arkansas Legislature.*

[24] *Ibid.,* Map of Robert T. Browne, *loc. cit.*

what are now LeFlore, Sequoyah, Cherokee, Adair, and parts of Delaware, Mayes, Muskogee, Haskell, Latimer, and Pushmataha counties. The seat of government was temporarily located at Fort Smith.[25]

While the surveyed lands east of the Kiamichi were never sold to the settlers, the latter continued to increase in number. The location of the court authorized by the act creating Miller County in 1820, was established at a place[26] on the north bank of the Red River near where Fort Towson was afterward located. This station in the most thickly populated part of the county, was called Miller Courthouse, and here a post office of the same name was established on September 5, 1824,[27] which continued until December 28, 1838.

The white people of Mississippi were clamoring for the removal of the Choctaw Indians; and in 1818, to appease their demands, the Government began negotiations with the Indians. The next year Andrew Jackson, Colonel John McKee, Choctaw agent, and Colonel Burnett were appointed commissioners to treat with them, and they offered the Indians a tract of country west of Arkansas in exchange for their land in Mississippi.[28] Preliminary to this offer, General Jackson, as commanding officer of the Southern Division, gave orders to Major William Bradford in command at Fort Smith, to remove all the settlers

[25] The county seat of Crawford County was later moved about twenty miles down the river to Billingsley's Settlement which became known as Crawford Courthouse.

[26] This earliest court in Oklahoma was at first to "be holden at the house of John Hall, in Gelleland's settlement in said County" (*Acts of Arkansas Legislature*).

[27] Records of Postmaster-General; John Fowler was the first postmaster (*American State Papers*, "Post Office Department," p. 180). On November 30, 1824, Miller Courthouse Post Office was made the official channel of correspondence for Fort Towson (AGO, OFD); on May 8, 1822, Congress established a post road from Little Rock by Clark Courthouse to Natchitoches, and one from Clark Courthouse by Hempstead Courthouse to Miller Courthouse (3 Stat. L. 706).

[28] *American State Papers*, "Indian Affairs," II, 229 ff.

who should be found west of a line drawn from the source of the Kiamichi to the Poteau.[29]

With half a dozen soldiers, Bradford set out from Fort Smith on May 16, 1819, in company with Thomas Nuttall, the botanist,[30] and found about two hundred families in the proscribed territory, some of them growing crops; many of them were living on Gates Creek and the Kiamichi River.[31] Major Bradford read the order to the heads of the families, and directed them to remove at once, except those who had crops[32] growing, whom he permitted to remain until October. The order was

[29] Secretary of War Calhoun, on December 15, 1818, directed Jackson to cause these settlers to be removed (*U. S. House Document No. 263,* Twentieth Congress, first session, p. 7).

[30] Thwaites [ed.], *op. cit.,* XIII, 206; Foreman, *op. cit.,* p. 37. Nuttall wrote an interesting account of his visit to this section (Thwaites, *op. cit.,* p. 206 ff.). They were accompanied by two Cherokee named Rogers, who served as guides and interpreters. On the way they passed numbers of buffaloes. Near the mouth of the Kiamichi, Nuttall, in search of botanical specimens, became separated from Major Bradford's party who left for Fort Smith without him. Nuttall was hospitably entertained at the home of Mr. Stiles nearby for several weeks, until he found an escort of white men setting out to the north to recover horses stolen by Cherokee Indians. Stiles who had only recently located in the vicinity, had brought his family and a loaded wagon over the mountains on the same route as that pursued by Nuttall; they had "been obliged to remove from the settlement of Mulberry creek on the arrival of the Cherokees." When Nuttall took his leave, his host, "knowing from the first my destitute situation, separated from pecuniary resources, could scarcely be prevailed upon to accept the trifling pittance which I accidentally possessed. I shall always remember, with feelings of gratitude, the sincere kindness from these poor and honest people, when left in the midst of the wilderness." William Stiles was subsequently the victim of the Osage who, on October 13, 1820, entered his home and stole clothing and bedding, and carried off his horses, for which he filed a claim for $750 (OIA, RCF, "Special File" No. 191). Some of Stiles's descendants still live on the Red River.

[31] *American State Papers,* "Indian Affairs," II, 557; *Arkansas Gazette,* March 3, 1825, p. 3, col. 4.

[32] "The people appeared but ill prepared for the unpleasant official intelligence of their ejectment. Some who had cleared considerable farms were thus unexpectedly thrust out into the inhospitable wilderness. I could not sympathize with their complaints, notwithstanding the justice and propriety of the requisition" (Thwaites [ed.], *op. cit.,* XIII, 214).

obeyed, many of the families crossing over into Texas; and later those who had remained to harvest their crops were removed by Captain Coombs stationed at Natchitoches, who had received a similar commission, and executed it in the vicinity of the Red River, in some instances burning houses and destroying crops.

James Pitchlynn was employed by Jackson to circulate among the Choctaw and endeavor to convert enough to the measure for removal to insure the making of the treaty before calling the conference. He represented to them that nearly a third of the tribe had removed to the West and therefore they should exchange their old home for the new land offered them, where those who wished to live the lives of hunters could remain while those who preferred to live by agriculture would be secure in their homes.[33] Further, he communicated Jackson's threat that unless they agreed to this program, Congress would pass a law compelling the members of the tribe who were living in the West to return to their old home; this, he urged, would result in overcrowding the ancestral domain which would be objectionable to both factions of the tribe, each of which desired to have nothing to do with the scheme of life adopted by the other.

Jackson's persuasions made no impression on the two principal chiefs, Pushmataha and Mushalatubbe, who replied in emphatic language[34] that they were determined to remain where they were. The former said:

> We wish to remain here where we have grown up as the herbs of the woods, and do not wish to be transplanted into another soil. Those of our people who are over the Mississippi, did not go there with the consent of the nation; they are considered as strangers; they have no houses or places of residence; they are like wolves; it is the wish of the council that the president should direct his

[33] *American State Papers*, "Indian Affairs," II, 229, Jackson to McKee, Choctaw agent, April 22, 1819.
[34] *Ibid.*, p. 230.

agents to the west to order these stragglers home, and, if they will not come, to direct them where he pleases. I am well acquainted with the country contemplated for us. I have often had my feet sorely bruised there by the roughness of its surface.

Nothing was accomplished that year; but the people of Mississippi induced Jackson to make another effort, and a commission was issued to him in July, 1820.[35] After the necessary preparations, he and his party arrived at Doak's Stand on September 20, but it was until October 10 that a sufficient number of headmen could be induced to attend. Edmund Folsom was employed to circulate among the Indians, and he succeeded in bringing in fifty-two warriors of the Six Towns parties of the Chickasawhay and Concha on October 6. Until Folsom approached them the Choctaw had refused to attend the treaty conference.[36] Several days of deliberation and argument resulted in a treaty[37] on October 18. By its terms the Choctaw ceded a large part of their lands in Mississippi in exchange for a vast tract in the West,[38] embracing substantially all the land between the Arkansas and Canadian rivers on the north and the Red River on the south, extending west as far as the source of the Canadian, and bounded on the east by a line running from the mouth of the Little River northeast to the site of Morrillton, Arkansas; by this agreement, territory comprising what are now ten Arkansas counties and parts of nearly ten more was granted to the Choctaw. This area, which embraced also

[35] *Ibid.*, p. 231.

[36] Folsom and Mackey to Commissioners, October 6, 1820, OIA, RCF, "Choctaw."

[37] Kappler, *op. cit.*, II, 133.

[38] On the recommendation of General Jackson a commission was issued by the Secretary of War on March 27, 1821, to Edmund Folsom appointing him agent to collect the Choctaw who wished to migrate west of the Mississippi and conduct them to their new home. The following November he reported that his efforts had achieved nothing but the bitter hostility of the Indians; that he was opposed by the fullbloods, the headmen, and the whites living among them, but he hoped for some success with the half-breeds the next year (*American State Papers*, "Indian Affairs," II, 394, 395).

settlements now in southeastern Oklahoma, included about five thousand white settlers with many valuable farms and other improvements.[39] The enraged people whom it was proposed thus incontinently to disposses, charged that Jackson had been outwitted by the shrewd Choctaw chiefs and had permitted the stupid treaty to be executed in disregard of the rights of the people in the West, through his zeal to serve those in the East.[40]

Some of the indignant settlers made preparations to remove to Texas;[41] their delegate in Congress, Henry W. Conway, presented to the President their remonstrance ".... against the odious terms of the treaty with the Choctaws and he assured them that another treaty would be negotiated to rectify the one of October last."[42] By authority of the President,[43] Governor Miller published a proclamation notifying the people affected that they would not be disturbed in their possessions on account of the Choctaw treaty; but that a new arrangement would be made with them so as to locate the Indians west of the white settlements.[44]

[39] Much of the grant on the Red River was very fertile "and in a fine state of cultivation.....It is a well known fact, that there are fine farms, dwelling-houses, cotton gins, and mills of various descriptions, on the land which was ceded to us" (*ibid.*, p. 551).

[40] Robert Cole, Pushmataha, and other Choctaw chiefs said they had visited the western country before 1820 and knew that white people were living there; they informed General Jackson of that fact and he said the Government would remove them; but they complained in 1824 that no effort had been made to keep that promise (*ibid.*, p. 549).

[41] "....If this treaty is ratified, nearly, if not all, the families which fall within the limits of the cession in this Territory, will remove to the Spanish province of Texas, and seek that protection under a foreign monarch, which is denied them in their native country" (*Arkansas Gazette,* January 6, 1821, p. 3, col. 2). Governor Miller on December 10, 1820, wrote the President that "....it will be necessary to drive all these white citizens from their humble homes prepared by many years hard labor, to give place to savages."

[42] *Arkansas Gazette,* May 12, 1821, p. 3, col. 1; *Louisiana Herald,* June 16, 1821, p. 3, col. 1.

[43] *American State Papers,* "Indian Affairs," II, 394.

[44] *Arkansas Gazette,* June 30, 1821, p. 3, col. 1.

Thus encouraged, without waiting for congressional authority, surveyors Downs and Woodward in the employ of Arkansas proceeded to establish a new line, from the mouth of the Canadian River southward to the head of Jack's Fork of the Kiamichi, and down it to its mouth.[45] Immediately the white people who had been removed by the military, together with a considerable influx of immigrants, reoccupied the country east of this new line.[46] Information of this having reached the Government at Washington, Colonel Arbuckle at Fort Smith was ordered in May, 1823, to remove the settlers to the east side of the line connecting the sources of the Kiamichi and Poteau, and they were notified to move by December 1; they complied with the order and again established themselves on the east side of these streams.[47] Lieutenant Richard Wash, who was directed to see that these orders were obeyed, carried them to the settlers also on the south side of the Red River.[48] He found squatters living here for a distance of forty miles above the Kiamichi, and ordered them to remove by December 1.[49]

Congress provided in March, 1823,[50] for running a new line from the southwest corner of Missouri due south to the Red

[45] Downs reported in 1821 that white people were settled on the Arkansas almost as high up as the Canadian, and on the Red River quite up to the Kiamichi (*American State Papers*, "Indian Affairs," II, 395, 549).

[46] *American State Papers*, "Indian Affairs," II, 557; *Arkansas Gazette*, March 8, 1825, p. 3, col. 4.

[47] *American State Papers, ibid.*, AGO, ORD, 10 S 24; Arbuckle to Calhoun, August 15, 1823, AGO, ORD, WDF.

[48] In this part of what are now Bowie, Red, and Lamar counties, Texas, the inhabitants who believed they were within the limits of Miller County, Arkansas, subsequently set up a sort of local government, and until 1837 paid taxes at a place called Jonesborough, on the south bank of the Red River, opposite the mouth of Clear Creek (*U. S. Supreme Court* "No. 4 Original" *Records, United States v. Texas*, p. 1328); Miller Courthouse on the north bank of the river was first established and county offices were apparently removed to Jonesborough as the population here was increased by those evicted from the Choctaw country.

[49] AGO, OFD, 10 S 24.

[50] Act of Congress, March 3, 1823, chap. xxiv, sec. 3, iii, *Stat. L.* 750.

River; news of this was received with much favor until an investigation disclosed that this line would still leave nearly two thousand whites west of it.[51] This evoked another memorial from the Legislature of Arkansas on October 18, 1823, protesting, through their delegate, Mr. Conway, against the proposed line, in which it was said the section in dispute

> .... has been justly considered as one of the most choice tracts of land in our territory—the pride, the boast of Arkansas. Indeed, the line, as established will transfer to the Choctaw Indians[52] more than one-half of the respectable inhabitants of Miller, which is now a well organized community, located upon the public lands already surveyed.[53]

They urged that the line should extend from the southwest corner of Missouri to the Falls of the Verdigris and from there to the mouth of the Kiamichi.[54]

[51] *American State Papers,* "Indian Affairs," II, 555.

[52] Upon the removal of the Choctaw from the East, after the passage of the Indian Removal Act in 1830, they were beneficiaries of the labors of the white people; but many of them were enabled at once to occupy cleared fields and improvements that saved them much labor and delay in establishing themselves; indeed, this situation accounted in a measure for the dense settlements of Choctaw in McCurtain County directly on their removal.

[53] *American State Papers,* "Indian Affairs," II, 556; AGO, ORD, Conway to Secretary of War, January 30, 1824.

[54] Congressional Library, Manuscript Division, "Senate Files" No. 346.

XII

MASSACRE OF WHITE HUNTERS AND SETTLERS BY THE INDIANS, 1817-23

IN 1816 there were three families living at the mouth of the Poteau, and another small settlement was located on the north side of the Arkansas a few miles above.[1] Soon after the acquisition of Lovely's Purchase from the Osage in 1818, white people began to frequent that country in large numbers; General Atkinson reported to the Secretary of War that Acting Governor Crittenden had given permission in violation of law to at least two hundred citizens to go over into the Indian country to hunt and trap and that others were engaged in trading with the Indians on the Arkansas River.[2] A few weeks later, Cherokee Agent Lewis reported to the Secretary of War that the white people were attempting to settle this country, and he requested that the commanding officer at Fort Smith be directed to prevent it. He added that there were three valuable springs within fifteen miles of the mouth of the Illinois River in the new purchase, and the Cherokee, assuming that the country belonged to them were planning to operate the springs for the manufacture of salt. Mark Bean, he said, was at the time erecting an establishment at one of them.[3] Orders were then issued[4] to prevent white settlement on this land in the present eastern Oklahoma,[5] as it was intended to provide the western outlet promised to the Cherokee.[6]

[1] David Musick to Governor Clark, August 1, 1816, AGO, ORD, WDF. In his map accompanying his report, Musick shows these settlements and legends "Saltworks" on the north side of the Arkansas, a short distance above the mouth of the Canadian River.

[2] Atkinson to Calhoun, January 2, 1820, *ibid.*

[3] Lewis to Calhoun, January 21, 1820, *ibid.*

[4] April 30, 1821.

[5] *U. S. House Document No. 263*, Twentieth Congress, first session, p. 26.

The protection afforded by Fort Smith brought settlers to the vicinity, and when Colonel Arbuckle took command there in February, 1822, he ordered some white people, living on the Choctaw land on the south side of the Arkansas River between the Poteau and Canadian rivers, to remove below Fort Smith. During the succeeding March and April, while Colonel Arbuckle was absent on furlough, several more families from Missouri settled in the same neighborhood and began planting corn; others soon followed them, and by the end of the year Arbuckle reported[7] that the settlement extended forty or fifty miles up the river from Fort Smith and that it was much exposed to depredations by warring Osage and Cherokee. Again the chronicles of the missionaries supply a contribution to the history of this settlement. From the time of the arrival of the missionaries at Union in February, 1821, these emigrants formed a familiar sight as they passed the mission over the road that carried them through what are now Mayes, Wagoner, and Muskogee counties on the west side of the Neosho River; part turned east to locate along the Arkansas River and others crossed that stream and continued south to the Red River and beyond.[8] The Union Mission journalist recorded December 3, 1821:

> Several families arrived in waggons from Missouri. They came by way of Harmony..... These people have been expecting to settle on this side of the Arkansas between this and Fort Smith, but the late official orders for people to leave this part of the country wholly disconcerts their plans. They have encamped for a few days near this establishment. [The Little Osage stole nine of their horses, and on the twelfth] part of the Missouri people have moved forward yet they know not which way to go nor

---

[6] "No one has been permitted to settle on the route between this post [Fort Smith] and the Salt Works occupied by Messrs. Sanders and Bean ...." (Arbuckle to Calhoun, October 27, 1823, AGO, OFD, 64 A 23).

[7] Arbuckle to Secretary of War, January 12, 1823, AGO, ORD, WDF.

[8] Union Mission Journal.

where to settle, for it is not yet decided how much of the Territory is to be ceded to the Choctaws.

Similar entries were made from time to time.

The Dwight missionaries, also stationed on a road traveled by these adventurers, observed in October, 1822, that not less than thirty families had passed them within three months on their way up the Arkansas; two months later they reported that

.... six wagons and twice that many families have passed within a few days. Generally they are all in a miserable condition and call on us for assistance.[9]

.... In the years 1817,-18 and 19 from four to five hundred families moved to the Red river and Arkansas country .... they had settled on public land but .... they had seen Indiana, Illinois, Missouri, parts of Louisiana, and Alabama, settled in the same way, ... [and supposed their improvements would be secured to them by the same right.[10] In 1822 it was reported that] .... a great number of families are emigrating from the Missouri across to the Arkansas, and are settling on the south side of that river, in Crawford County.[11] They cross the country from about Fort Osage[12] and strike the Arkansas above Fort Smith, and we understand are flocking in, in great numbers between the Poto and Canadian, as well as below Fort Smith. The roads in that neighborhood are said to be literally swarming with emigrants to that country—and we learn from White River, that they are coming in from that quarter by hundreds.[13]

[9] American Board of Commissioners for Foreign Missions, Manuscript Library, Vol. II, Dwight Mission Journal.

[10] *Arkansas Gazette,* February 3, 1821, p. 3, cols. 1, 2, 3, 4.

[11] This section of Oklahoma had been incorporated in Crawford County.

[12] Near where Kansas City now is.

[13] *Arkansas Gazette,* November 20, 1822, p. 3, col. 3. In the Bancroft Library at the University of California is the interesting journal of George Nidiver whose family removed to Missouri in 1816, when he was fourteen years of age. In 1820 his family and six others including twenty men, left Missouri for the Six Bulls of Neosho, where they intended to join some of their neighbors who had preceded them; as the latter had been ordered to leave the Neosho, the whole party continued south to the Arkansas, and located near Fort Smith. In this party were persons named Mathers, Bleven, and Harril. In 1828 Nidiver

Other emigrants recruited in Kentucky and Tennessee[14] loaded their goods in keel boats, let the current of the Mississippi carry them down to the mouths of the Arkansas and Red rivers, and ascended those streams to points decided upon in advance or dictated by the state of navigation.[15] But the great majority of them came overland, and the movement increased. Taking the testimony of the Union Mission journalist again in April, 1823:

> .... Another company of travelers passed by today. This appears to be the best route from the western part of Missouri to Red River and the country west of Fort Smith. [In September he reported] .... Several people pass by us on their way to Missouri from the Arkansas. Their returning to Missouri is owing to an order of ejectment from the lands west of the Poteau, where a number have settled within a year. Gave some provisions and a number of tracts. [Again[16]] .... Yesterday several families passed us on the way from Red River and the Arkansas to Missouri. Today 20 people are passing by on their way from Missouri to Arkansas. Thus are they going to and fro in pursuit of a better country.

A party of forty from Illinois, traveling with six heavy wagons,

and Alex Sinclair "went up the Canadian fork of the Arkansas and began the building of a large raft of cedar logs, which we intended to float down to New Orleans to sell. We were engaged with a few men we hired, nearly a year in making the raft. When everything was ready and we were about to start down the river the Cherokees to whom that section had been ceeded attempted to seize our raft, but taking advantage of a freshet we sailed down in the night beyond their reach and escaped them. This availed us but little however, for at the mouth of the fork the raft ran aground, was broken up, and we abandoned it." Nidiver then became a hunter, and he related many thrilling experiences with the wild Indians before he became a resident of California.

14 The *Arkansas Gazette* spoke of the emigrants from Tennessee and Kentucky who were passing up the river in their keel boats (February 24, 1821, p. 3, col. 2). When Nuttall came up the Arkansas River in 1819, he noted the recent arrivals of the white people along that stream (Thwaites [ed.], *op. cit.*, XIII, 105 ff.).

15 As noted by Nuttall and the missionaries.

16 October 14, 1823.

and a great number of horses and cattle, stopped a few days at the mission; they were bound for the settlement above Fort Smith.

In the summer of 1823 Bean and Sanders, who operated the salt works on the old trail near its crossing of the Illinois River,[17] solicited Robert Crittenden, acting-governor of Arkansas Territory, to permit some of these arrivals to settle on that trail between the salt works and Fort Smith.[18] That expanse, Arbuckle said, was a wilderness of fifty miles, and he agreed with Crittenden that the presence of white people there would "certainly much increase the convenience of traveling."[19] Crittenden thereupon gave permission for four families to settle at two points on the trail, and Colonel Arbuckle solicited the approval of the Secretary of War in spite of instructions to the contrary.[20]

Washington was far away; and as the white population increased, the people of Arkansas pressed on Congress their demands to be allowed to settle this beautiful and valuable country on the north bank of the Arkansas. They found a champion in Senator Benton of Missouri, chairman of the Committee on Indian Affairs. The people of his state were becoming restless from the rapidly increasing number of Indians settling there, and were sympathetic with the problems of their neighbors on the south. With the assistance of Senator Benton, an act[21] was passed by Congress fixing the west boundary line of Arkansas so as to include the limits of Crawford, Pulaski, and Miller counties. At a point forty miles west of the southwest corner of Missouri it started south, crossed the Arkansas

[17] On Salt Creek about seven miles north of Gore, Oklahoma.

[18] This old trail, approximately that of the military road from Fort Gibson to Fort Smith constructed in 1827, was on the north side of the Arkansas in Lovely's Purchase.

[19] Travelers between Fort Smith and Union Mission and the trading settlement at the Three Forks employed this trail.

[20] Arbuckle to Calhoun, June 22, 1823, AGO, ORD, WDF.

[21] Act of May 26, 1824, *U.S. Statutes at Large*, III, 40.

River just above the mouth of the Verdigris, and reached the Red River a short distance above the Kiamichi.[22]

This new line took from the Choctaw Indians and gave to the white occupants a great extent of their best land, and the Indians immediately protested vigorously against it. Negotiations were thereupon reopened; the tribe sent to Washington a delegation including Apuckshunnubbee, who was called the Great Medal Chief, Pushmataha, Mushalatubbe, Robert Cole, Nitakechi, and David Folsom, with John Pitchlynn as interpreter; two of these chiefs were destined never to return. The party traveling by stage, reached Maysville, Kentucky, on Wednesday, October 13, 1824, and supped at an inn; some time later Apuckshunnubbee, who was said to have been trying to make his way to the river, fell over the abutments of the road to the pavement fifteen or twenty feet below. He received injuries to his head from the fall which rendered him unconscious; in this condition he lingered until Friday evening when he died. The sympathetic people of Maysville did everything possible for the venerable chief, and on his death showed him the most distinguished marks of respect:

> On Saturday his remains were accompanied to the Methodist meeting house by the Maysville Light Infantry, under Capt. Lee, united by a part of Capt. Nicholson's troop of horse, dismounted,

---

[22] This line, surveyed by John C. Sullivan and Joseph C. Brown in 1825, was described by them as follows: "Commencing at the southwest corner of the state of Missouri and running west 21 miles, crosses—Grand River and thence 19 miles making 40 miles west from the place of beginning, which point is established as the northwest corner of the territory of Arkansas. From this point the line runs due south. At 43 miles it crosses the Verdigris and five miles further the Arkansas river, about two miles above the mouth of the former. At 82 miles the line crosses the Canadian river, at about 140 miles, crosses the Kiamichi at Jack's Fork, at 170 miles, crosses the Kiamichi again about 6 miles from its mouth, at 176 miles, which is the whole length of the line, strikes Red river at a point about five miles above the mouth of the Kiamichi and more than 8 miles west of the surveyed lands, in range 39 miles west of the 5th principal meridian" (*Missouri Intelligencer,* June 25, 1825, p. 3, col. 1). The people of Arkansas felicitated themselves on the new line thus: "We are gratified to learn

together with the largest concourse of citizens and strangers ever assembled in this place on a funeral occasion. An appropriate sermon was preached by the Rev. Richard Corwine, after which the remains were conveyed to the "narrow house of the grave" and interred with military honors.[23]

Robert Cole, who accompanied the party, was named by the other members to succeed Apuckshunnubbee as a member of the delegation. Apuckshunnubbee was very old; when the Indians met to make the treaty of 1820 the headmen and warriors of "the District of the Upper Towns" represented to the commissioners

> that their present Chief Puck-She-Nubbee being old & infirm & anxious to retire that they have held a meeting for the purpose of consulting upon the subject of appointing his successor & that they have unanimously determined to appoint Capt. Robert Cole a young and active man of said District & they pray you to consider & acknowledge him as such.[24]

After their arrival in Washington on December 24, the second member of the delegation, the great Chief Pushmataha, died in Tennison's Hotel. His death was the occasion for an impressive funeral and eulogy pronounced in the Senate by John Randolph.[25] An interesting expense account rendered

that the line runs a little more than three miles west of the Cantonment [Gibson] and about one mile west of the mouth of the Verdigris; and that it leaves all the most valuable part of the bottoms of the Six Bulls, or Grand River, and the principal part of the most important Salt Springs, (which are very abundant in that country, and the waters of the strongest quality), within the limits of our Territory" (*Arkansas Gazette,* May 10, 1825, p. 3, col. 1).

[23] *Maysville Eagle* account, copied in *Kentucky Gazette* (Lexington), October 28, 1824, p. 3, col. 2. A bill for the sum of $15 was rendered by Dr. W. Coburn, of Maysville, for medical attendance on the chief; the following account for funeral expenses reflects the simple tastes of the Indians: five yards cambric, $1.87; tape, $.12½; barber's bill, $.37½; grave, $1.50; coffin, $7.00 (OIA, RCF, "1824 Choctaws, John Pitchlyn").

[24] Estonuckee and others to commissioners, October 20, 1820, OIA, RCF, "Choctaw Treaty Ground."

[25] For an account of Pushmataha, see *Handbook of American Indians,* II, 329.

Mad Buffalo or Skitok (Tcha-tó-ga) Osage Chief. Painted by George Catlin, 1836. Courtesy of Smithsonian Institution, Bureau of American Ethnology.

against this delegation during their stay in Washington gives a picture of their self-indulgence in that city that helps to explain not only the deaths of the two chiefs, but the strong desire of Indians to be sent to Washington in those days, and the condition produced in them, so favorable to the machinations of government agents seeking to overreach them. At Tennison's Hotel their bar bill was $2,149.50; board and lodging,$2,029.50; refectory bill, for oysters and liquor, $349.75; clothing, a suit each, $1,134.74; jewelry, $398.75; besides other smaller items, their washer-woman's bill was $25.71; the Secretary of War allowed Tennison's bill after deducting about thirty per cent from the amount.[26]

Over the bitter opposition of the whites a new treaty[27] was concluded with the Choctaw on January 20, 1825, fixing the eastern line of the Choctaw country approximately where it now is,[28] running south from Fort Smith to the Red River.[29]

[26] OIA, RCF, "1824 Choctaws, John Pitchlin."

[27] Kappler, *op. cit.*, II, 149.

[28] While negotiations were under consideration for the new treaty, the legislature of Arkansas again memorialized the President to establish the Poteau and Kiamichi as the boundary so as to protect three thousand white settlers on those streams in their property and improvements (Memorial of the Legislative Council and House of Representatives of Arkansas Territory, inclosure with letter of Henry W. Conway to Secretary of War, December 13, 1824, OIA, RCF).

[29] This line was surveyed under the supervision of United States Commissioner Henry D. Downs, of Mississippi, by J. S. Conway, who began the work at Fort Smith with his company of surveyors on November 2, 1825. He was accompanied by Maj. John P. Pitchlynn and Mr. Wall, the Choctaw commissioners. Conway felt much sympathy for the white people living on farms west of this line, who would be compelled to remove. (Conway to Governor Izard, November 2, 1825, OIA, RCF). Conway finished his work on January 7, 1826. He found sixty or eighty white families on the Poteau River in Crawford County, west of the line, which placed in the Choctaw country "the whole of the inhabitants of the populous county of Miller" except eight or twelve families. "On the 105th mile the Choctaw line crosses a line of the public surveys, 14 chains west of the corner of sections 35 and 36, of township ten south, in range 33 west of the 5th principal meridian" (*Missouri Intelligencer,* January 18, 1826, p. 3, cols. 1 and 2). This line was found to be too far west and in

Following the establishment of this line many white people west of it removed from the country, and the resultant scarcity and increased cost of pork and other provisions that had been furnished by these farmers greatly inconvenienced the garrison at Fort Towson.[30]

The large white population of the new line were vehement in their indignation. A memorial signed by about three hundred people, living on the land involved, said with much truth that the settlements had not been commenced on the lands of the Choctaw Indians but upon the lands of the United States; that under the assurance of protection, they had enlarged their improvements, planted orchards, and increased their stock, and that to have to abandon their plantations would be ruinous; that they were living on lands surveyed for the purpose six years before, since which time "Civil Government and Civil Jurisdiction has been extended to them, and Courts of Law established, and held within the tract of country lately ceded and confirmed to said Choctaw Indians."[31]

Claybourn Wright, as sheriff and assessor of Miller County, prepared a statement at his office at Miller Courthouse on July 10, 1825, showing that in Miller County, thus given to the Choctaw, there were the following people and taxable property: 2,500 white people owning 8,500 head of horses, 55,000 head of meat cattle, 10,000 hogs, 6,000 acres of land in cultivation,[32] 500 acres of which was in cotton. One cotton gin that cost

---

later years was resurveyed so as to reach the Red River a few miles lower down. The Choctaw charged that the error was deliberately committed in 1825 to save for white settlers some valuable salt springs located between the lines.

[30] Commissary General of Subsistence, "Letters Received," Vol. IV, 1825-1827, No. 1031, Maj. A. Cummings to Commissary General, July 6, 1826.

[31] *American State Papers*, "Indian Affairs," II, 555 ff.; Petition of inhabitants of Miller County, Arkansas (OIA, RCF). In this petition the scrivener spells the two rivers mentioned, "Kia Miche" and "Poto."

[32] Nuttall said in 1819: "The wheat planted here produced about 80 bushels to the acre, for which some of the inhabitants had the conscience to demand three dollars and a half per bushel, in consequence of the scarcity of last season" (Thwaites [ed.], *op. cit.*, XIII, 221).

$2,000 had been in operation "for a long time," and two others were in course of construction. Besides horse mills there were two water mills for grinding grain, one of which on Clear Creek[33] had been in operation for more than six years. John H. Fowler,[34] as clerk of the Circuit Court for Miller County at Miller Courthouse,[35] certified as to the official capacity of the sheriff.[36]

Many of these adventurous white settlers had for years braved untold dangers on that frontier now in eastern Oklahoma. In February, 1817, George C. Sibley reported a list of murders and robberies committed on the Arkansas River by the lawless Cheniers of Arkansas Osage; farmers named Geterlan, Williams, and Milmon, and one other had been murdered and robbed in 1815. The next year, below the mouth of the Canadian, these Indians killed and scalped an old man, robbed and beat an old Frenchman, and stole three horses from that section which had become known as the "American Settlement."[37]

The *Arkansas Gazette* published a summary of outrages committed by the Osage on the white people living near the Red River. In the summer and fall of 1815 these Indians stole sixty horses from the whites along that river; Jacob Barkman and Abraham Anthony were attacked between the Boggy and Kiamichi, and Anthony was killed. In 1816 a party of white

[33] Clear Creek empties into the Red River, southwest of Valliant, Oklahoma. Until recent years a water mill on that creek was in operation that is said to have been constructed before the memory of any living person.

[34] Fowler had formerly been the government factor at Sulphur Fork near Natchitoches.

[35] "The Clerk's office in Miller County, Arkansas, was entirely destroyed by fire on the night of the 10th ult, and was supposed to have been the work of an incendiary. All the records and papers belonging to the office since the organization of the county, together with the papers belonging to the Post-office which were kept in the same building were destroyed" (*National Banner* and *Nashville Whig* [Tennessee], December 12, 1828, p. 2, col. 3).

[36] OIA, RCF.

[37] *Missouri Gazette,* March 15, 1817.

hunters were encamped on the left bank of the Kiamichi, about fifteen miles from its mouth; one of the party named John Smith Achils was killed near camp by the Osage, who cut his head off.

On June 28, 1817, William Scritchfield, Wyatt Anderson, Johnathon Anderson, Joshua Anderson, James Thompson and a negro slave, all living at the Clear Creek Settlement about six miles below the mouth of Kiamichi, passed up the latter river about 20 miles to procure some buffalo meat for support of their families; on their return the day following, a party of Wasasah [Osage] waylaid them, fired on them, killed, sculped [*sic*], and beheaded Scritchfield ....[38]

and wounded Anderson. Early in the following December another party camped on the Red River were awakened by a shower of arrows.

The next year the Osage came to the house of Joseph English on Clear Creek and stole a number of his horses. They also raided the home of Adam Lawrence near the mouth of the Kiamichi and "robbed it of all the clothing and many other things, and left a respectable family in a deplorable condition, in a wilderness and frontier country."[39] Other citizens in the neighborhood suffered the loss of their horses to the Indians.[40] At the April, 1820, term of the Southern Circuit of the Territory of Arkansas, the Grand Jury of Hempstead County addressed an interesting memorial to Governor Miller in which they catalogued a long list of outrages committed on the white people in southwestern Arkansas by Cherokee, Osage, and Caddo Indians.[41]

A party outfitted by Frederick Notrebe of Arkansas Post

[38] Matthew Moss to the Secretary of State, August 4, 1817, AGO,ORD,WDF.

[39] Adam Lawrence was later killed by the Indians.

[40] *Arkansas Gazette*, February 26, 1820, p. 2, col. 1.

[41] OIA, RCF, "Commanche & others, Hempstead Co., Arkansas Grand Jury, April Term, 1820."

and headed by Antoine Barraque[42] of the same place had located on De L'eau Bleu [Blue Water River], a favorite stream for beaver, about thirty miles above the mouth, in what is now Bryan County, Oklahoma. This party, composed of more than twenty American and French white men and half-breed Quapaw Indians, was engaged in hunting, trapping, and trading with the Indians. To avoid being mistaken for an Indian camp and therefore involved in the quarrels between the Osage to the north and the Indians below the Red River, a flag was flown over the camp and most of their horses wore bells while grazing.

On November 17, 1823, a band of two hundred Osage warriors headed by their chief, Mad Buffalo[43] or Skitok, who had been on a raid against the Caddo Indians,[44] reached the Blue River near which on other occasions they had battled their enemies, the Choctaw and Caddo. Approaching the white hunting camp through the screen afforded by the cane along the stream, one hundred yards from camp, they effected a surprise attack on the hunters; and after a fierce battle Major Curtis Welborn of Hempstead County, three other men named Sloan, Lester, and Deterline, and a negro named Ben, belonging to Mr. Barraque, were killed, their heads cut off, and their bodies

---

[42] Antoine Barraque, a Frenchman, was appointed by Governor Izard in 1827 to pilot the Quapaw Indians to their new home on the Red River to see that justice was done them in getting their rations (*Arkansas Gazette,* March 6, 1827, p. 3, col. 3).

[43] Mad Buffalo affixed his name (by mark) to the Treaty of 1822, with the Cherokee as "Skitok or Mad Buffalo." He was the son of Clermont, "The Builder of Towns" (*Arkansas Gazette,* June 22, 1824, p. 3, col. 1). His name was written also Kiatica Washinpichai (*U. S. Senate Document No.512,* Twenty-third Congress, first session, III, 356).

[44] On the thirteenth they stole twenty-four horses from a Mr. Rose and other settlers at the mouth of the Kiamichi (Arbuckle to Gaines, December 22, 1823, AGO, OFD, 40 S 24). In October preceding, the Osage of White Hair's band made a raid on the Pawnee, in which they killed nine of the latter and took fifty horses with the loss of one Osage (P. L. Chouteau at "Ni on sho," February 14, 1824, OIA, RCF, "1824 Osages").

shockingly mangled.[45] Their camp equipment, kettles, rifles, clothing, peltries, and thirty horses were carried off by the Indians; the survivors fled to the settlements on the Red and Arkansas rivers and reported the atrocity.[46]

This outrage produced great excitement and uneasiness

[45] The details of this affair are to be found in "Graham Papers," Missouri Historical Society, Arbuckle to McNair, December 5, 1823; Arbuckle to Gaines, February 1, 1824, AGO, OFD, 40 S 24; H. Smith to Adjutant General, February 24, 1824, *ibid.;* Philbrook to Calhoun, December 9, 1823, AGO, ORD, WDF; *St. Louis Enquirer,* January 13, 1824, p. 2, col. 5; *Missouri Intelligencer,* January 15, 1824, p. 1, cols. 4 and 5; p. 2, col. 1; *ibid.,* March 13, 1824, p. 3, col. 2; *ibid.,* November 27, 1824, p. 1, col. 3; *Arkansas Gazette,* October 26, 1824, p. 3, cols. 1 and 2, *report of the trial; ibid.,* December 4, 1823, *Louisville Public Advertiser,* January 31, 1824, p. 3, col. 3; February 4, 1824, p. 2, col. 4; March 13, 1824, p. 3, col. 2.

[46] Other members of the hunting party were Isaac Pennington who lived on the Arkansas River, John McElmurray, Francis Imbeau, and Mitchell Bone. Pennington, who thought he was the only survivor, brought to the settlements a thrilling tale of his escape; he concealed himself in the cane, and after the battle recognized the body of "old Major Welborn" (*Arkansas Gazette,* December 9, 1823; *Missouri Intelligencer,* January 15, 1824, p. 1, col. 4; p. 2, col. 1). They "also stole a number of horses from Judge Brice's company of mustang hunters, whom he fell in with" (*Louisville Public Advertiser,* February 4, 1824, p. 2, col. 4). McElmurray, who seems to have been one of the proprietors of the party, settled at Cadron prior to 1818 (Thwaites [ed.], *op. cit.,* XIII, 156, 157).

"Barraque was licensed by Governor Miller of Arkansas to trade with the Indians. He therefore filed with the Government a claim to cover his losses, which he inventoried as follows:

'2,000 deer skins	@ 75 cents	$1,500
24 beaver skins	@$4.00	96.
32 traps	@ 3.00	96.
6 fine blankets	@ 6.00	36.
1 new saddle		15
7 brass kettles	@ 6.00	42
30 lbs. powder	@ .75	22.50
80 lbs. lead	@ .12½	10.
2 axes	@ 2.	4.
Shirts and other clothing,		15.' "

His papers were placed in the hands of Henry Conway, delegate from Arkansas Territory in Congress but when the latter was killed by Robert Crittenden in a duel they were lost; and in 1843 Barraque was still pressing for payment (OIA, Osage file, A 1402)."

among the missionaries at Union, and a number of their employees deserted and fled the country. The white settlers organized for defense;[47] and Colonel Arbuckle at Fort Smith was called on to bring the offenders to justice. Under his direction Major Alexander Cummings went to the trading house of Colonel A. P. Chouteau to demand of the Osage the surrender of the murderers. Clermont, Mad Buffalo, and Moi-neh-per-sha met him there, and on his orders had brought in twenty-one of the horses taken from the camp of Mr. Barraque;[48] five other horses, beaver skins, and other stolen property were being col-

[47] A company of cavalry was organized in Crawford County; fifty men volunteered under Capt. Frederick Fletcher; fifty swords and fifty pistols from the public stores at Little Rock were sent up the river on the steam boat "Florence." Another company was being recruited in the Peconery settlement, lower down the river (*Arkansas Gazette,* March 12, 1824, p. 3, col. 1). A company of cavalry was also recruited in Miller County for protection against the Indians (*ibid.,* September 28, 1824, p. 3, col. 1). The officers of the Miller County militia, Ninth Regiment, were Jacob Pennington, colonel; John Clark, lieutenant colonel; and Nathaniel Robbins, major, all commissioned June 10, 1823 (*ibid.,* June 14, 1825, p. 3, cols. 1 and 2). William Bradford was brigadier general of militia for the state. On October 7, 1819, on the requisition of Governor Miller, then on his way to assume his post in the West, the United States issued to the Territory of Arkansas a quantity of munitions of which he brought with him to Arkansas Post, 400 muskets, 40,000 rounds of ammunition, and "fifty horsemen pistols" (Governor Miller's message to the Legislative Council, February 10, 1820, State Department). Prior to December 31, 1821, two hundred cavalry sabers, four hundred "horsemen pistols," twelve drums, and twelve fifes were added to the martial equipment of Arkansas (*American State Papers,* "Military Affairs," II, 485). They were distributed to different parts of the territory, and on June 11, 1845, with the approach of the Mexican War, Solon Bourland, Adjutant General of the State, advertised for their return to him (*Arkansas Intelligencer,* August 9, 1845, p. 3, col. 1). Col. John Nicks, postmaster and sutler, at Fort Gibson, was appointed Brigadier General of the Arkansas militia in 1828 (Izard to Secretary of War, February 2, 1828, AGO, OFD, 7 I 28).

[48] Missouri Historical Society, Chouteau Manuscript Collection, A. P. Chouteau to Melicour Papin, December 11, 1823. Barraque's men arrived at Chouteau's trading house on the evening of the tenth of December, to claim their property (*ibid.*). December 19, Major Cummings passed Union Mission on his way to the Osage Village where he called a council of the chiefs and demanded the murderers (Union Mission Journal). An express passed the mission on February 14, carrying orders concerning the situation to Colonel Arbuckle from General Atkinson at Council Bluffs (*ibid.*).

lected to be surrendered. The chiefs assured Major Cummings that they were much distressed about the encounter, and that the leaders of the band who took part in it did not know until after they fired that the camp was occupied by white men. Clermont promised to call his people together and ascertain their sentiments on the subject of surrendering the leaders of the attack.[49]

With slight hope that the Osage would deliver the murderers, Colonel Arbuckle continued his effort.[50] Some of the Indians who promised to come and discuss the situation with him went on a buffalo hunt instead. A number of Cherokee came to Fort Smith and sought to join in the chastisement of the Osage, but Colonel Arbuckle declined their offer and ordered them[51] to return home. A party of Osage had just returned to the Verdigris with a large number of horses, which they said they had taken from the Pawnee Indians but Colonel Arbuckle thought they were stolen from the white people on the Red River.[52] He recommended that if the Government should decide to chastise the Osage the campaign should be launched in the spring or early summer, and that eighty or one hundred horses should be provided; he said also that in the event of a rupture with the Osage, "it would be indespensibly necessary that a supply of subsistence, ordinance stores &c should be established on the Grand or Verdigris river."[53]

[49] Cummings to Arbuckle, December 22, 1823, AGO, OFD, 40 S 24.

[50] Arbuckle to Gaines, December 22, 1823, *ibid.*

[51] Arbuckle to Atkinson, January 7, 1824; Arbuckle to Adjutant General, January 3, 1824, AGO, OFD, 10 A 24; Union Mission Journal.

[52] "Chongaismonnon's people have stolen horses from the Charaquees, and the Charaquees from Clermonts band they ware propering on both sides for hostilities. Colonel Arbuckle has stop them and made them agree to bring they horses lately stolen to Fort Smith and their exchange them" (P. L. Chouteau on "Indian Murders," February 14, 1823, OIA, RCF). Chouteau, the Osage agent, wrote in his imperfect English that the news of the murder "wase so contradictory thrue the Indians that a taulk proper today writing you until I could assairtain the fact, I have wrought the same to General Clark" (*ibid.*).

[53] Arbuckle to Gaines, January 19, 1824, AGO, OFD, 40 S 24).

However, on the twenty-fifth, Clermont, Tallai, and a few other Osage came to Fort Smith and conferred with Colonel Arbuckle.[54] They expressed their regret at the outrage on the whites and said that the leaders of the party had tried in vain to restrain their young warriors. Colonel Arbuckle said he believed the military were able and determined to chastise them if they refused; but until they were able to make good their threat that a demand for the offenders would be met with reprisals on the missionaries, traders, and other whites living near them. Accordingly he postponed making it until a more propitious occasion.[55]

Upon receipt of this information, General Winfield Scott, in command of the Western Department, at his headquarters at New Orleans, on March 8, 1824, ordered Colonel Arbuckle to remove his five companies from Fort Smith to the mouth of the Verdigris[56] and take a new position there. This move was dictated in part, he said, by the great amount of sickness among the troops at Fort Smith. Before Colonel Arbuckle received his orders, however, he had sent word by Colonel A. P. Chouteau to Clermont's band to meet Major Cummings at the Falls of the Verdigris[57] on March 13, when a final demand would be made on them for the leaders of the guilty Indians; but he had little hope of success.[58]

Colonel Arbuckle's messenger to the Osage was Nathaniel Philbrook, who traveled the route from Fort Smith past Bean's Salt Works; later his horse and personal effects were found

[54] Captain Pryor had induced Tallai to attend the conference and they passed the mission on their way, January 23 (Union Mission Journal).

[55] Arbuckle to Gaines, February 1, 1824, AGO, OFD, 40 S 24.

[56] Scott to Adjutant General, March 8, 1824, *ibid.*, 43 S 24.

[57] Falls of the Verdigris, about four miles above the mouth of that stream; now under the bridge of the Kansas, Oklahoma and Gulf Railroad.

[58] Arbuckle to Smith, March 14, 1824, AGO, OFD, 7 S 24; Arbuckle to Adjutant General, March 18, 1824, *ibid.*, 61 S 24; Arbuckle said in this letter that ". . . . should the Government not determine to chastise them, it will be very difficult to restrain the Cherokees . . . ." who, he said, wanted to make war on the Osage.

near the mouth of the Grand River, and it was reported that he had been drowned while crossing that stream.[59] Several weeks afterwards, however, his body, pierced by a bullet, was found in the Arkansas River nearly two hundred miles below; who murdered him remained a mystery, but suspicion indicated the Osage.

None of the Osage met Major Cummings at the Verdigris, except Clermont[60] who said he was not prepared to answer the demand for the guilty ones; he had not conferred with his people, as they were all either hunting or at war. Most of the Indians were unwilling to meet in council or to vote to surrender the murderers, which would make them unpopular among their people. Major Cummings said that in the event of war he thought the Osage of Big Hill (Grosse Côte) or White Hair's village would take no part in it, so that they would have to oppose only Clermont's band which probably contained about five hundred warriors.[61] Early in April, Tallai and other leading Osage went to the mouth of the Verdigris to seek counsel of Colonel Chouteau; but he had descended the river with a cargo of skins and they returned to their home.

[59] Foreman, *op. cit.*, p. 83; *Missouri Intelligencer*, May 24, 1824, p. 2, col. 5; Union Mission Journal.

[60] In this correspondence his name is usually spelled by the army officers "Clarimore."

[61] Cummings to Arbuckle, March 17, 1824, AGO, OFD, 61 S 24. The Osage chief, Black Dog, treated the notice with contempt, and immediately started out on a hunt. Most of the chiefs gave themselves little concern about the matter, "thinking that Clarimore [Clermont] ought to settle it, as the outrage was committed by his band."

XIII

FORT SMITH GARRISON INVADES THE OSAGE COUNTRY, 1824

COLONEL ARBUCKLE received his orders to remove his force on April 2, and immediately made his preparations to leave. Eight or ten men under the assistant commissary, Lieutenant Bonneville,[1] were left in charge of the buildings temporarily, and the remainder of the command departed from Fort Smith April 9. Part of the troops went by land with the wagons belonging to the command, and the remainder proceeded by water with the military stores in their two keel boats.[2] Five companies of the Seventh Infantry on April 21[3] occupied the site of the new post on the east side of the Neosho[4] or Grand River about three miles above the mouth,[5] which was

[1] For an account of Bonneville, see Washington Irving, *Adventures of Captain Bonneville* (New York, 1868); Foreman, *op. cit.*, pp. 243 ff.

[2] Arbuckle to Adjutant General, April 7, 1824, AGO, OFD, 61 S 24; *Missouri Intelligencer*, May 24, 1824, p. 2, col. 5; these keel boats were part of the equipment of Fort Smith and Fort Towson for transporting provisions and supplies.

[3] Arbuckle to Jones, December 11, 1834, AGO, ORD, *Fort Gibson Letter Book 1834-36*, p. 23. April 22, Arbuckle reported the establishment of his new position (AGO, ORD, "Headquarters Western Department," Scott to Arbuckle, June 18, 1824). For some months the station was known officially as "Grand River Arkansas (Galt to Arbuckle, June 18, 1824, AGO, ORD, "Little Rock" No. 6, p. 69). It was later named Fort Gibson and when it was discovered that the style of the name violated one of the departmental orders, it was changed to Cantonment Gibson (Butler to Arbuckle, May 12, 1827, AGO, ORD, "Western Department," Letter Book No. 2). On February 8, 1832, the name was again changed to Fort Gibson (AGO, Reservation Files).

[4] This was at the crossing of an ancient trail that continued northwest to the trading post just below the Falls of the Verdigris.

[5] Arbuckle found but two good boat-landings in the vicinity in which he was directed to locate; and he selected a site for the post where a wide ledge of rock made an excellent landing. In later years the Cherokee demanded the vacation of the Fort Gibson reservation so this boat-landing could be turned over to the tribe. The other landing place was on the east side of the Verdigris about four miles from the mouth, where the Creek Agency and the trading settlement were located.

subsequently named Cantonment Gibson. Here the troops, at first quartered in tents, began the erection of log huts to house the men and stores until the completion of permanent quarters surrounded by a stockade.[6]

Soon after their arrival at the new station, with the continued assistance of Captain Pryor who had great influence with the Osage, and because of the alarm occasioned by the proximity of the troops, the accused persons were surrendered.[7] David Barber, a former trader who had been made subagent to the Osage in place of the late Mr. Philbrook, brought word from his charges on May 29 that they would be at Cantonment Gibson in ten days.[8]

The surrender was witnessed by Mr. Vaill, Mr. Chapman, Mr. G. Requa, and Mr. Vaill's oldest son.

They left Union on Monday at three o'clock P.M. in a canoe and reached Cantonment on Tuesday morning. The council took place at two o'clock P.M.[9] the result of which was the delivering to Colonel Arbuckle of 6 Osage warriors to be tried by the Govt. of the U. S. for the murder of a party of whites as mentioned in the journal for Dec. last. It would exceed the usual limits of a Journal to notice in detail the interesting transaction. To see six Brave men come forward, and voluntarily submit to become prisoners; to be put in irons; and sent away to be tried for their lives; to see this done with firmness and decision, by the unanimous consent of the Nation, and without a single sign from their affectionate wives—to see the sense of honor manifested on the part of the criminals, and the desire to do justice in the Nation, was indeed affecting to every spectator. And as it was more than we have expected it was to us a surprising event. . . . . The next

[6] By the end of the year 1824, sufficient log barracks had been erected to house the garrison, and it was surrounded by a strong stockade for its protection. This crude post composed of log houses was so far completed in March, 1828, as to win the approval of Gen. Winfield Scott who visited it on a tour of inspection. His arrival at the post was greeted by the roar of cannon (*Arkansas Gazette,* March 12, 1828, p. 3, col. 1; *ibid.,* March 19, p. 3, col. 2).

[7] Galt to Adjutant General, June 7, 1824, AGO, ORD, Headquarters Western Department, "Letter Book" No. 2, p. 61.

[8] Oklahoma Historical Society, Union Mission Journal.   [9] June 7, 1824.

day was spent in Council on some minor affairs and in delivering to them presents of beef, pork, and flour. There were not less than 500 men around the Fort all friendly and harmless. The next day, Thursday, was appointed for the Colo and Sub Agent Mr. Barber to meet the Chiefs and Warriors at their Encampment near the falls of the Verdigris to assist them in forming some civil regulations.[10]

Colonel Arbuckle and the Osage agent undertook to organize a form of government among the Osage; the whole of Clermont's band was assembled near the Falls of the Verdigris, and they were much pleased with the plan proposed. Thirteen persons were named to constitute a national council, and of this body Clermont was elected president and Tallai vice-president. The duty of the council was to legislate on all important matters, and a national guard of forty warriors was selected to carry into effect the decisions and laws of the council.[11] This was probably the first attempt to establish a government among the Osage; unfortunately there is no record of its having survived. After finishing their business the Indians indulged in races and games for the entertainment of the officers at Cantonment Gibson. In one of these races, two of the horses ran together, throwing Clermont's son from his horse with such force that he was almost instantly killed.[12]

The surrendered Osage, having missed passage on Colonel Chouteau's keel boat which had started down the Arkansas with a load of furs,[13] proceeded under a guard of soldiers commanded by Captain John Philbrick; and although one of the prisoners escaped the first night after they left Cantonment Gibson, the remainder were delivered to Acting-Governor Crittenden at Little Rock on June 25.[14]

---

[10] Union Mission Journal.   [11] *Ibid.*   [12] *Ibid.*

[13] This boat left the Verdigris for New Orleans loaded with 38,757 pounds of furs and skins (Foreman, *op. cit.*, p. 83).

[14] *Arkansas Gazette,* June 29, 1824, p. 3, col. 1; Acting-Governor Crittenden to Calhoun, September 12, 1824, OIA, RCF. The prisoners were accompanied by Pierre Beatte who was employed by the agent to act as interpreter for them at their trial. In 1834 Beatte served Washington Irving and Henry L. Ellsworth as guide on their western tour. Irving frequently mentioned him in his book, *A*

The five Osage were indicted, and in November were brought
to trial in the Superior Court of the United States for the Territory of Arkansas, sitting at Little Rock, charged with the murder of Major Curtis Welborn. The defendants were Mad Buffalo, Little Eagle, Little Rattlesnake, Little Bear, and Caddo
Killer, all of whom were indicted by both their Indian names
and English equivalents.[15] Mad Buffalo was tried separately
and convicted; the other four were tried together, Little Eagle
was convicted and the remainder acquitted.[16]

When Mad Buffalo was asked what cause he had to show why
sentence of death should not be passed upon him, he made a long
speech to the court, in the course of which, he admitted that he
belonged to the party that committed the murder, but denied
having any agency in it himself. He said that he was some distance
off in a cave at the time of the attack, and that he had remon-
strated against it; that he was friendly to the Americans, and
wished to preserve peace and harmony with them.

The Chief appears to be considerably advanced in years, is
large and well proportioned, of fine and commanding mien, and
shews from his interesting countenance and manner that he possesses a superior mind and great intelligence, for one of his race.

Tour on the Prairies. During this association Beatte told Irving of his services
with the Osage prisoners for which Arbuckle had promised him two dollars a
day that had never been paid. When Irving returned to Washington from Fort
Gibson he brought and presented to the commissioner of Indian affairs Beatte's
claim supported by statements made by General Arbuckle and Col. A. P. Chouteau relating to his service. In the claim the scrivener spelled his name "Pierre
Beyatto."

[15] Mad Buffalo bore the Osage names of Cha-to-kah-wa-she-pe-she and Ski-
tok; Little Eagle was Wa-na-sha-shinger; Little Bear was Wa-sa-ba-shinger,
Little Rattlesnake, Sha-gu-shinger, and Caddo Killer was He-sha-ke-he-ree
(*Arkansas Gazette,* October 26, 1824, p. 3, cols. 1 and 2).

[16] The Osage were tried before Judge Andrew Scott and prosecuted by Sam
C. Roane, United States District Attorney, assisted by A. H. Sevier; they were
defended by Robert C. Oden and T. Dickinson (*ibid.*). The trial which consumed one day excited much interest; as nearly all who were called for jury
service had heard of the murder and expressed opinions of the guilt of the
prisoners fifty were rejected for cause; a large number of witnesses were examined; the jury was out only ten minutes (*Arkansas Gazette,* account in *Missouri
Intelligencer,* November 13, 1824).

The sentence of death he received with the greatest composure, and without betraying the slightest emotion of fear. The mode of his death is all that he objects to, and we understand, he declared to the interpreter that he would kill himself before the day appointed for his execution arrives. Indeed so determined is he to avoid the ignominious death that awaits him, that on Friday evening last, he made an attempt on his life by stabbing himself with a small penknife (which had been given to him for the purpose of cutting tobacco), in his left breast, opposite his heart. The blade of the knife, however, was too short to effect the object which he had evidently intended, and only inflicted a pretty deep wound, which is not considered dangerous.[17]

Mad Buffalo and Little Eagle were sentenced to be hanged on December 21. Before that date, however, Colonel Arbuckle wrote the War Department that he thought clemency ought to be extended to the convicted Indians; he said that a pardon, based on justice, would be productive of good results.[18] Acting-Governor Crittenden of Arkansas Territory opposed this recommendation, but under instruction of the War Department he postponed the execution to February 24.[19] He was later directed to furnish the Secretary of War a statement of the evidence on which the Indians were convicted, on receipt of which the War Department again directed a postponement of the execution; the imprisoned Indians chafed under the uncertainty and declared they would rather be hanged than suffer confinement any longer.[20]

Governor Alexander McNair, the Osage agent,[21] went to Clermont's Town and then to Fort Gibson, where he convened the Osage Indians in a council on January 24 to urge them to agree to remove from the Verdigris and rejoin the remainder

---

[17] *Missouri Intelligencer,* November 27, 1824, p. 1, col. 3; *Arkansas Gazette,* October 26, 1824, p. 3, cols. 1 and 2.

[18] Arbuckle to Nourse, November 4, 1824, OIA, RCF.

[19] Crittenden to Calhoun, December 25, 1824, *ibid.*

[20] *Ibid.,* January 29, 1825.

[21] Alexander McNair, former Governor of Missouri Territory, was appointed agent to the Osage on June 1, 1824; he died in that service in the spring of 1826.

of the tribe on the Neosho.[22] He found the Indians very poor
and learned that they had impoverished themselves in order to
pay attorneys to defend their tribesmen in the court at Little
Rock. Governor McNair, moved by deep sympathy for the
condition of the Osage people, wrote to the President[23] saying
that there was a very general sentiment among the army officers
and the better class of white settlers along the Arkansas that
the convicted Osage should not be executed. The Indians said
that a few years before, some of their hunters were killed by
white people on the Missouri River, and the Government did
nothing about it;[24] and the killing on the Blue River, of the
white hunters who were trespassing on the Osage hunting
ground, was only in satisfaction of the unsettled account. The
Indians thought it unjust to punish them and not punish the
whites who had wronged them. Moved by these considerations,
President Adams pardoned the Indians March 21, 1825.[25] Set
at liberty May 15,[26] they started at once for their home on the
Verdigris, but not traveling together. Mad Buffalo was much
exhausted by the fatigue and hunger he endured during his
journey through the wilderness, and was almost starved on
arrival at his home. He and Little Eagle related to their people
a ludicrous account of their trial, imprisonment and treatment
while in Little Rock.[27]

[22] McNair to Clark, March 14, 1825, OIA, RCF. Besides Clermont's Town,
that called Grosse Côte (Big Hill) was located a few miles higher up the Verdigris. McNair was directed to secure the removal of both Osage towns to the
Neosho.

[23] McNair to President Monroe, January 30, 1825, Department of State,
368 Bureau of Indexes and Archives, Miscellaneous.

[24] In the summer of 1820, nine Osage returning from a war excursion against
the Iowa were passing through the white settlement on the north side of the
Missouri River near where Kansas City now is; they stopped at the house of
Mr. McIlree and attempted to steal some horses; a fight resulted in which two
Indians were killed and two whites wounded with tomahawks (George C. Sibley
to Governor Clark, "Fort Osage 25th July 1820," AGO, ORD, WDF).

[25] U.S. Department of State, "Pardons," IV, 123.

[26] *Arkansas Gazette,* May 3, 1825, p. 3, col. 1; *ibid.,* May 20, 1825, p. 2,
col. 2; *Louisville Public Advertiser,* June 4, 1825, p. 3, col. 4.

[27] *Arkansas Gazette,* June 7, 1825, p. 3, col. 1.

XIV

FORT TOWSON ESTABLISHED ON THE RED RIVER, 1824

THE Cherokee having located on both sides of the Arkansas River, those on the south side were ordered to remove to the north.[1] Resentful of the efforts to disturb them and compel them to move again, a band of the boldest of them, under the leadership of The Bowle, had

> .... left those on the Arkansas and gone to the Red River, where a banditti of outlaws are forming with whom I expect trouble. They are in the constant practice of stealing horses from the white people. This banditti consists as I am informed, of a strolling party of Cherokees, Delawares, Shawnees, Choctaws, Creeks and Coshattahs, and all backed by the Caddos, who are a very considerable tribe, and their principal chief, I am told holds a Spanish commission as Colonel.[2]

On May 22, 1820, a band of these Indians stole some horses from Pecan Township, and were pursued by Captain Nathaniel Robbins and a posse; after a pursuit of one hundred miles the Indians were captured, and admitted having stolen the horses in company with The Bowle. ".... The Cherokee that was taken is known by the name of Hog in The Pen, and on

[1] *U. S. House Document 263,* Twentieth Congress, first session, p. 7, Calhoun to Lewis, July 22, 1819. Not all of those who were living on the south side of the Arkansas left with The Bowle; and it was necessary the next year to order Governor Miller to remove them; refusing to obey, in 1823, Acting-Governor Crittenden, in compliance with the wishes of the white people, again ordered the Cherokee to vacate the land on the south side of the river, or be removed by force (*Missouri Intelligencer,* August 12, 1823, p. 2, col. 4). Some Cherokee had removed from Arkansas to the Red River prior to 1818 (Morse, *op. cit.,* Appendix, p. 258).

[2] Governor Miller to Secretary of War, June 30, 1820, OIA, RCF. It was reported that sixty Cherokee warriors had joined the Caddo confederacy in the winter of 1819-1820 (*Niles' Weekly Register,* October 28, 1820, p. 133).

his way to justice was rescued by about 40 Cherokees and a few Caddoes, who came and took him by force of arms."[3]

In 1821, when four companies of the Seventh Infantry moved to Natchitoches to complete the occupation of the Southwest Frontier, these troops were not far enough up the Red River to protect the people in the vicinity of the Kiamichi[4] from depredations by bands of predatory Indians on both sides of the stream, whose presence was largely responsible for the incursions of the Osage with whom they were continually at war. The Arkansas House of Representatives and Legislative Council, on October 18, 1823, memorialized the Secretary of War to remove the military establishment from Sulphur Fork up to the mouth of the Kiamichi; they said that 1,500 of their citizens living below the Kiamichi were exposed to depredations by Indians who were crowding upon their frontier, and they complained particularly of fresh incursions by the Osage who frequently descended upon them.[5] This memorial was presented to the War Department by their delegate, Mr. Conway, who suggested that the troops at Fort Smith be removed to the mouth of the Verdigris and those at Natchitoches be stationed at the mouth of the Kiamichi.

Lieutenant Richard Wash had reported to Colonel Arbuckle, after his visit to the Red River:

.... From information obtained in the settlement, the laws of the United States are but little regarded relative to the introduction of slaves into that section of country. A number of inhabitants on the south side of Red River consider themselves as Spanish subjects, and have elected a commandant and other civil officers and consider themselves no longer subject to the laws of the United States.[6] [Army headquarters at Louisville had reported to Washington that] .... The evils existing on our Spanish border

---

[3] Letter from Governor Miller, *Arkansas Gazette,* July 15, 1820, p. 3, col. 1.

[4] This word is spelled also "Kiamitia" but the weight of authority seems to favor the spelling in the text.

[5] Conway to Secretary of War, January 20, 1824, AGO, ORD, WDF.

[6] Wash to Arbuckle, October 31, 1823, AGO, OFD, 10 S 24.

and mentioned by Colonel Arbuckle had been carried to a great extent. No question exists, but that (in addition to frequent quarrels in that neighborhood, among the parties of different nations of Indians), the laws of the United States relative to the introduction of slaves and to trading with the Indians are set at perfect contempt and daily and extensively violated. In addition to this, a band of lawless marauders have established themselves on the Red River above our post [Jesup], and are in habits of committing the most outrageous acts of robbery, violence and murder. These evils the general [Scott] thinks can be corrected, by the establishment of a post at (or near) the junction of the *Kiamitia* and Red Rivers and proposes, with this view, to detach to that place a company of the 7th Regt. . . . .[7]

The War Department on February 8, 1824, referred all the correspondence to Major General Winfield Scott, in command of the Western Frontier, with discretion to act immediately upon the whole matter.[8] Accordingly, after a tour of inspection of the Red River, General Scott on March 8 ordered one company from Fort Jesup to join one at Sulphur Fork, and take a position at the mouth of the Kiamichi.[9]

The troops reached the Kiamichi in May[10] and established what was later named Cantonment Towson, under the command of Major Alexander Cummings. By June there were present one hundred men belonging to companies D, A, I, and F, engaged in building barracks which were completed by the end of the year.[11] Early in April, Lieutenant Stephenson with fifty men in two keel boats left Natchitoches with provisions and ammunition for the new post; but they encountered such

[7] Smith to Adjutant General, January 16, 1824, AGO, ORD, Headquarters Western Division, "Letter Book" No. 2, pp. 18, 19.

[8] Letter from Henry Conway, February 12, 1824, in *Arkansas Gazette,* March 23, 1824, p. 3, col. 1.

[9] Scott to Adjutant General, New Orleans, March 8, 1824, AGO, ORD, Headquarters Western Division, "Letter Book" No. 2, p. 40; AGO, OFD, 43 S 24.

[10] Their encampment was known for a time as "Kiamechia"; "Camp Towson near the mouth of Kiamichi"; "Camp Towson, near the Kiamitia River."

[11] Cummings to Many, January 4, 1825, AGO, OFD, 14 C 25.

difficulties in passing up the river through the Great Raft that the journey required more than two months.[12]

The troops were much needed on the Red River; vagabond Indians there carried raids as far north as the Arkansas River; the Choctaw, who had in 1822 attacked the Osage on the Canadian, killed two and took captive two children, proceeded to the Osage villege and robbed them of a number of horses, and returned to the Red River bringing other horses belonging to Colonel Chouteau and the Cherokee chief, Black Fox. For some of these they found a market with the whites, who carried them to the Spanish Country.[13] These same whites were destined to give the troops nearly as much trouble as the Indians.

The commanding officer at Fort Towson endeavored to enforce the laws of the United States against unlicensed persons occupying and hunting upon Indian land, unpopular measures with the whites. Several distilleries were operating near the post; the owners sold whisky to the soldiers, and traded it to Choctaw and other Indians for the horses they were encouraged to steal from the Osage.[14] In November, 1824, Major Cummings, in command at Fort Towson, reported to the district attorney

12 War Department, Quartermaster's Corps, Commissary General's Files, "Letters received," Vol. III, No. 706; *ibid.,* Vol. IV, No. 1039. Fort Towson was a lonely outpost with an irregular mail by way of Miller Courthouse. Maj. Alex. Cummings wrote to the Adjutant General: "Dear Col. Amusements rather scanty with us a game of chess or backgammon occasionally is all we have to drive away dull ennui. While you are gratified daily with news from all parts of the world, we have not received a mail at this post for the last six weeks. Our mail carrier deserves hanging" (Cummings to Jones, May 2, 1827, AGO, OFD, 86 C 27).

13 War Department, AGO, OFD, 10 S 24. Lieutenant Wask reported to Colonel Arbuckle that sixty Choctaw Indians living on the Red River were responsible for all the outrages committed by the Osage on that settlement (Arbuckle to Adjutant General, October 31, 1823, *ibid.*).

14 The Osage went boldly upon their hazardous expedition to the western Indians, and stole large numbers of horses, which they brought to the Verdigris and disposed of to the unscrupulous and pusillanimous whites who would not risk what the Indians did to secure them. When the Osage returned from their buffalo hunts, their hundreds of horses were turned loose near the hunting camps, to recover if possible from their hard riding; and after a sufficient time

at Little Rock a number of violators of the law who were thereby incensed against the officer.[15]

Several soldiers who were gathered at one of the stills five miles from the post, were involved in a difficulty with civilians who came in considerable force on the morning of January 20, 1825, bound them, and started to the home of Squire Ewing, a justice of the peace, the mounted captors snapping their guns and beating the soldiers they were driving on foot. On learning of the predicament of his men Major Cummings sent a force to rescue them.[16] In March a citizen who had a claim against a soldier sued in a justice of the peace court, and after what was called a mock trial[17] got an award for $15. A constable assaulted the defendant and attached the horse he was riding; a sergeant and four men were sent to recover the horse, which they did after whipping the constable. His friends rallied to his defense and imprisoned the soldiers. On hearing of this, Lieutenant Stephenson was sent with a larger force which rescued the soldiers.[18] Then citizens under the leadership of Pennington, Brice, and Bowman, engaged in levying a force to attack and destroy Fort Towson.[19] Two hundred men congregated on February 2 at the home of Joseph English on Clear Creek, for this purpose.[20]

Cummings furnished to Sam B. Roane, United States district attorney for Arkansas Territory, a list of the ringleaders in

had elapsed the Indian owners would return for them. The animals became known as "tired horses," and the whites on the Red River made a practice of invading the Osage pastures and stealing them, which kept alive the animosity of the Indians (Arbuckle [Fort Smith], September 3, 1823, to Adjutant General, *ibid.*, 58 A 23).

[15] Letter from Major Cummings, January 4, 1825, *ibid.*, 14 C 25.

[16] Cummings to Many, January 30, 1825, *ibid.;* Crittenden to Calhoun, February 14, 1825, *ibid.*, 15 C 25. The citizens charged that Cummings' men marched in the courtroom of Squire Ewing with bayonets presented, and rescued the prisoners (*Arkansas Gazette,* June 26, 1825, p. 3, cols. 2, 3, and 4).

[17] *Arkansas Gazette,* April 26, 1825, p. 3, col. 1.

[18] *Natchitoches Courier,* March 21, 1825, p. 1, col. 1.

[19] Cummings to Atkinson, April 8, 1825, AGO, OFD, 30 C 25. An incendiary burned the buildings at Fort Towson in 1829 (Foreman, *op. cit.,* p. 61 n.).

[20] *Natchitoches Courier,* March 1825, p. 1, col. 1.

these disturbances, and lists of white men who were hunting west of the "Kiamishy in violation of the 2d & 3d sections of Act of March 30, 1802."[21] Roane came to Miller Courthouse and from there wrote to Cummings that he would not prosecute the persons named adding that they were going to Little Rock to have Cummings and some of his officers indicted.[22] This they did, and orders were given to deliver the accused men to the civil authorities of Arkansas.

Major Cummings, who had tried in vain to suppress a distillery conducted near the post by men named Brice and Cheek, who were selling whisky to the soldiers and Indians, was relieved of his command[23] and succeeded by Captain R. B. Hyde. After assuming command of the post, Hyde had Jesse Cheek arrested and taken before a justice of the peace near Fort Towson. During the trial Cheek attacked Hyde in the courtroom with a club and attempted to kill him; the justice fined him $15 and turned him loose. Cheek then fled to Little Rock. He was described as a desperate character—a peddler from St. Louis who had absconded with some goods.[24]

The Osage and Quapaw Indians were among the very few of the tribes found by the Government on the Louisiana Purchase west of the Mississippi who were recognized by treaty as owners of the soil on which they lived. The Quapaw, a branch of the Arkansas tribe of Indians, claimed all the country between the Red and Arkansas rivers and westward from the Mississippi; and the Osage claimed a vast section extending north from the Arkansas River and westward from the Missis-

21 "There is about one half of the inhabitants of the country engaged in hunting & trading with the Indians; there are a large number out at this time who might be taken on their return to the settlement" (Hyde to Governor Izard, October 11, 1825, AGO, OFD, 41 C. 25).

22 Cummings to Atkinson, April 8, 1825, *ibid.*, 30 C 25; *Natchitoches Courier*, June 7, 1825, p. 1, col. 4.

23 Cummings was ordered before a court martial to convene at Fort Towson on April 20, for "resisting the civil authority of the Territory of Arkansas" (Order 27 of the Adjutant General, March 18, 1825).

24 *Arkansas Gazette*, August 30, 1825, p. 3, col. 1.

sippi. The Government took cessions from these two tribes of over eighty million acres of land, for a trifle.

Since 1818 Indian emigrants from the north had been forcing their way into southwestern Missouri, until by 1824, there were said to be more than eight thousand of them.[25] In that year the Senate Committee on Indian Affairs, whose chairman was Senator Benton of Missouri, made a report[26] recommending the purchase of the country lying west of Missouri and Arkansas, on which to locate the Indians in those states as well as those who might remove from east of the Mississippi. Accordingly treaties were made with a number of western tribes, including the Quapaw and Osage. In 1818 the Quapaw had ceded by treaty[27] to the United States all that great domain lying between the Red River and the Arkansas and Canadian rivers and westward from the Mississippi, except a tract on the south side of the Arkansas lying between Little Rock and Arkansas Post. For this cession they were paid in goods to the value of $4,000, and an annuity of $1,000. In 1824 they gave up the remainder of their land lying in the center of Arkansas Territory[28] for $6,000 and an annuity of $1,000 for eleven years, which was at the approximate rate of one dollar for 1,000 acres, or the twelfth part of a cent for an acre. This same treaty reserved to James Scull, a trader, two sections of land in satisfaction of a claim he had against the Quapaw tribe for $7,500, which put a value of about $6.00 an acre on the land. Reservations of good tracts of land were made to halfbreeds with French names, the French having freely intermarried with the Quapaw as with the Osage. As if taking this great tract of land from these weak people for nearly nothing was not enough, it was provided further in the last treaty that they should thereafter be concentrated and confined to the

---

[25] Abel, *op. cit.*, p. 362.

[26] *American State Papers,* "Indian Affairs," II, 512; *Missouri Intelligencer,* June 12, 1824, p. 2, cols. 3 and 4.

[27] Kappler, *op. cit.*, II, 112.   [28] *Ibid.*, p. 147.

district inhabited by the Caddo Indians on the Red River, and form a part of that tribe.

They were accordingly removed to the Red River, but the Caddo Indians refused to receive them; and they were so located that the overflow caused by the Great Raft in that stream covered their lands and destroyed their crops two of the three years of their residence there,[29] and they were on the point of starvation. In June, 1827, Governor Izard of Arkansas Territory made a visit[30] to these unfortunate people to investigate reports that some of them had actually died of starvation, which he found all too true. He reported that they had been grossly neglected by the government officials and mistreated by the Caddo Indians. Some of the citizens of Hempstead County came to their relief with food and sent word of their wretched condition to the Governor, who took prompt steps to supply them with corn and at once reported their condition to the Government. It was truly a shameful situation. The Government had secured from these harmless, weak people an empire as large as Arkansas, for almost nothing; and having taken from them the fertile lands from which they had made their living and the forests that provided them with game, had driven them off to starve, apparently indifferent to their destination and suffering.

Subsequently the Quapaw wandered back in small parties to the Arkansas, trying to sustain life on their ancestral domain, to the great displeasure of some of the whites. General Clark devised the plan of merging them with the Osage, who agreed to the suggestion, provided some of the land that they had so thoughtlessly given to the United States should be restored to them.[31] The Secretary of War approved of Clark's

[29] George Gray, Indian agent, to Secretary of War, June 30, 1828, OIA, RCF, "1828 Red River Agency." Gray said the timber in the Great Raft below his [Caddo] Agency, had been increasing yearly since he had been stationed there. Gray, a native of Kentucky, died at his Agency on November 4, 1828.

[30] Izard to Secretary of War, June 6, 1827, *ibid.*

[31] Clark to McKenney, February 24, 1828, OIA, RCF.

proposal and directed that the merger be carried into effect.[32] The humane Governor Pope wrote that the Quapaw chief, Saracen

> .... called on me and made, I believe, a very sincere and certainly a feeling representation of his sufferings and misfortunes in the Caddean Country and the desire of his tribe to remain here in peace with us on some inferior lands, and appealed in a very impressive manner to the justice and humanity of his Great Father the President and the White People whose blood his nation had never shed. They are a kind of inoffensive people and aid the Whites in picking out their cotton and furnishing them with game. I have heard but one sentiment expressed in this territory with regard to this tribe, that of kindness and a desire that they should be permitted to live among us; I would be particularly gratified to be authorized to assign them a township on this river, in the vicinity of their permanent residence. The residue of this tribe are now on their return from the Caddean to join their friends here— they will all be united on this river and they would prefer death to be driven from the land of their fathers.[33]

With the aggressive Osage, however, the condition was quite different. While by the treaty they made in 1808 they yielded the land in Arkansas and Missouri, they continued to range over much of it, contesting the right of whites and other Indians they found there. By the treaty of 1818 they professed to give up more land extending west to the Verdigris River, and still they fought the Cherokee Indians whether they found them there or farther east. Following the Benton report a treaty[34] was negotiated, in 1825, with the Osage, by which they ceded to the United States all their lands except a tract fifty miles wide and extending east and west in what is now southern Kansas. The government officials bent their efforts for many years to compel the Osage to locate on this tract, but met with the most obstinate resistance.

[32] *Ibid.*, July 3, 1828.
[33] Pope to Secretary of War, June 22, 1829, OIA, RCF.
[34] Kappler, *op. cit.*, II, 153.

XV

IMMIGRANT INDIANS FORM AN OFFEN-
SIVE AND DEFENSIVE ALLIANCE
1823-26

AT an early day the Indians whose habitat had been east of the Mississippi began to realize the menace of two hostile forces enveloping them—the white men east of them and the savages to the west. The Cherokee on the Arkansas who wished to live in peace on their little farms were opposed by the predatory Osage who, unlike the former, had nothing to lose and all to gain by their raids on the herds and fields of the immigrant Indians. The leading men among the Cherokee had a vision of a confederacy of immigrant tribes, united for their common good to oppose the wild tribes to the west and by force of numbers to promote their own aggressions and exact more favorable treatment at the hands of the whites.

In the campaign against the Osage in 1817 a union of the tribes was already functioning; and the next year Tahlonteskee informed Governor Clark that in consideration of the assistance rendered in that campaign by the Shawnee and Delaware, he had agreed to solicit the Government for a tract of land on which his people, their allies, and other small tribes might locate and be governed by the same policy and where they could promote each other's interest. He said:

> My object in wishing the junction of the Shawnees and others in the same boundary is to form regulations for our government; we could be materially assisted by the whites who are intermarried among us and them. . . . . This course would promote the improvement of our conditions and enable us all to live more happy, under such improvements and regulations as we may be enabled to effect.[1]

[1] Tahlonteskee's speech to William Clark, February 21, 1818, OIA, RCF, "Cherokees West."

A delegation of Cherokee headed by Tahlonteskee presented these views to the President, who promised his assistance in bringing about the removal of eastern Indians desired by them.[2]

The movement of emigrant Indians toward the Osage frontier was to have a lasting influence on the western country; some of the Delaware were already living west of the Mississippi under permission given by the Spaniards in 1789. Parts of the Shawnee and Delaware tribes were in possession of a tract of land about twenty-five miles square near Cape Girardeau, Missouri, under an arrangement with the same government, given them by Baron de Carondelet on January 4, 1793, and recorded in the office of the Recorder of Titles at St. Louis. In 1815 the Delaware abandoned this location, leaving cultivated fields and improvements. These and recent arrivals from the East[3] were moving westward across southern Missouri. The Indian agent, Richard Graham,[4] was directed in 1821 to locate them and remnants of Kickapoo, Shawnee, Miami, Piankashaw, and Wea as far west as possible next to the Osage. He was instructed first to make peace between them and the Osage; pending this preparation, they had stopped and raised a crop on the Current River in 1821; Graham induced chiefs of the different tribes to agree to meet him in St. Louis on October 10, and enter into a treaty of friendship.

2 Secretary of War to Clark, May 8, 1818, *ibid.*

3 In June, 1820, Pierre Menard at Kaskaskia reported $525 expended for provisions and ferriage for Shawnee and Delaware emigrants crossing the Mississippi into southern Missouri (Missouri Historical Society, "Graham Papers," Menard, June 30, 1820): during the autumn of 1820 a considerable number of Delaware from the White River in Indiana were crossing the Mississippi at Kaskaskia, bound for the Arkansas River (*Arkansas Gazette,* December 2, 1820, p. 2, col. 4). Another party of Delaware on their way from Ohio and Indiana to join their western brothers were forced by sickness to spend the winter of 1820-22 near Vincennes where they were naked and starving (Missouri Historical Society, "Graham Papers," Menard to Graham, Kaskaskia, January 3, 1822).

4 Richard Graham was appointed agent of Indian affairs in the Illinois Territory July 14, 1815, and directed to report to Governor Edwards at Kaskaskia (*ibid.*).

The consent of the Delaware and Shawnee was reluctant, as they had been inflamed by the experience and influence of the Cherokee; and they failed to appear at the appointed time. The Great Osage were present, however, anxious for peace, three of their chiefs had just died from a fever that had swept off many of their number, and Graham said they were the objects of pity and charity. They were disappointed that the Cherokee, Delaware, and others were not present, and they asked Graham not to bring them to St. Louis again to make peace with the Cherokee, in whom no faith could be placed. They and the Little Osage were willing, however, that the Arkansas Osage should be punished by their enemies, for bitter jealousy had long existed between them; these Indians of Clermont's Town and Grosse Côte, higher up the Verdigris, living in the fine hunting grounds of what is now eastern Oklahoma, nearer the buffalo, were believed to be more prosperous than those of the old settlement. The chiefs of the old village complained that by the time they could reach their hunting ground, the Cheniers (Clermont's band) had driven the buffaloes off and they were obliged to advance farther among their enemies, the Pawnee, to find game. They begged that Clermont should be made to return to his village,[5] and were willing that their tribesmen should receive "a good whipping from the Cherokees, believing that would drive them back to their village."[6] Colonel Menard was sent to bring the Delaware chiefs in; and they answered that they could not make a peace, as their chiefs had all gone on their winter hunt and the Cherokee were angry with them for not taking up the tomahawk against the Osage.

The agent warned Anderson and the other Delaware chiefs against joining the Cherokee in their warfare with the Osage; but the chiefs seemed to have little control over their young men who, they said, had seemed "like bloodhounds in the

---

[5] Missouri Historical Society, "Graham Papers," Graham, November 12, 1821.
[6] *Ibid.*

leash" since they heard of the victory of the Cherokee over the hunting party of Clermont's band.[7]

This winter's hunt has given the emigrating Indians an idea of the great riches of the Osage Country and they openly avow their intentions of taking possession of it. Hunting parties of the Delawares are equipped for war ready to strike if they fall in with any Osages. If they go to war the Kickapoo will join them, tho they have a fine country, none superior, yet they are anxious to exterminate or drive the Osages off. One half of the Kickapoos are still in Illinois and are unwilling to remove, but say they will come in the spring. They have between two & three hundred warriors on the Osage River. The following will be something like the number of warriors that can be brought against the Osages—from the east—Cherokees 600, Delawares 600, Kickapoos 400, Shawnees, Peorias,[8] Wias, Michigamans, Piankashaws, 500, making a total of 2100. In the west about 2000 Pawnees and others. To meet this force the Osages can bring into the field 1000 warriors, and the Kansas 250, making a total of 1250. There is a treaty I believe offensive and defensive between the Sacs & Foxes & Osages as it respects the Pawnees, but the Sacs & Foxes will not take up the tomahawk against the Delawares who have an extensive control over all these Indians now residing east of the Mississippi. A party of Pawnees have taken three lodges of Little Osages, & another party of the same nation consisting of 11 warriors were all killed by the Kansas, this latter party had gone out for the purpose of stealing horses.[9]

It was the autumn of 1822 before Graham could induce the Delaware and Shawnee to enter into a treaty of peace with the

---

[7] The massacre of Osage women and children in October, 1821.

[8] ".... the Peorias have been residing in the Missouri Territory these Forty years past, and the Piankeshaws ever since 1814" (*ibid.*, Menard to Graham, Kaskaskia, June 13, 1820). The Shawnee ".... who reside westward of the Mississippi .... separated from their nation and moved there immediately after the revolutionary war under the advice and direction of a noted incendiary named Loramie" (*ibid.*, John Johnston, Indian agent, Piqua, Ohio, to Secretary of War, September 24, 1822).

[9] *Ibid.*, Richard Graham, February 7, 1822.

Osage and get his remnants of tribes started again to the lands allotted them on James Fork of the White River in southwestern Missouri. Located here near their allies, the Cherokee, adjoining the lands of the Osage which they coveted, there began in spite of their treaty a new era of bloodshed and fierce contest for dominion over eastern Oklahoma that left its impress on the history of the country.

The next summer Colonel Arbuckle reported:

> I am informed that a Dispute took place about 15 or 20 days since between a party of Delaware Indians who reside on the waters of the White River and a party of Osages, which resulted in the Delawares killing Seven Lodges of the Osages, and it has also been reported that the Comanchy Indians had a short time since killed Twenty or Twenty five Osage Warriors.[10]

The Cherokee exercised considerable influence, and their plans for organized defense and aggression were favorably received by the fragments of other immigrant tribes who were drifting to the White and Neosho rivers where they were obliged to meet the hostility of the savage Osage on their hunting expeditions. They had been sadly treated by the whites and felt the need of a protection that the Government did not give them. Early in 1823 a general council was held[11] by representatives of the Cherokee, Delaware, Shawnee, Wea, Kickapoo, Piankashaw, and Peoria tribes. Tahlonteskee was then dead and the venerable and astute Chief Takatoka and the Shawnee chief, Captain Lewis, were the leaders in the movement for a union of tribes for their mutual benefit. A controlling motive, which was seldom mehtioned, was their plan of aggression by which they hoped to wrest from the Osage the fine hunting and agricultural land of the present eastern Oklahoma, with its salt springs and lead mines.

For several years the eastern and western tribes had been

[10] Arbuckle to Adjutant General, August 2, 1823, AGO, OFD, 54 A 23.
[11] Crittenden to Calhoun, September 28, 1823, OIA, RCF.

carrying on a correspondence by means of wampum on the subject of the removal of the eastern tribes to the west of the Mississippi.[12] The council decided to extend to their red brethren in the East a formal invitation to remove west of the Mississippi and join them in the proposed confederacy. Their chief, Captain John Lewis, was deputized to carry white wampum to his tribe in Ohio and inform them of the action of the council that sent him; he was told to request the eastern tribes to arrange a council where the Cherokee would explain the inducements to live in the West, the benefits to be derived from a union of the tribes, and extend a formal invitation to join the projected confederacy.[13]

On his journey to Ohio, Captain Lewis stopped at St. Louis where he visited General Clark and explained the purpose of his mission. The late Indian council had decided that a general council should be held at Wapakoneta by deputations of the Shawnee, Delaware, Cherokee, Kickapoo, Piankashaw, Wea, and Peoria from west of the Mississippi, and of the Shawnee, Wyandot, Ottawa, Miami, and Tuscarora from the East.

> The principle object of the Council is to form an Alliance, and to propose a general peace among all the Indians, and to enforce it on those nations who may be disposed not to listen to reason and justice, to perfect the removal and Settlement of all the Indians East of the Mississippi and south of the lake, to the west side, or on such land as they may obtain from the United States, for which they will exchange the land they now Possess. The reasons which has led to a call of this Great Council (as stated to me) is *First* the Indians Settlements in Indiana, Ohio and New York have become surrounded and hemed in by a dense white population, leaving no lands to hunt on and affording too great a facility to the introduction of ardent spirits which is so distructive to the Indians and *Secondly*, to give to Indians forming this Council a

[12] Missouri Historical Society, "Graham Papers," Clark to Calhoun, September 5, 1823.

[13] OIA, RCF, "Cherokees West & Shawonees—Wm. Clark. Council at St. Louis," January 11, 1825.

settlement by which they may exact and enforce their own law and regulations necessary towards the agricultural life, which they are extremely anxious to exchange [for] that of the hunters; so precarious of the means of subsistence and so little to be depended on in future.—*Thirdly*, to receive among them Teachers and Husbandmen, to prepare themselves in every way to enjoy the same blessings which they see industry and agriculture extends to the white man, to endeavour to enjoy these blessings themselves and to extend it to other nations of their influence.

In this late Indian Council it has been decided that a deputation of each Tribe shall go on to the City of Washington with Lewis immediately after the Great Council at Sandusky, to state their views and wishes, exchange their lands, and make arrangements to move to and occupy such lands as they may receive in exchange, and conclude all arrangements which may be necessary. The General outlines of their views and wishes having been communicated to me, soliciting my assistance and advise, I have stated to that Agent Col. Lewis that I think favorably of the objects of the several Indian treaties as communicated through him, and think it probable that the Government will be inclined to favur the views of the Indians in promoting any measure calculated to facilitate their welfare and future happiness. . . . . It is believed that the number of Indians composing this Deputation to the seat of Government will be about 19 selected from the different tribes as follows—2 from the Cherokees, 2 from the Showones, 2 from the Delawares, 1 from the Pottowatomies, 1 from the Weas and 1 from the Peorias, of the West side of the Mississippi, 2 from the Senecas, 2 from the Wyandots, 2 from the Miamias and two from the Ottoways.[14]

General Clark was so much impressed with the importance of the project of the Indians that he immediately communicated the information to the Secretary of War; their plans coincided so nearly with the desires of the Government[15] that

[14] Missouri Historical Society, "Graham Papers," Clark to Calhoun, September 5, 1823.

[15] After Secretary Calhoun received General Clark's letter, he wrote to Agent Graham: "The object is considered an important one and meets the entire appro-

every encouragement was given them. Major Graham, Indian
agent, was directed by General Clark to accompany Captain
Lewis and his delegation to Ohio, where he joined them in explaining to the Shawnee the purpose of the mission and gave
it governmental sanction.[16]

Whether the movement had its origin in the mind of Tahlonteskee or Takatoka, the latter was active in promoting it; he
had visited many of the Indians in what are now Oklahoma,
Missouri, Arkansas, and Texas, both indigenous and intrusive,
who gave it their approval. Acknowledging his authority and
capacity for constructive leadership, the Ohio Indians requested
that he accompany them to Washington and contribute his
information and influence to the negotiations they wished to
conduct with the President looking to their exchange of lands
and removal to the West. Renewed difficulties with the Osage
delayed the Cherokee in starting and their delegation did not
reach St. Louis until December, 1823. They wished to continue
to Ohio and Washington, but General Clark told them the season was too far advanced and directed them to return home
and come back the following May.[17]

In the spring as the Cherokee did not appear in Ohio according to their agreement, the Shawnee and Seneca sent messengers to St. Louis to ascertain whether they had been misled by
the promises of their agent, Lewis.[18] But trouble with the Osage
again delayed the Cherokee in taking their departure, and it
was not until autumn that they were able to begin their journey. On October 27, 1824, the Cherokee in full council issued

bation of the government"; and Graham was directed to accompany a delegation
of Indians to Washington when they should be ready (Calhoun to Graham,
September 27, 1823, OIA, RCF, "Letter Book" E, p. 492; First Annual Report
of the Indian Office, November 10, 1825, OIA, RCF, 1825 Miscellaneous).

[16] OIA, RCF, "1825 Cherokees West & Shawnees," William Clark, "Talks
Relative to Delegation."

[17] *Ibid.*

[18] The Seneca messenger was instructed by his people not to return home
without the Cherokee deputation (*ibid.*).

to their Beloved Man, as Takatoka was called, a formal commission in writing authorizing him in the name of the Cherokee Nation to assist in the council because, they said, the Cherokee Nation felt a deep solicitude for the success of the negotiations as being intimately connected with the happiness and prosperity of the red people generally. Takatoka was accompanied by the Spring Frog, Young Glass, the Witch, Tassell, Tah-lone, and Young Duck, minor chiefs of the tribe, as councilors, and John Drew as interpreter.[19] A few weeks after their departure, E. W. DuVal, Cherokee agent, wrote the Secretary of War concerning Takatoka:

.... I have reason to believe that .... he has a more extensive acquaintance and greater influence with the Red People generally than any other known individual among them and that the government could further any views that it may have in relation to them more pacifically and certainly thro him than any other, or others. He is a man of good sense and I would place more reliance on his word than on that of any other Indian I have ever seen.[20]

[19] *Ibid.,* "1825 Cherokees West, John Jolly to Gov. Izard."

[20] *Ibid.,* "1824, Cherokees West, E. W. DuVal," November 28, 1824. Two years earlier Takatoka was seen in Georgia by a Scotch missionary who was much impressed by his appearance and personality; he first saw him ".... an elderly Indian, attired in an ancient costume, and his travel-worn pony hitched at the gate .... just arrived" at an Indian home. When others approached ".... He rose to his feet to receive them revealing a figure rather below the common height; but I can truly say that seldom, if ever, have I met a person who so greatly impressed me at first sight with native urbanity and graceful dignity as that dark-skinned Indian. No one could look upon his broad forehead, flashing eye, and expressive face without feeling that he was a born chief; .... his object in visiting the Nation East was to persuade all his people to remove to Arkansas, there to unite with other friendly tribes in a great confederation, which should be strong enough to demand of the United States that the Mississippi River should be made the boundary forever between the white and red races. For this purpose he visited many of the tribes, and never ceased his efforts until his death. When Takatoka learned that the missionary was a British subject, he became very cordial, for he had fought on the side of the British in the Revolution and in the War of 1812 (Rev. F. R. Goulding, *Sal-o-quah; or Boy-life among the Cherokees* [Philadelphia, 1870], pp. 234 ff.).

Takatoka's deputation left in October for Kaskaskia; there they were to be met by the representatives of the Ohio tribes who were anxiously awaiting them in anticipation of the aid to be given by the great Takatoka. But upon arrival at this place the venerable Beloved Man fell sick and died; and with his death perished his scheme of an Indian confederacy, since there was no one capable of taking his place. However, so intent was he on the success of his undertaking that on his deathbed he urged his followers to continue; they accordingly went on to St. Louis and reported to General Clark. Takatoka had labored industriously and systematically, and the delegation exhibited to Clark wampum from nineteen eastern tribes that had been sent to him to indicate their approval of his overtures to them.[21] The delegation was joined at Kaskaskia by Captain Lewis and the Sandusky chief; and they united in such strong terms in soliciting Clark to provide the means for

[21] OIA, RCF, "1825 Cherokees West, Delegation Papers, etc., Council House, St. Louis, Jan. 6, 1825." "The deputation of Cherokees exhibited a number of strands and bunches of Wampum with several white Wampum belts which that nation had received at different times from the various Tribes of Indians residing East of the Mississippi which had been delivered to them with talks in relation to their removal to the West and occupying a Country convenient to each other for the purpose of union and support of regulations calculated to govern the whole, and promote the culture of the earth and a tendency to civilization." The wampum included a long white belt from the Six Nations of New York, a white belt from the Connewango, a white belt and several strands from the Shawnee of Ohio, one each from the Choctaw and Chickasaw and a bunch of blue wampum from the Choctaw warriors; white and blue wampum from the Creeks, three bunches of white from the "Nottoway," two from the Shawnee, and one each from the Wyandott, "So-wa-ke-la," Miami in Ohio, Potawatomi, Ottawa, Chippewa, Sauk, Foxes, Kickapoo, Wyandot of New York, and Delaware. And, showing further the prodigious energy and systematic labor employed by their Beloved Man in laying the foundation for his cherished scheme, "A string of white beads encircled and curiously connected attached to a piece of tobacco received by the Cherokees from eighteen villages of the Tribes residing between the Arkansas Territory and New Mexico acknowledging the talks of the above tribes which had been communicated by the Cherokees and through him inviting those Tribes to come and be their neighbors. In presence of W. B. Alexander, Sub Indian Agent" (*ibid.*).

them to continue their journey to Washington where they might lay their plans before the President, that he authorized the Indian agent, Pierre Menard, to accompany them and look after their wants.

The delegation, numbering seventeen persons, mounted on horseback, proceeded by way of Wapakoneta, Ohio, to Washington where they arrived on February 19.

> They were agreably surprised on learning what the President had said on the subject in his message to Congress, at the opening of the session; "Our Great Father" said they to General Clark, "must have been inspired by the Great Spirit, or have studied well our miserable situation, with a view to our future happiness, to have enabled him to speak to the great council, so exactly in agreement with the wishes of the Indians, as he had in his talk to Congress." Thus it would seem a movement is begun, upon the plan now before Congress, for bettering the condition of our Indians, by *Indians Themselves*. This certainly augurs favorably to its ultimate completion.[22]

After remaining in the capital a month and receiving approval by the President of their project,[23] the deputation departed from Washington on March 21[24] and returned to Ohio where a council was begun at Wapakoneta on May 11. Gover-

[22] *Daily National Journal* (Washington), February 8, 1825, p. 3, col. 4.

[23] A tactless request of the Secretary of War came near to destroying the good feeling the Indains brought with them; he told them the Government wished the Cherokee to give up some of their land and remove farther west. The Cherokee were incensed and astonished at the suggestion: "We have made known that our desire is to concentrate the Shawnees and others on our western boundary; if this is effected, the strangers who come into our country are to be fed from our table. We can not consent to remove our eastern boundary . . . . we present before you two medals which were given to two of our *chiefs* by Mr. Jefferson during his administration. The Glass and Dick Justice were their names, but they now sleep in death on the Arkansas. These medals are returned to the government that such a disposition of them may be made as though best" (OIA, RCF, "1825 Cherokees West-Delegation").

[24] *Arkansas Gazette*, May 3, 1825, p. 3, col. 3.

nor Cass was present, but he did not arrive in time to prevent much adverse advice and influence which was exerted by designing white men upon the Indians present;[25] and in spite of the foundation that had been laid for inducing their removal, but few of those present would agree to go. They had been told that the movement was designed by the Government to get possession of their land. Governor Cass told them that this was not true, that the movement had originated with the Cherokee as they and the Shawnee west of the Mississippi wished their eastern brethren to remove to the West where they would be neighbors;[26] but he told them he was authorized to say that the Government would make them just and liberal offers for their lands.

The Indians then proceeded to St. Louis where another council was held with General Clark on November 10. The Cherokee chief, Wy-sa-o-she-ka, spoke and showed General Clark the wampum that was sent to them at the meeting in Wapakoneta:

> .... This is from the Mingoes, this the Wyandotts, this the Delawares, this the Senecas, this the Oneidas, this the Ontarios, and this from the woman begging us to pursue in our undertaking and not to give it up; this large wampum of white is a stran from each of the tribes mentioned to make the road clear..... [Captain Lewis of the Shawnee spoke and said:] .... I shall move over the Mississippi for my people now with me will not return—those who are not on their way will soon commence their journey..... The Prophet was invited to attend the Great Council, supposing he had learned some sense by this time, and have a wish with the other Indians to live altogether..... We have a large party of Showonees and Senecas with us; we will make our fires for the present among the swamps near the Mississippi and try to sustain our-

[25] Even the agent for the Shawnee discouraged the effort and attacked Captain Fields as dishonest and lacking in influence with the tribe (Johnson to McKenney, Piqua, April 11, 1825, OIA, RCF).

[26] OIA, RCF, "1925 emigration, Gov. Lewis Cass, Journal of council with Shawnees & Cherokees West, May 24, 1825."

selves until we hear from you. I hope you will take pity on us and afford us some aid, in corn, lead & powder this winter.[27]

The plight of the Shawnee, who had crossed the Mississippi and continued to southwestern Missouri, was pathetic; they appealed for assistance:

> My Father Clark—You know that when we were residing on land near Cape Girardeau wee were happy and you know what has made us left it; Father—We have never injured our white Brother, Wee are sorry to say that they have stolen from us our horses, our cattle, our corn and even the tools we work the ground with, our ploughs &c; For several years you ask us to exchange our land. With paine wee have consented to and upon your word we have left them. Father—since we have left them we are more than poor. We are miserable wee are dispersed like turkeys and if you had not asisted us with corn, several of us would have died of hunger. . . . .

They asked Governor Clark to assist them to reach Washington so that they might solicit the President to pay them for their land and improvements abandoned at Cape Girardeau, and for the property stolen from them by white people.[28]

[27] Clark to Secretary of War, November 15, 1825, Report of Council, "1825 Cherokees of Arkansas and Shawnees." An emigrant party of 255, all Shawnee but one family of Seneca, camped in the Big Bottom twenty miles below Kaskaskia during the winter of 1826 while waiting to cross the Mississippi (Missouri Historical Society, "Graham Papers," Menard to Graham, January 17, 1827).

[28] OIA, RCF, "1824 Shawnees from Cape Girardeau." The year before, Matthew Adams, a justice of the peace for Independency Country, Arkansas Territory, made a statement for General Clark concerning the destitution of the Shawnee Indians on the White River: " . . . . they are now & have been for a considerable time in a suffering situation; this I am enabled to say by seeing their children skinning off the bark of Trees & making use of sap, procuring roots, weeds &c which their Chiefs told me was their only alternative to support life" (Clark to Calhoun, June 5, 1823, AGO, ORD, WDF). Three villages of "the dispersed Indians" of the Shawnee, Delaware, and Creek tribes were living between the forks of St. Francis River; they were located at a place called Big Prairie on land slightly elevated above the surrounding vast expanse of water covering the lands inundated by the subsidence in the

The Delaware recently located on the White River were also in desperate straits for food. When they were being removed there, the white people stole nearly all their horses and seriously incapacitated them to care for themselves. In February, 1824, William Anderson, the head chief, Black Beaver, Natcoming, and other Delaware addressed a pathetic letter to General Clark:

> Last summer a number of our people died just for the want of something to live on. . . . . We have got in a country where we do not find all as stated to us when we was asked to swap lands with you and we do not get as much as was promised us at the treaty of St Marys neither. . . . . Father—We did not think that big man would tell us things that was not true. We have found a poor hilly stony country and the worst of all no game to be found on it to live on. Last summer our corn looked very well until a heavy rain come on for 3 or 4 days and raised the waters so high that we could just see the tops of our corn in some of the fields and it destroyed the greatest part of our corn, punkins and beans and a great many more of my people coming on and we had to divide our little stock with them. Last summer there was a few deere here and we had a few hogs but we was obliged to kill all of them and some that was not our own but this summer there are no game nor no hogs and my old people and children must suffer. Father— You know its hard to be hungry, if you do not know it we poor Indians know it. Father—If we go a great ways off we may find

earthquake of 1811. This isolated country abounded with game and for some time these people were happily free from intrusion by whites. They were " . . . . inoffensive, useful, and in some degree industrious. They raise good stocks of horses, cattle, and hogs, and make a sufficiency of bread stuffs for home consumption. No charge of dishonesty has ever been, even colorably sustained against them, and the little trade they furnish in fur, peltries, beaver, oil, &c is extremely acceptible to our small community from its vicinity . . . . It seems as if providence in consideration of their misfortunes had directed them hither, where white men will not live." Friendly people living at Point Pleasant, New Madrid County, Missouri, protested against threats to break up these settlements and drive the Indians out (Francois Lesieurs & Son to Pierre Menard, August 4, 1825; S. G. Hopkins to Maj. R. Graham, August 6, 1825, Missouri Historical Society, "Graham Papers").

some deere but if we do that we cannot make any corn and we must still suffer. Father—We are obliged to call on you onst more for assistance in the name of God. . . . . Father—We expect a great many more of our people here this spring to make corn; . . . . we wish to gether all of my people onst more to Gether cass I know I cant live always; Father—If you will give us any help you will please let us know as soon as possible by writing to our friend Pierre Menard, if you do not we cannot make much corn this summer.[29]

This picture of the destitution of the immigrant tribes driven to southwestern Missouri next the Osage, over whose country they were compelled to hunt in the search for food, will help to explain a period of bloody contest between those Indians, that made Oklahoma a battle ground for several succeeding years— a struggle for existence if not for supremacy that was forecast by Takatoka's conception of a confederacy of the immigrant tribes.

[29] OIA, RCF, "1824, Delaware on White River." Just a few years earlier this country abounded with game. In November, 1818, Henry R. Schoolcraft visited the country on both sides of the line between the present states of Arkansas and Missouri. He went as far west as the site of Springfield, Missouri, and on his return descended the White River to where Batesville is situated. In his interesting journal he recounts frequently seeing bear, deer, and beaver. Hunters were moving into the country, slaughtering these animals, buffaloes, and elk and shipping furs down the White River to the Mississippi; from that time hunters came in increasing numbers and with the Cherokee and other immigrant Indians soon made short work of the vast numbers of wild animals that flourished in that country. On Swan Creek within the present Christian County, Missouri, Schoolcraft passed three Osage camps, "now deserted, all very large, arranged with much order and neatness, and capable of quartering probably 100 men each"; and he gives a minute description of their houses (Schoolcraft, *op. cit.*). Anderson lived until 1831.

XVI

THE OSAGE, CHEROKEE, AND DELAWARE
AT WAR, 1826

THE country on which these Indians had been located answered the requirements that they be got as far as possible
from the white settlements, but it had been hunted over so
much that it was almost destitute of game and they were compelled to go far to find meat. It contained a lead mine that was
being worked under a Spanish grant by some white people, and
a considerable number of squatters from Boone's Lick neighborhood were settled there. These people had been removed;
and as a result they were resentful of the immigrant Indians,
the innocent cause of their inconvenience, and the Indians
feared them. Pierre Menard visited them in February, 1824,
and found them destitute, the hunters all having left to hunt
in the Osage country for food to support their families.[1] Natu-
rally the Osage regarded with bitter animosity these invaders
of their ancestral hunting grounds who killed the game they
relied upon to feed their wives and children. The Delaware,
Cherokee, Shawnee, and Kickapoo, both separately and in co-
operation, embarked often on hunting and war expeditions
across what is now Oklahoma to the Red River and to the
western prairies; conflicts with the Osage[2] were frequent and
blows were struck in reprisal over a wide range of territory.

In the autumn of 1824, Anderson's[3] son had left with a party

[1] Missouri Historical Society, "Graham Papers," Menard to Clark, February
15, 1824.

[2] The Chickasaw were harassing the Osage by stealing their horses (*ibid.*,
Menard to Clark, February 15, 1824).

[3] The Delaware Chief, Anderson, lived at a settlement called variously
Anderson's Village, James Fork, and sometimes Delaware Village. The Delaware, Kickapoo, Piankashaw, Peoria, and Wea living nearby, were known

for an extended hunting expedition across Oklahoma to the Upper Red River. The next year "about roasting-ear time," on their return, a party of Osage stole some of their horses and while they were trying to recover them Anderson was killed, This grieved and incensed the old chief, and his warriors launched a bloody campaign of revenge. The Osage killed a Delaware boy the next winter south of the Canadian River, and made off with twenty-six horses he was driving. In February, near the Red River, they killed George Bullet, George White Eyes, and some other Delaware.[4] A month later, in March, 1826, within three miles of the place where the boy was murdered, a hunting party of ten Delaware and ten Kickapoo killed five Osage, whom they encountered there; the Osage, who said they were returning from war with the Pawnee, invited the Delaware and Kickapoo to camp with them.

.... They did so, in the night the kickapues proposed to the dellewars to kill them the dellewares replied saying that there chief and there agent had told them that they must not doe any mischief while on their hunt—but before daylight they all concluded to join and tomhock them, which they did accordingly, they justify this act because the horse belonging to andersons son hoo was killed was seen amongst the Osages, another reason they assign that the Cherrokea chief told them that the osages had killed eleven of his people last fall and one shawny and one delleware boy, the Cherrokea chief is now collecting all his wareors and intends striking the blow in about fore weaks, there was when this young man left Marshalls trading house on red river about eight hundred collected from the different tribes about six weeks

collectively as "the White River Indians," and they were under the supervision of subagent John Campbell (Missouri Historical Society, "Graham Papers," Campbell to Graham, July 25, 1825). Batesville, Arkansas, reported an alarm from the "disorderly movement of Shawnees and Delawares on White River who have been removed there within the last two or three years" (*Missouri Intelligencer*, May 22, 1824, p. 2, col. 5).

[4] Missouri Historical Society, "Graham Papers," Menard to Graham, April 17, 1826.

since the Osages have killed five dellawares among them was George White his father, one woman, and two boys, for soon as this news reached Natcoman on red river he started with five men determined to have scalps, the Indians have all left red river on there way home so soon as they arrive I shall be able to get all the particulars, and will communicate them to you.[5]

This called for retaliation by the Osage, a party of fifty or sixty of whom invaded the Piankashaw and Delaware settlements in the latter part of March, and killed and scalped Joe Elliot, a Delaware. Most of the warriors being away from home, the remainder fled. When Pierre Menard heard of this raid, knowing that the Delaware had no ammunition, he sent them from Kaskaskia a cart with six kegs of powder, three hundred pounds of lead, and five hundred gun flints, and sent a mechanic to repair their arms so that the Delaware could defend themselves.[6]

During sugar-making time[7] a party of Osage warriors, returning from the Pawnee villages, killed a Delaware woman, two men, and a boy, destroyed six hundred skins, and took eight horses. On March 19, fifty Osage warriors attacked a Delaware hunting camp of three men, three women, two girls, and a child on the Robideau fork of the Gasconade. Two men and two women made their escape; the balance were killed and mutilated, and the child was thrown into the fire. On March 28, a party of Delaware returning from the Red River killed another Osage, a member of Clermont's band, near Bean's Salt Works above the mouth of the Illinois River.[8] These Delaware

---

[5] *Ibid.*, Letter from John Campbell, subagent, written at Delaware Village, March 16, 1826.

[6] *Ibid.*, Menard to Graham, April 17, 1826.

[7] When the Frenchman, Cortambert, visited the Osage in 1835, he reported (Louis Cortambert, *Voyage Au Pays Des Osages* [Paris, 1837], p. 37) that they not only appropriated the wild honey of the forests, but also made maple sugar.

[8] The Illinois River in Oklahoma. This was at the crossing of the old Osage trail.

then joined a large party of Cherokee camped below Fort Smith, where they prepared for an attack on the Osage.[9]

The Delaware were determined on a war of vengeance against the Osage, and had solicited the Cherokee, Kickapoo, Sauk, and other tribes to join in a general campaign of extermination. It was feared in some quarters that the opposition would in fact destroy the Osage, after which the combined forces would turn upon the whites and carry out a general plan of insurrection. This Governor Izard believed to have been the purpose of the proposed federation promoted by Takatoka. He wrote the Secretary of War that it would take considerable time to assemble a force of militia, and that the territory had not a single piece of artillery and only a few boxes of musket ammunition scattered at various points where they were deposited for safe-keeping in merchants' stores.[10]

Colonel Arbuckle and other government officers exerted themselves to prevent the Indians from involving a large extent of country in hostilities, and secured an agreement by the Osage and Cherokee to meet at Fort Gibson in May, 1826, the Delaware refusing to attend, or consider any overtures of peace. The Cherokee chiefs arrived on May 3 and the chiefs of Clermont's band about a week later. The Osage refused to go into council with their enemies, as their agent, Governor McNair, had recently died and they would not go into conference with only a subagent to represent them. The Cherokee likewise refused to meet them in council until the Osage had delivered the warrior who had killed Red Hawk, the nephew of Tom Graves, several years before. In fact the Cherokee came to Fort Gibson armed, with the intention of taking their revenge at that time, and were with difficulty dissuaded from that course.[11] As the great obstacle to peace lay in the unsettled question of punish-

---

[9] Arbuckle to Lowndes, April 4, 1826, AGO, OFD, 30 A 26; Arbuckle to Clark, May 14, 1826, OIA, RCF.

[10] Izard to Secretary of War, January 30, 1826, OIA, RCF.

[11] DuVal to Secretary of War, May 31, 1826, *ibid.*

ment for the killing of Graves's nephew, Colonel Arbuckle and the agents of the tribes finally induced the belligerents to agree to return home and cease their hostilities for three moons pending determination by General Clark, the superintendent of Indian affairs at St. Louis, of the question whether the Osage would be required to surrender the murderer to the Cherokee for execution,[12] pursuant to the treaty of 1822.

Hostilities, which were increasing to an alarming extent, were complicated by the death of Governor McNair, the Osage agent.[13] Other Indian agents were sent to the Delaware with little success. Lieutenant Thomas Johnston was sent from Fort Gibson by Colonel Arbuckle to warn them that if they persisted in their plans to go to war, troops would be sent to chastise them; but this and the offer of the agent to adjust the differences between them and their enemies had no effect. The Delaware said that, solely to please their White Father, they had frequently made peace with the Osage, well knowing all the time that the Osage would break the treaty; that during peace they were never safe but were murdered and robbed on all occasions by their treacherous foes; and that as brave men their only alternative was to be exterminated in battle or to destroy their enemies. Disregarding the warnings of white officials, they continued their preparations for war; their young men were ordered out on a hunt of twenty days to procure meat to subsist them.[14]

---

[12] Arbuckle to Clark, May 14, 1826, *ibid.,* "1826 Delaware and Osage"; Arkansas Gazette, May 23, 1826, p. 2, col. 1; *Missouri Intelligencer,* June 16, 1826, p. 2, cols. 2 and 3.

[13] Clark to Secretary of War, May 6, 1826, OIA, RCF, "1826 Delaware & Osage."

[14] Johnston to Arbuckle, June 7, 1826, OIA, RCF. The allies solicited help from east of the Mississippi; on July 12, 1826, a Sauk warrior exhibited to the Indian agent at "Rocky Island," Illinois, "wampum, tobacco, and an Osage scalp, accompanied with a speech from the Shawnees, Delawares & Kickapoo Indians, inviting the Sauk & Fox Indians of this country in a pressing manner to make war against the Osage Indians . . . . as soon as the corn is in roasting ears." A few weeks earlier, Thomas Forsythe, the Sauk and

When this and other information reached General Gaines, commander of the Western Military Department, at his headquarters in Cincinnati, he reported to the Secretary of War his plans to meet the situation. Ten Delaware, he said, had been killed by the Osage within nine months; the Delaware had killed five Osage "and they claim the privilege of killing five others, to fill up the measure of their revenge." The truce with the Cherokee secured by Colonel Arbuckle did not bind the Delaware, and was only temporary, and a war on a large scale impended. It was supposed that with the allies of both, six hundred to a thousand warriors on each side would be involved, and there were not more than three hundred soldiers at Fort Gibson to restrain either party or protect the frontier settlers who would be certain to suffer.

General Gaines therefore directed four companies of the First Infantry, under Major Kearney, and four of the Sixth Infantry to be held in readiness to take the field on the Arkansas River in the event that the anticipated hostilities should make it necessary; and in order to cope with the Indians he recommended that these troops be mounted. Concurring with the views of General Clark, he added that a military post should be established on the Missouri River near the western border of the state.[15]

The Osage chiefs, alarmed at the forces combining against them, asked that the Delaware join them in St. Louis on September 15 in a peace conference; the Delaware agreed upon

Foxes agent, irritated by a rumor that his charges were going to war against the Osage, wrote that the Osage agent "ought to know better than to suppose that the Sauk & Fox Indians would join any people against their friends the Osage Indians, for it is very well known that a strict alliance took place between the Sauk and Fox Indians on the one part and the Osage Indians on the other part some years ago, and if I am well informed you recommended the understanding to take place between the above mentioned parties" (Thomas Forsythe to William Clark, June 27 and July 13, 1826, Wisconsin Historical Society, Draper Manuscripts, T 50 and 51).

[15] Gaines to Barbour, July 20, 1826, AGO, ORD, WDF. The establishment of Fort Leavenworth the next year followed.

condition that the Cherokee be included.[16] However, a new complication with this tribe had arisen; there resided in the Cherokee Nation an outstanding chief named Tahchee, or Dutch, as he was usually called. He was among those who located on the south side of the Arkansas River and who were required by the Government in 1824 to remove to the Cherokee lands on the other side of the river. Dutch refused to go and was so incensed with both the Government and the members of the tribe who complied, that he vowed he would leave them for the Spanish provinces and never return. Late in the autumn of 1825 he attended a council of the Cherokee, where he made known in a formal manner his intention to separate from the tribe; and with a company of his followers he departed in September[17] from the Arkansas and removed to the Red River, where he settled above the mouth of the Kiamichi. There he became known as the fearless leader of his lawless band of Cherokee and Kickapoo, who made war on the Tawakoni and other tribes, including of course the Osage, always the objects of bitter enmity.

Dutch had been urged by the other members of the tribe not to leave them; and after he had taken his departure the chiefs, knowing his restless disposition and fearful that he might commit some lawless act which would involve the tribe, passed a resolution in the national committee disfranchising and renouncing Dutch and all who had joined him on the Red River who should not return to the tribe within fifteen days. They further declared that the tribe would not be responsible for any acts committed by the renegades. As they feared, while the situation was at the tensest, Dutch and some of his companions came with reckless daring to the vicinity of Fort Gibson on a horse-stealing expedition; and the evening of July 18, 1826, he darted in among a number of Osage within a few feet

---

[16] Clark to Barbour, July 17, 1826, OIA, RCF.

[17] John Jolly to E. W. DuVal, December 4, 1826, OIA, RCF: DuVal to Clark, December 6, 1826, *ibid*.

of Colonel Chouteau's trading house on the Verdigris, and killed and scalped an Osage man.[18]

Dutch successfully eluded pursuit and reached the Red River with the Osage scalp; here a Delaware obtained possession of it and brought it to the Cherokee settlements, where the gruesome trophy was the occasion for dancing and rejoicing.[19] The impudence of this adventure almost under the guns of Fort Gibson created much excitement; and it required many disavowals and several interesting documentary showings to relieve the tribe of the charge of violating their armistice. It

[18] Arbuckle to Butler, July 29, 1826, AGO, OFD, 61 A 26. On this expedition Dutch's party stole horses from white people also, and two of his band were killed. The editor of "The George Catlin Indian Gallery" embellishes a good story by saying that Colonel Arbuckle had offered a reward of five hundred dollars for the capture of Dutch and that the latter performed this exploit to show his contempt for the government offices (Smithsonian Institution, *Annual Report to July 1885* [Washington, 1886], Part V, "The George Catlin Indian Gallery," p. 207). There is no official confirmation of this statement; officers at these posts had no funds to offer as rewards for the capture of outlaws; that was one of the duties of military posts. The editor, perhaps copying from the sketch with the McKenney and Hall picture of Dutch, equally erroneous, says also that Dutch went to the Red River *after* the treaty of 1828 (*ibid*).

Dutch lived with his band of Cherokee in Texas until 1831, when they were removed, with the help of the tribe living on the Arkansas, to the mouth of the Canadian. John Smith, Edwards, Ignatious, N. and Ogden Chisholm and forty other men with their horses were employed for ninety-five days in removing Dutch's party to a point near the mouth of the Canadian (OIA, RCF, "Cherokee D," 436). Here Dutch built up a handsome plantation surrounded by an extensive settlement of Cherokee who continued to challenge the Osage wherever they met them. His great force of character, his extensive knowledge of the frontier and resourcefulness made him a valuable guide and hunter on numerous missions performed by the Government. The Cherokee living in the West long held him in the highest respect for his service as a warrior and leader against their dread enemy the Osage. Capt. William Dutch, as he was then known, died November 12, 1848, in Flint District of the Cherokee Nation (*Fort Smith* [Arkansas] *Herald*, November 22, 1848, p. 2, col. 4). For further accounts of Dutch, see Grant Foreman, *The Five Civilized Tribes*.

[19] Arbuckle to Butler, November 4, 1826, AGO, OFD, 97 A 26; Jolly to DuVal, *ibid*.

"An Osage Scalp Dance." Painted by John Mix Stanley, 1845. Courtesy of Smithsonian Institution, Bureau of American Ethnology

was said in some quarters that Dutch had been hired to kill the Osage to avenge the death of Graves's nephew.

General Clark did not give the Cherokee notice of the conference with the Osage at St. Louis, which was contrived so that only the Delaware met them. It resulted in a treaty in October, 1826, between the Osage and Delaware, and peace was at last declared between those tribes.[20] The Osage were late in arriving at St. Louis; all but one of the horses purchased by the agent for them to make the journey on, were killed by prairie flies.[21]

The feud between the Osage and Cherokee burned with a fiercer heat from the fuel added by Dutch's killing of the Osage at the mouth of the Verdigris. Upon the appointment of J. F. Hamtramck as Osage agent, Clermont's band held a council with him at Fort Gibson and on August 24, 1826, surrendered the murderer of Graves's nephew, who was confined at the garrison. The Cherokee then demanded possession of him so that they might put him to death. When the commanding officer refused to comply with their request, the relentless Tom Graves, accompanied by Captain James Rogers, went to St. Louis to press their demands on General Clark. He held that the treaty of 1822 gave him no authority to order the Indian turned over to them.[22] The Osage said that they would deliver the prisoner to the Cherokee if the latter in turn would deliver Dutch to them to be executed for his murder of the Osage on the Verdigris. To this the Cherokee refused to agree, and so the matter stood.

The armistice with the Cherokee had given the Osage opportunity to resume their normal activities in other quarters; in

[20] Clark to Secretary of War, January 4, 1827, OIA, RCF. The Osage delegation in St. Louis included Mad Buffalo, Sans Nerf, the Old Corn, La Montre, and Tallai; Noel Mongrain acted as interpreter (*New York Spectator*, November 13, 1826).

[21] Hamtramck to Clark, September 1, 1827, OIA, RCF.

[22] Clark to DuVal, January 2, 1827, *ibid.*; Atkinson to Jones, January 9, 1827, AGO, OFD.

July, 1826, while Dutch was making his raid near Fort Gibson, a band of thirty Osage appeared in the country near Fort Towson, and drove out a small hunting party of whites. They captured two of the white men and stripped them of their clothing, then stole a number of horses at the settlements within four miles of Fort Towson, including some belonging to the officers at the post.[23] At the end of their hunt in the following autumn, a party of Osage crossed the Red River, killed seven Kickapoo, and took as captives a woman and child of that tribe; they then returned to their home on the Verdigris, stopping at Fort Gibson on the way to boast of their exploit.[24] A band of White Hair's village brought in two women and a girl prisoner and eighteen Pawnee scalps. The Little Osage returned from their hunt with a number of horses stolen from the same tribe. During the same hunting season, about November 15, five Osage were attacked on one of the branches of the Arkansas; one was killed and three fatally wounded, and their horses were stolen. Their antagonists were supposed to have been Kickapoo and Delaware from the Red River.[25]

In February the Cherokee determined in council to send twenty or twenty-five select warriors, most of them relatives of Graves, to make another attack on the Osage near Union Mission. Their purpose was to take one life to even the score between them; they said if that could be accomplished without loss of life on their side, they would be satisfied and would be ready immediately to take the Osage by the hand and renew with them their friendly relations.[26] They had proceeded as far as Fort Gibson when Walter Webber, who had pursued on a fast horse, overtook them and with the influence of Captain Pryor, succeeded in inducing them to abandon the attack.[27]

23 *Missouri Intelligencer*, September 7, 1826, p. 2, col. 3.

24 Maj. A. Cummings to Arbuckle, March 4, 1827, AGO, OFD, 74 C 27.

25 Hamtramck to Clark, February 8, 1827, OIA, RCF.

26 DuVal to Arbuckle, February 3, 1827, OIA, RCF.

27 Congregational House (Boston), Manuscript Library, Vol. XXXIV, No. 59, Palmer to Evarts, February 12, 1827.

The Cherokee chiefs at Fort Smith then sent a message to the Osage by Nathaniel Pryor, to the effect that they were willing to declare peace if the Osage would say that the prisoner who had been surrendered by them was expected to be delivered by the military to the Cherokee for punishment.[28] The Osage responded that such was their intention; but they added that since the prisoner had been surrendered and confined at Fort Gibson, Dutch had scalped one of their people and sent the scalp to the Cherokee who, by dancing round it, received it as the scalp of an enemy. They then demanded the capture of Dutch and submitted the whole matter to the President, saying they would abide his decision; but they protested that they ardently joined with the Cherokee in the desire for peace.[29]

Then the Osage prisoner escaped from Fort Gibson. Next a small band of Cherokee, without the authority of their chiefs, set out early in March to attack the Osage. Colonel Arbuckle thereupon sent a command, under Lieutenant Edgar S. Hawkins, up the Grand River to prevent hostilities, but the Cherokee did not come so far.[30]

The Osage having shrewdly negotiated a separate treaty of peace with the Delaware in 1826, the Secretary of War directed that the Osage and Cherokee be assembled at Fort Gibson for the purpose of making another attempt to establish peace between them. The Osage delegation with their agent, Mr. Hamtramck, appeared at Fort Gibson September 15, 1827, the time appointed; but the Cherokee were not present. Instead, they presented two letters through Colonel Arbuckle in which they continued their attitude of quibbling. As described by an Osage chief, one of the letters

> sounds the fierce yell of war, & the other the honied & parasitical words of adulation, all of which is attributed by the Osages to the

[28] Rogers and Webber to the Osage, February 9, 1827, OIA, RCF.

[29] Clermont and other Osage chiefs at Cantonment Gibson to the Cherokee chiefs, February 25, 1827, *ibid.*

[30] Arbuckle to Butler, March 26, 1827, *ibid.*

duplicity of the Cherokees.[31] [A report reached the East that] three or four hundred Cherokees are planning to proceed against the Osages. . . . . The Cherokees use the rifle in war, and the Osage the bow and arrow almost entirely and always fight on horseback. The woods therefore would suit the former much better than the prairies, where they would have to meet the latter.[32]

[31] Hamtramck to Clark, November 1, 1827, *ibid*.
[32] *Niles' Weekly Register*, August 25, 1827.

XVII

WHITE INTRIGUES ON THE RED RIVER
1823-29

TRADING parties frequently crossed Oklahoma to reach the prairie Indians. In February, 1823, a party from St. Louis, under General Thomas James and John and Robert McKnight, passed up the Canadian River to the Comanche country; there John McKnight was killed by the Comanche.[1] The survivors returned downstream as far as the mouth of the Illinois River where they remained for a time and then descended the Arkansas, part of them going overland to St. Louis and the remainder traveling by canoe, arriving at Little Rock on July 18, 1823.[2]

Other parties were passing from time to time, carrying goods for traffic with the Indians and Mexicans. In May, 1825, a company of forty passed through on their way to Santa Fe; part of them set out from Jackson, Tennessee, and were joined by others at Memphis. Each man on horseback led one or more loaded pack horses. Their route took them past Fort Smith and west from there.[3] The next year a trading outfit under Pierre Menard of Kaskaskia, Illinois, with five wagons and twenty pack horses loaded with Indian goods, passed through on their way to the Comanche country.[4]

A company of these adventurers was involved in a bloody affair south of the Canadian River. A party of twelve men of Miller County were hunting wild horses on the Washita, when

---

[1] Gen. Thomas James, *Three Years Among the Indians and Mexicans*, ed. Walter B. Douglas, p. 98; Foreman, op. cit., p. 54.

[2] *Arkansas Gazette*, July 22, 1823, p. 2, col. 2.

[3] Account from Little Rock in *Missouri Advocate and St. Louis Public Advertiser*, May 20, 1825, p. 2, col. 2.

[4] *Arkansas Gazette*, November 21, 1826.

they were attacked on April 17, 1826, by a band of 150 to 200
prairie Indians. The hunters, who were divided into two parties, were attacked separately and pursued until they either
escaped or were killed by the savages, armed with bows and
arrows and guns. Five of the hunters were killed, including
Adam Lawrence and his sons, John and Henry Lawrence, all
of whom lived near the mouth of the Kiamichi. The Indians,
or some of them, wore Spanish uniforms, from which it was
deduced that they were Comanche or Pawnee; the hunters lost
all their possessions, including twenty-five mustangs they had
taken.[5] During the following summer a party of twenty from
Hempstead County on a trading expedition to Texas were besieged for fifteen days by Comanche Indians.[6]

The hostilities of the Indians were adding their burden to
the already discouraging conditions affecting Union Mission.
William C. Requa and E. Chapman had removed their families
in the spring of 1824 to a point four miles above the mission
on the east side of the Grand River, and called the station
Hopefield.[7] There they gathered about them a few Osage under
a chief named Moi-neh-per-sha and undertook to teach them
how to cultivate the soil, at the same time instructing them in
religion and letters. In September, 1826, high waters overflowed
their settlement at Hopefield, carried off ten log houses and all
their possessions, washed away the cornfield of eighty-five
acres at Union Mission, and drowned their cattle and hogs.
The next March floods again caused them losses. In May Mrs.

[5] *Ibid.*, May 23, 1826, p. 2, col. 1; *Missouri Intelligencer*, June 16, 1826, p.
2, col. 1.

[6] *Arkansas Gazette*, January 16, 1827, p. 3, col. 3.

[7] Mr. Chapman died soon afterward; before his young widow sorrowfully
departed for her home in Connecticut, she erected over her husband's grave a
neat monument of native stone that bears the only legible inscription to be
found in that little, rocky burying ground covered with brambles, near the
site of Union Mission: "In Memory of Rev. Epaphras Chapman who died
Jan. 6, 1825. Aged 32. First Missionary to the Osages. 'Say among the
Heathen, the Lord Reigneth.'"

Requa and three children died at Hopefield. Their cattle and horses were perishing from the swarms of prairie flies and they had no recourse but to turn their stock loose in the thickets. The hostilities of the Indians caused the Hopefield settlement to be abandoned several times, and the settlers there fled to Union Mission.

> .... The Frenchmen who had Osage wives and some children in school, would also come with their families to the number of five or six at once, and spend whole weeks around us, fearing to go away until Colonel Arbuckle kindly took them into the Garrison.[8]

In the summer of 1828 a white man, two half-breeds, and two Indians came to Union Mission to avenge the death of a relative who had been killed on the Red River by the Osage. Two of the men were named Roberts.[9] On the east side of the Grand River, across from the mission, they encountered, killed, and scalped The Bird, one of the early Osage settlers at the mission. The alarm being given, the Osage near the mission crossed the river and pursued the attackers, whom they overtook; they killed them all and brought their scalps to the mission.[10]

Disorder increased in 1827. Conditions were complicated by events south of the Red River, and by the undetermined question of sovereignty over the country adjoining that stream on the south. There was launched in Edwards Colony, at Nacogdoches, the "Republic of Fredonia," sponsored by a band of white Americans and two hundred Cherokee Indians living in Texas. Their Treaty of Union, League, and Confederation, a compact to prosecute a war of independence, and divide the province of Texas between them, executed on December 21,

---

[8] Letter from Rev. W. F. Vaill, Union, July 14, 1827, *Missionary Herald* (Boston), October, 1827, p. 311.

[9] *Arkansas Gazette*, July 21, 1828, p. 2, col. 2.

[10] Letter from John Montgomery to *New York Observer*, copied in *Cherokee Phoenix*, October 8, 1828, p. 2, col. 5.

1826, inaugurated the short-lived "Fredonian Rebellion."[11] The two leaders of the Indians in this movement, Richard Fields and John D. Hunter, were treacherously assassinated at the instigation of the Mexicans by the agency of the Cherokee chief, The Bowle.[12] For this service General Austin memorialized the Government recommending a reward to The Bowle; and in response the governor commissioned him a colonel and sent him a complete set of regimentals. Hard Mush, the next in command, was given a civil badge.[13] Soon after the killing of Fields, a number of his followers left Texas and located in Miller County on the Little River, about twenty miles from Fort Towson, adding to the complication in that quarter.[14]

In March, John Bowman and James Roberts killed a Cherokee on the south side of the Red River, and the whites prepared to defend themselves against an expected attack by the Indians. The next month the Osage killed Luke Roberts, a white man, on the same side of the river; and the white people began crossing to the north side in great alarm. Major Cummings at Fort Towson reported to Colonel Arbuckle: ".... For the last two or three weeks, this post has been much harrassed with detachments made from it in pursuit of marauders and murderers; I have only two officers subject to details of this kind, and they are nearly worn out with it."[15] Captain Bonneville was sent

[11] *Courrier des Natchitoches,* January 2, 1827, p. 2, col. 1; *ibid.,* January 16, 1827, p. 2, cols. 1 and 2; *Arkansas Gazette,* February 10, 1827, p. 3, cols. 1 and 2; *ibid.,* March 27, 1827; American Historical Association, *Annual Report for 1919* (Washington, 1924), "Austin Papers," II, 1527 ff.

[12] *Courrier des Natchitoches,* January 30, 1827, p. 2, col. 1; *Arkansas Gazette,* May 29, 1827, p. 3, col. 3; H. Yoakum, *History of Texas,* II, 246 ff.; Gaines (Baton Rouge) to Taylor, March 14, 1827, AGO, ORD, "Letter Book" No. 4, p. 233. Richard Fields was one-fourth Cherokee; John Dunn Hunter was a white man, the author of *Memories of a Captivity Among the Indians of North America* (London, 1823), a book that excited much controversy. In England Hunter had many friends, but in this country he was charged with being an impostor.

[13] *Handbook of American Indians,* I, 163.

[14] Arbuckle to Adjutant General, January 10, 1827, AGO, OFD, 12 A 27.

[15] Arbuckle to Adjutant General, May 4, 1827, *ibid.,* 50 A 27

from Fort Gibson to the Red River to investigate the Indians along that stream; in July, Major Cummings sent Lieutenant Williams S. Colquhoun to the Indians in the vicinity, to request them to visit Fort Towson and meet the officers of the Government and chiefs of the Osage, for the purpose of entering into a treaty of peace. Colquhoun went to the Indian villages on Pecan Bayou on the south side of the river, and at the cabin of Walkama, a Shawnee chief, met about thirty chiefs of the Shawnee, Delaware, and Kickapoo tribes, who had removed there from the White River. They refused to make any agreement to consider a treaty of peace with the Osage, against whom they were bitter. They said it was no use to make peace with them, as they would rob and kill them "up on the Big Prairie after they had made peace." But they agreed that in one moon an Indian would go to Fort Towson to give their answer to the invitation to the meeting at the post, where they were promised a feast of bread and meat and a frolic. They heard with disapproval the information delivered by Colquhoun that Colonel Arbuckle and General Clark desired them to return to their villages on the White River.[16]

Colquhoun states in his report that the Shawnee had raised good crops that season and the night before his arrival a green corn dance had taken place in their village, which he described as well watered and tolerably thriving. There were two Delaware villages containing one hundred warriors about twenty miles south, on Sulphur Fork. The Shawnee, numbering 150 warriors, had two villages and both tribes had numerous straggling parties living about in camps. The Kickapoo, who claimed 150 warriors, lived on the Sabine River, except a small party on Pecan Bayou. He thought there were five hundred warriors in that section among the Shawnee, Delaware, Kickapoo, Koasati, Cherokee, "Poiles," Creeks, and a few Choctaw. "When I told them the chiefs of the Cadois and Quapaws would attend the Council they laughed and made no reply." There was much

---

[16] Colquhoun to Cummings, August 1, 1827, *ibid.*, 184 C 27.

drunkenness among them, and they said they bought their whisky north of the Red River. The obvious necessity of having a large force of troops to maintain order at the proposed peace council—a force that was not available—and the conviction that the Indians were opposed to making peace induced Cummings to recommend the abandonment of the proposed meeting at Fort Towson.[17] This news had hardly reached Colonel Arbuckle at Fort Gibson when he was informed by Colonel Chouteau that four hundred braves of Clermont's band had marched forth to war, one party of two hundred of whom had proceeded to attack their enemies on the Red River. Colonel Arbuckle thereupon decided to abandon all efforts to make peace between the Osage and the Indians on the Red River. While he did not believe reports that the latter would attack the whites on the north side of the river, he thought the whites on both sides would be responsible for frequent disorders among the Indians.[18]

In fact some of the whites were doing all they could to embroil the Indians in difficulties for their personal gain. In the early part of July, Nathaniel Robbins of Miller County, who represented himself to be a colonel in the Mexican service, and Dr. Lewis R. Dayton, claiming to be commissioners on the part of the government of Texas, endeavored to persuade a portion of the inhabitants south of the Red River to throw off their allegiance to the Government of the United States,[19] and form a provisional government under the authorities of Texas.[20] For

[17] Cummings to Arbuckle, August 3, 1827, *ibid.*

[18] Arbuckle to Adjutant General, August 27, 1827, AGO, OFD, 92 A 27.

[19] On February 20, 1827, Robbins and Dayton at Pecan Point wrote to the Mexican authorities complaining that officers of the United States exacted taxes from them and asked for relief from their demands and the depredations of the Indians. In reply they were informed under date of April 19, 1827, that until the boundary line was established the Mexican Government could do nothing for them; but it was suggested that, pending that time, they might form a provisional government (American Historical Association, "Austin Papers," 11, 1633).

[20] It had been undetermined whether this section belonged to Spain or to

this purpose they exhibited a paper, purporting to be signed by Jose Antonio Sausedo, Chief of the Department of the Province of Texas, containing instructions for the formation of a provisional government.

While this scheme was being agitated, Charles Burkman, living in the settlement at Pecan Point, representing himself to be a captain in the Mexican service, issued a proclamation on June 12, giving notice to the inhabitants that he was authorized by the Mexican Government to conduct an expedition against the Comanche Indians,[21] and invited recruits to join him. He offered to every man who would arm and equip himself and join the expedition a handsome compensation from the Mexican Government, and a share of the plunder to be taken from the Indians. It was expected that many Indians on the Red River would join him. The Caddo Indians had been solicited to join the expedition, but they discreetly sought the advice of their agent who warned them to have nothing to do with it.[22] The citizens who were not in sympathy with these enterprises were much alarmed at the possibility that their defenseless situation would expose them to reprisals, and there was great excitement

the United States, but the population claimed it was part of Miller County, Arkansas, and that their allegiance was to the United States. Because of this uncertainty it had become a lawless community. When Col. Josiah H. Vose came to Fort Towson in 1833 he said the settlements on the south side of the Red River extended up as far as the Boggy, and they maintained a county seat at a place below Fort Towson, called Jonesborough, where there was a considerable number of inhabitants. The greater part of this population he said " . . . is of the very worst kind—men who have fled from justice and who are now engaged in kidnapping negroes—horse racing, gambling, and selling whiskey to soldiers and Indians" (Vose to McCombs, June 5, 1833, AGO, OFD, 23 V 33).

21 Governor Izard notified the War Department that Burkman and Robbins were planning an expedition against the Comanche Indians in Texas (Izard to Barbour, July 31, 1827, Department of State, B1A, Miscellaneous); his letter was referred to the State Department, and Henry Clay wrote to him that any citizen of Arkansas planning to join in this illegal enterprise would be prosecuted (Secretary of State to Izard, September 6, 1827, Department of State, 399 BIA, Domestic).

22 Gray to Barbour, July 3, 1827, OIA, RCF, "1827 Red River Agency."

on both sides of the river.[23] The alarm on the southwest frontier was communicated to the Legislative Council of Arkansas, which appointed a committee on October 5 to investigate the trouble. A report was made a few weeks later,[24] which exhibited in an interesting manner the events and written documents involved in these difficulties. When the conviction became fixed in the minds of most of those who had enlisted that the real purpose of the enterprise was to plunder caravans conveying silver from Santa Fe to Mexico City, they disbanded and the expedition collapsed.[25]

Upon receipt of information of the movement to set up a Mexican government, Major Cummings sent Lieutenant Colquhoun from Fort Towson to investigate. Colquhoun went to Pecan Point and warned the leaders that they would be treated as enemies of the United States if they persisted in their efforts. They informed him that, as they did not know to which country they belonged and believed that when the boundary should be run it would place them under Mexican jurisdiction, they were desirous of establishing a provisional government in the meantime; but as they were constantly calling on the troops at Fort Towson for protection against the Indians, the majority of the population preferred to continue this dependence, and the projected provisional government made little progress. The leaders in the movement promised to do nothing more until the boundary line was run.[26] Steps were taken soon after by officials of Texas to survey the lands on the south side of the Red River,

[23] *Arkansas Gazette*, November 6, 1827, p. 4, col. 1.

[24] *Ibid.*

[25] Governor Izard to Henry Clay, October 16, 1827, Department of State, 400 BIA, Miscellaneous.

[26] Cummings to Adjutant General, June 21, 1827, AGO, OFD, 124 C 27. The schemes of these freebooters were not wholly abandoned however; for the next March Col. Peter Ellis Bean of the Mexican Republic complained to Governor Izard that Dayton was engaged a short distance above Cantonment Towson in raising a force of men to start as soon as grass rises on a plundering and murdering expedition in his country (Bean to Izard, March 4, 1828, OIA, RCF).

of which notice was given to the Secretary of State who wrote that he had "requested Colonel Tornel to interpose his good offices in preventing Colonels Milan and Bean" from surveying lands in Miller County.[27]

Miller County, one of the most important in the territory, continued to furnish news. In the summer of 1827 an armed body of fifty-six men from New Orleans commanded by Captain LeGrand, who had a passport from the United States, passed through the settlement on their way to Santa Fe with the alleged object of surveying a large grant of land belonging to a company in London; but the chronicler thought they were concealing the real purpose of their mission.[28] Correspondence from that section indicated that notwithstanding other distractions, the agitation of politics commanded considerable attention in what is now McCurtain County, Oklahoma. During the summer John H. Fowler was elected to represent the county in the General Assembly. Isaac Pennington was elected from Clark and John Dillard from Crawford County.[29] While the Miller County settlement was located on the Red River, it was denied the benefit of the navigation so great a stream should have afforded, by the Great Raft which in 1827 was said to be growing at the rate of three or four miles each year. There was much agitation to secure governmental aid in removing it.

[27] Secretary of State to Governor Pope, October 11, 1830, Department of State, 477 BIA, Domestic.

[28] *Arkansas Gazette,* July 24, 1827, p. 3, col. 1.

[29] *Ibid.,* August 21, 1827, p. 3, col. 1; John Dillard lived at Fort Gibson which was within the limits of Crawford County as bounded in 1820.

XVIII

THE CONTEST BETWEEN THE CHERO-KEE AND WHITES FOR LOVELY'S PURCHASE, 1826-28

THE western limits of the Cherokee country in Arkansas were not defined in the treaty of 1817 and could not be until the exact acreage of the cessions in the East had been determined; but in 1822 a delegation waited on Secretary Calhoun and asked him to have their boundaries marked. Making a rough guess at the amount of land they represented in the East, as one-third of the whole, Calhoun instructed Governor Miller to lay off a proportionate area in Arkansas. The survey was begun in 1823 under the direction of Acting-Governor Crittenden, who ordered the Cherokee on the south side of the Arkansas River to remove to their land on the north side or be removed by force.[1] The Indians were dissatisfied with the boundaries proposed by Crittenden; and they sent a delegation composed of Black Fox, Walter Webber, James Rogers, and John McLamore to Washington to protest; they told Calhoun that they wanted a survey that would show the western outlet promised them by the Government.[2]

The white people of Arkansas and the legislature memorialized the President, asking for permission to settle upon Lovely's Purchase. In no wise deterred by repeated refusals, they continued to filter into what are now Sequoyah, Muskogee, and Wagoner counties, but they were frequently ejected by the troops from Fort Gibson.[3] At the instance of the Arkansas dele-

---

[1] *Missouri Intelligencer,* August 12, 1823, p. 2, col. 4.

[2] Cherokee Delegation to Calhoun, February 26, 1823, OIA, RCF; Calhoun to Miller, March 4, 1823, OIA, "Letter Books," Series I. E., p. 396.

[3] Arbuckle to Nourse, July 31, 1826, OIA, RCF, "1826 Cherokee West."

gate, Congress passed an act April 5, 1826,[4] directing that the
land in Lovely's Purchase be surveyed and advertised for sale.
The Secretary of War then rescinded the order of inhibition of
1818,[5] and settlers began removing into the country in great
numbers.[6] Most of them came from south of the Arkansas and
Canadian rivers; they had been living upon the lands lately
given to the Choctaw, whence they were compelled to remove.
By 1827 it was said that three hundred families had removed
from the Choctaw country into Lovely's Purchase.

It was reported that

> Lovely's Purchase is fast settling up. At the last term of the Craw-
> ford Circuit Court[7] three townships were laid off, named Nicks,
> Hope, and Prospect.[8] A considerable body of land is also open for
> settlement in the Fork of the Canadian and Arkansas, and is filling
> with steady and respectable emigrants.[9] This is not attached to
> any county, and of course, civil jurisdiction is not held over it.[10]

The population here increased to such an extent that the Legislature of the Territory, on October 13, 1827, enacted a law
creating Lovely County out of "all that portion of the County
of Crawford called and known by the name of Lovely's Purchase."[11]

[4] *U. S. Statutes at Large,* IV, 153; *U. S. House Document No. 263,* Twentieth Congress, first session.

[5] Jones to Arbuckle, October 10, 1826, OIA, RCF, "1826 Arkansas Adjutant General."

[6] *Arkansas Gazette,* December 19, 1826, p. 3, col. 1.

[7] Held at Crawford Courthouse a few miles below Fort Smith.

[8] Nicks Township included the area surrounding Marble City, Oklahoma,
near where Nicksville, the county seat of Lovely County, was established in
1827 (Foreman, *op. cit.,* p. 66).

[9] *Arkansas Gazette,* April 10, 1828, p. 3, col. 1.

[10] The 1820 boundary line of Crawford County followed the Canadian to
its mouth, and then ascended the Arkansas, and so excluded a wedge-shaped
territory between those streams, upon which is the site of the present town
of Webbers Falls.

[11] Wm. McRee to George Graham, February 23, 1827, OIA, RCF; Lovely
County was bounded in the Act as follows: "Beginning at the upper Cherokee
boundary line, on the north bank of the Arkansas River, thence running up

The creation of Lovely County brought to a crisis the efforts to negotiate a new treaty with the Cherokee, and created a favorable opportunity for government officials to operate on the Indians. Governor Izard, who was interested in removing the Indians from Arkansas, submitted to the Secretary of War a letter from a citizen at Fort Smith stating that it would be very difficult to make a treaty with them and would require

.... a great deal of management to effect it; in the first place there must be a delegation of chiefs to Washington which would require considerable funds judiciously employed in the selection of the delegation. To hold a treaty here would be fruitless as the whole nation would be to contend with whereas if they were to go on to Washington there would only be a select party to contend with and these should be well prepared before they started and if I undertake to select them I must have something to grease the hinges with, at least two thousand dollars and must enjoin the strictest confidence on you in this matter; if it was known it would cost me my life and should you succeed I shall expect to be handsomely rewarded.[12]

Governor Izard expressed his belief that an exchange of their lands for Lovely's Purchase was uppermost in the minds of the influential half-breeds, who hoped to acquire the valuable min-

and with the meanders of said river to the mouth of the Canadian Fork, thence up the Canadian Fork to the Western limits of the Territory of Arkansas; thence north with that line to the northwest corner of the territory of Arkansas; thence east to the southwest corner of Missouri, thence east to the Fiery Prairie or Brown's line, thence south with Brown's line to the Cherokee line, and thence with the Cherokee line to the place of beginning" (Acts of the Arkansas General Assembly). These limits today would include Sequoyah, Adair, Cherokee, and parts of Delaware, Mayes, Wagoner, and Muskogee counties, Oklahoma. On October 24, Legislative provision was made for commissioners to locate the seat of justice for Lovely County; the commissioners appointed were John Alexander of Prospect Township; John Simpson of Hope Township; John Nicks of Nicks Township; and Benjamin Weaver (*Arkansas Gazette,* December 11, 1827, p. 1, col. 2). The commissioners selected Nicksville as the county seat; it was within what is now Sequoyah County, Oklahoma (Foreman, *op. cit.,* p. 66), and near Marble City.

[12] Izard to Secretary of War, July 6, 1827, OIA, RCF.

"A Buffalo Hunt on the Southwestern Prairies."   *Painted by John Mix Stanley, 1845.*
Courtesy of Smithsonian Institution, Bureau of American Ethnology.

eral lands there. Just how much influence was exerted on the Cherokee the records do not disclose; but they became much alarmed by a memorial submitted to Congress by the Arkansas Legislature which insisted on the rights of white people to settle Lovely's Purchase. It charged that the Cherokee

> are a restless, dissatisfied, insolent and ambitious tribe engaged in constant intrigues with neighbouring tribes, to foment difficulties, produce discord, and defeat the great object of the government, in promoting the civilization of the Indians, and preserving peace among them. Your memorialists have long entertained the belief that the most effectual measure to defeat their designs and paralize their wicked efforts was to surround them by white settlements and confine them to their own lands.

This proposal, so at variance with the treaty obligation that they should have a free outlet to the West with no whites in that direction, together with the recent orders requiring the whites to remove from the Choctaw lands and giving them permission also to settle on Lovely's Purchase, greatly alarmed the Cherokee. The chiefs and headmen met in council and on December 28, 1827, appointed a delegation composed of The Black Fox, John Rogers, Thomas Graves, Thomas Maw, George Morris, Tobacco Will, and George Guess to go to Washington. Their credentials[13] authorized them to solicit from the Government a performance of the unsettled matters pending between the Government and the Indians; particularly they were directed to request a survey of their lands in Arkansas as promised in their treaties.[14]

The arrival of the delegation in Washington aroused the jealousy of the white people of Arkansas.

> They believe the Indians have come hither to obtain a tract of country on Arkansas River known by the name of "Lovely's Pur-

[13] John W. Flowers was attached to the delegation as counselor, David Brown as secretary, and James Rogers as interpreter (E. W. DuVal, "certificate" January 1, 1828, *ibid.*).

[14] John Jolly and other chiefs, December 28, 1827, *ibid.*

chase.". . . . Lovely's Purchase was lately by the Arkansas legislature organized into a separate and distinct county, and contains at this time upwards of three thousand souls and is daily increasing in population. This tract of country is bounded on the east by the Cherokee Nation and is much the most healthy, populous, and wealthy portion of Arkansas. . . . . Upon the petition of our citizens that country was surveyed by the United States;[15] upon the petition of our citizens an act of Congress was passed two years ago attaching that section of country to the Lawrence land district in Arkansas. What stronger assurances than these could they have that in making these settlements then, they would not be disturbed in their possession by Indians; especially when, by *the Government* the Indian boundary had been run and west of that boundary our citizens had settled. Though the people of Arkansas have repeatedly been the victims of Indian negociations I claim nothing of you for them on the score of sympathy. They have repeatedly been driven from their farms and improvements to make way for Indians; they were driven from the very ground that the Cherokees now occupy to make room for the Cherokees—and afterward by a treaty made with the Choctaws by General Jackson and Hinds upward of five thousand of our citizens were bartered away; three fourths of whom moved to Texas and are lost forever to the United States. Many of the residue have removed to Lovely's purchase and many of them by *your* kind indulgence for which they are thankful, have been permitted to remain & where I trust as there are but few Choctaws in our country they will be permitted to remain still longer.[16]

[15] A public survey of some of this land was begun in 1824 (DuVal to Secretary of War, December 25, 1826, *ibid.*). Again on November 15, 1826, a contract was made with Rene Paul, deputy surveyor, to establish a standard east and west line in Arkansas, passing approximately just north of Fort Gibson to the then western boundary of Arkansas (Wm. McRee to George Graham, February 23, 1827, *ibid.*).

[16] Sevier to Secretary of War, February 18, 1828, OIA, RCF; *Arkansas Gazette,* June 25, 1828, p. 3, cols. 3, 4, and 5. After the treaty was executed the *Arkansas Gazette* expressed the opinion that "with the exception of a few individuals who are engaged in the working of the *Salt Springs* and *Lead Mines* and a number who have made extensive improvements, that the people gen-

There is no doubt that the Secretary of War achieved a wise solution of the controversy when he negotiated with the Cherokee delegation a pretended treaty[17] by which they undertook to exchange their lands in Arkansas for those in Lovely's Purchase. All the parties to it knew that this treaty was wholly illegal, as the delegation had no authority whatever even to consider the subject of surrendering their land. Aware of this and familiar with the motives of some of the half-breeds who desired to promote their own interests by acquiring mines and salt springs on Lovely's Purchase, and conscious of the probability that bribes had been paid to members of the delegation, it is not surprising that news of the treaty caused the deepest resentment and indignation among the Indians at home who were about to be compelled to abandon their little farms and remove to a new country.[18] Poles were erected in front of the homes of James Rogers, the interpreter, and Thomas Maw, one of the delegates, as a threat that they would be hanged when they came home.[19] Flowers returned in the summer, but sensing the feeling toward him, hastily decamped.[20] A council was held July 18, but only two members of the delegation, Thomas Graves and George Guess, had the courage to face their countrymen. John Rogers wrote the Cherokee agent, DuVal, that he expected to attend the council "but did not, owing to false information."[21] The Glass, a prominent Cherokee, wrote on

erally will be satisfied with the treaty" (*ibid.*) as they were offered liberal inducements to remove from the Purchase.

[17] May 6, 1828, Kappler, *op. cit.*, p. 206.

[18] *Cherokee Phoenix,* October 29, 1828, p. 2, col. 3.

[19] *Ibid.*, August 20, 1828, p. 2, col. 4; October 15, 1828, p. 2, col. 3; *Arkansas Gazette,* July 21, 1828, p. 2, col. 1. "In May 1825 the Cherokees of Arkansas passed what they called a perpetual law with the penalty of death annexed against any person of their nation who shall propose the sale or exchange of their lands" (McKenney to Cocke, Chairman of Committee on Indian Affairs, December 15, 1826, OIA, RCF).

[20] Capt. James Rogers was by Article X of the treaty given $500 compensation for the loss of a horse and for his services in helping to bring about the treaty.

[21] *Cherokee Phoenix,* October 22, 1828, p. 2, col. 3.

September 1[22] that they were to have another council soon at which the delegation were to be tried for betraying the tribe.

The Treaty of 1828 contained some interesting provisions; according to the preamble it was to give the Indians

> a *permanent home,* and which shall, under the most solemn guarantee of the United States, be and remain theirs forever—a home that shall never, in all future time be embarrassed by having extended around it the lines, or placed over it the jurisdiction of a new territory, or a state, nor be pressed upon by the extension in any way, of any of the limits of any existing territory or state.[23]

The sum of $500 was promised to Sequoyah, or George Guess, in recognition of the benefits he had conferred on his tribe by the invention of his remarkable alphabet, and $1,000 to the tribe to set up a printing press for use by them in printing in their own language. A saline spring on Lee's Creek was given to Sequoyah, in lieu of one he would have to abandon in Arkansas.[24] There was given "also, one thousand two hundred dollars for the use of Thomas Graves[25] a Cherokee chief, for losses sustained in his property and for personal suffering endured by him when confined as a prisoner, on a criminal, but false, accusation."[26]

---

[22] *Ibid.,* October 29, 1828; *Arkansas Gazette,* November 25, 1828, p. 2, cols. 3 and 4.

[23] The "most solemn guarantee of the United States" was as ephemeral as the breath that uttered it, for that home of the Cherokee was long since overrun by the white men who made a jest of this, as of similar resounding promises to other tribes, by including it first in Indian Territory, then in the State of Oklahoma.

[24] Sequoyah had been living among the Arkansas Cherokee for many years. He enrolled for emigration from the East in 1818. Of the amount granted him he received only $150 in cash, 22 salt kettles of the value of $150, three saddles, and a small quantity of merchandise, in all representing less than $400 (Vashon to Herring, December 9, 1833, OIA, RCF, "Special File").

[25] The notorious white Cherokee, who escaped conviction for the murder of Osage children by reason of the fact that the crime was committed on Indian land.

[26] Kappler [ed.], *op. cit.,* p. 207, Article V.

The Arkansas boundary line was removed from where it was placed in 1824, forty miles eastwardly to where it now is. The Arkansas Cherokee were to be paid for the improvements they would have to abandon. This being another opportunity to promote removal from the East, the Government inserted in the treaty a promise to give to each head of a family in Georgia who would remove to the new home in the West, a rifle, a blanket, a kettle, and five pounds of tobacco.

The Arkansas Cherokee were not required by the treaty to remove from Arkansas until July, 1829, ". . . . but many of them were obliged to leave their places, long ago, as the whites would go into their houses, and crowd their families out";[27] and when they arrived in their new home some of the whites were still in possession of choice locations on the Illinois River and other places desired by the Indians.[28] However when the movement got under way in 1829 the Cherokee ascended the Arkansas River and settled principally along the north side of that stream above Fort Smith.[29] First there was the fertile bottom land along Lee's Creek, on which Sequoyah had his salt works, and which crossed the eastern Cherokee line before entering the Arkansas. Above that, at Skin Bayou,[30] Sanders and one of the Rogers, probably James, made a considerable settlement. At the mouth of the Saliseau, now called Sallisaw, George Justice had his establishment. Chief John Jolly built his home on the east bank of the Illinois River about a mile above the mouth; Walter Webber's place[31] gave his name to the falls

---

[27] Jolly, June 8, 1829, OIA, RCF, "1828 Cherokee West."

[28] *Ibid.*

[29] Some of them located on the military road running down from Fort Smith to Fort Gibson.

[30] This word "bayou" originated in the Choctaw *bayuk,* meaning a smaller river; it comes into English through the French from this or closely related Muskhogean dialect (*Handbook of American Indians,* I, 137).

[31] Webber was an influential and enterprising Cherokee; he was a merchant and owned a store at Nicksville where Dwight Mission was located in 1830. He died April 11, 1834, of "consumption." He was a half-brother of David Brown who was educated at Cornwall and Andover and became a zeal-

near by in Arkansas River. Other Indians, who left no record, located between these on the fertile lands of the river and its tributaries. From the mouth of the Canadian River west, the southern boundary line of the Cherokee country continued up and between the Arkansas and Canadian rivers a sufficient distance to make seven million acres. The Indians therefore proceeded to settle on both sides of the Arkansas above the mouth of the Canadian River; but as they neared the Verdigris, they found the river-bottom land on both sides already well occupied by the Creek Indians placed there by government officials. This entailed much ill feeling and subsequent negotiation. Settlements were also made on the Illinois[32] and Grand rivers.

As soon as the treaty was executed, the Government employed the interpreter, James Rogers, who had been active in promoting it, together with Thomas Maw, a member of the Cherokee delegation that signed the treaty, to circulate among the Cherokee in the East and present to them the inducements offered by the treaty to migrate—to the great exasperation of most of the members of the tribe both east and west. The

ous missionary in his tribe. When Nuttall met him on the Arkansas in 1819 he said, "Mr. Walter Webber, a metif, who acts as an Indian trader, is also a chief of the nation, and lives in ease and affluence, possessing a decently furnished and well provided house, several negro slaves, a large, well cleared and well fenced farm, and both himself and his nephew read, write and speak English" (Thwaites [ed.], *op. cit.*, XIII, 181). Webber then conducted a store at his home on the Arkansas five miles above Illinois Creek where the Indians could buy what they needed cheaper and of a better quality than the goods to be had at the government factory at Spadra Bluff (*American State Papers,* "Indian Affairs," II, 329). In 1824 his store burned with a loss of $10,000; he had then "amassed considerable wealth by his industry and enterprise" (*Arkansas Gazette,* March 9, 1824, p. 3, col. 1). When Webber settled at the falls in 1829 he appropriated a large amount of live stock belonging to a white man named Benjamin Murphy who had been located here. Senator Sevier vainly attempted to get a bill through Congress to compensate Murphy (*U. S. House Report No. 549,* Twenty-fifth Congress, second session).

32 "The Illinois is called by the Osages Eng-wah-condah, or Medicine Stone Creek," according to Captain Bell (Thwaites [ed.], *op. cit.*, XVI, 287).

Western Cherokee protested that they had not enough land[33] to divide with any more Indians, and objected strongly to the proposed migration.[34] The eastern members opposed it because it was intended to promote removal of the whole tribe.

A few small parties of Cherokee in the East were enrolled for removal on their own resources, and for them the Government contracted for the construction of seventy flatboats. Twenty-six of these boats were delivered to the emigrants who embarked in them with their families and personal effects for the long journey down the Hiwassee River to the Tennessee, down that stream, the Ohio, and the Mississippi to the mouth of the Arkansas, and up that river to the Cherokee Agency, a short distance above Fort Smith, and on to the mouth of the Illinois. They took with them also the guns, blankets, kettles, and tobacco issued to them as part consideration for their removal under the terms of the treaty of 1828.

In the summer of 1829, Moses Alberty, a white man with an Indian family, and Blueford West returned from exploring the western country, with which they were much pleased. They, together with Andrew Vann and Alexander Jourdan, all influential citizens with considerable white blood, began their preparations to remove in the autumn.[35] However, a great majority of the tribe were opposed to removal, and resorted to all manner of devices to intimidate those who desired to go.[36]

Upon the execution of the treaty of 1828 with the Cherokee, the white people of Lovely County who faced removal from the country given to the Indians waxed indignant, and at a

[33] Joseph Brearley, son of the Cherokee Agent, in 1828, surveyed the Cherokee boundary line running from Fort Smith to the southwest corner of Missouri (*Arkansas Gazette,* November 25, 1828, p. 3, col. 1).

[34] John Rogers wrote to the Secretary of War (Rogers to Eaton, January 4, 1830, OIA, RCF) that 200 emigrant Cherokee arrived from the East in the spring of 1829, and another party of 265 was then approaching, and he feared that this addition of 500 was going to crowd him.

[35] Montgomery to Eaton, August 31, 1829, OIA, RCF, "1829 Cherokee East."

[36] *Ibid.,* September 29, 1829.

[37] *Arkansas Gazette,* June 11, 1828, p. 3, col. 3.

meeting of citizens at their courthouse on May 27 adopted resolutions of protest.[37] However, Congress provided pre-emption rights elsewhere for those forced to remove,[38] and Governor Izard issued a proclamation on September 27 notifying them to remove east of the new line within ninety days or lose the right offered them.[39]

The Legislative Council of Arkansas was called in special session in October to adopt new lines for counties and judicial districts disrupted by the removal of the western boundary line of the territory.[40] By the act of October 17, 1828, Miller County north of the Red River was abolished and the remnant of that county east of the line was attached to Sevier County, then created. A Miller County south of the Red River was established with new lines. Lovely County likewise was wiped out, and the fragment that lay east of the new Cherokee line was incorporated in the newly created Washington County.[41]

[38] The offer was to those over twenty-one years, who had improvements west of the line on May 27; this opened the door to extensive fraud; " . . . . Pieces of paper with 21 years marked on them are placed in the shoes of children & witnesses innumerable can be & are found, who will swear, that said persons are over the age of 21 years & entitled to donation . . . . removals are made by crossing the line with a horse & then sworn to when the person returns to their own improvements. Boatmen, who were on the river on that day (27 of May) have also proven up their claims" (Wharton to Commissioner, August 15, 1828, Department of State, 419 GLO).

[39] *Arkansas Gazette,* September 30, 1828, p. 3, col. 4. An act of Congress of March 24, 1828, provided for a donation of two quarter sections of land to each head of a family, widow or single man over twenty-one years of age who resided west of the line at the time and who should remove east of it prior to making application for the donation at the land office; but no provision was made for those people south of the Arkansas River who were obligated to remove from the Choctaw country, and they bitterly resented this discrimination. If they were originally trespassers (squatters) they said, "they were so in common with half the territory. And yet their neighbors have been paid a bounty (by allowing them pre-emptions) for their violation of the law while the unfortunate citizens of Miller and Crawford, have been punished with the loss of all" (Memorial of Arkansas Legislature, November 2, 1831, OIA, RCF; *idem,* Department of State House Files).

[40] *Arkansas Gazette,* October 7, 1828, p. 3, col. 2.

[41] *Ibid.,* October 21, 1828, p. 3, col. 1; *ibid.,* November 11, 1828, p. 1. col. 1.

Following Governor Izard's notice, the white people of Lovely County began removing across the line to the new Washington County "into the flourishing settlements on the headwaters of the Illinois" which was claimed to embrace one of the best bodies of land in the western country, watered by springs. Emigration to it was taking place every day.[42] A post-office had been established at Nicksville, the county seat of Lovely County,[43] on April 25, 1828, with John Dillard as postmaster; but after the removal of the whites it was discontinued on October 2, 1829.[44]

When the immigrant Indians went out upon the prairies to hunt buffaloes, encounters with the prairie Indians frequently resulted. In the autumn of 1827, thirty-five Cherokee hunters met a band of Pawnee in a battle[45] in which three Cherokee, named Tee-le-tak-ta-gee, The Squirrel, and The Horse, were killed by the arrows of the western Indians. As the Cherokee were armed with rifles, they killed many more of their assailants.[46] The next june the Cherokee lost three more men in a similar encounter. The following winter thirty Cherokee warriors and a large body of Creeks went on a combined war, trapping, and hunting expedition in which many lives were lost.[47]

Sam Houston, coming up the Arkansas River on the steamboat "Facility," disembarked in March, 1829, at the mouth of the Illinois and went to the home of Chief John Jolly, who lived on the east side of that stream about a mile above the mouth. Houston called Jolly his "Indian Father."[48] In honor of

---

[42] *Arkansas Gazette,* October 21, 1828, p. 3, col. 1.

[43] Near where Marble City now is.

[44] United States Post Office Department, Old Records.

[45] So called by them; probably Pani Pique, or Wichita.

[46] *Cherokee Phoenix,* October 29, 1828, p. 2, col. 3.

[47] *Ibid.,* March 18, 1829, p. 2, col. 5.

[48] "My son (Gen. Houston or) the Raven came to me last spring. I was glad to meet him and my heart embraced him when he arrived at my wigwam; he rested with me and was as my own son. He has walked straight, and my heart has rejoiced in him" (Jolly to Jackson, December 3, 1829, AGO, ORD, WDF).

his brother, the late chief, the Cherokee council ground near
Jolly's home was long called "Tallunteskee." Houston had just
quitted his post as governor of Tennessee and departed from
Nashville in the company of H. Haralson for the Rocky Mountains.[49] They arrived at Fort Gibson in March, and soon after
he met some Osage at the post who invited him to a council at
Clermont's Town[50] to listen to a recital of wrongs they had
suffered. As Houston lingered at Fort Gibson, his interest in
the Rocky Mountains flagged in proportion as his sympathies
were aroused by the complaints of the Indians he met there.
The Creeks asked him to attend their council and there requested him to prepare a memorial to the President.[51] Soon
after Houston's arrival at Fort Gibson,[52] he established himself in a building about three miles northwest of the post, which
he called The Wigwam. Here he conducted a store[53] while he
cultivated the friendship of the Indians and prepared complaints against their agents.[54]

In the early part of July, 1829, a combined war dance and
council was held by Cherokee and Creeks at Bayou Menard,[55]
to plan another foray against their enemies of the western prai-

[49] H. Haralson to Secretary Eaton, June 23, 1829, OIA, RCF.

[50] Jolly and others, June 9, 1829, *ibid.*, "1829 Cherokee West."

[51] Arbuckle to Eaton, June 30, 1829, AGO, ORD, WDF.

[52] Arbuckle to Secretary of War, July 23, 1830, OIA, RCF.

[53] Thwaites says (*op. cit.*, XIII, 233 n.) that his store was near Webbers
Falls. This impression probably arose from the fact that Jolly's house where
Houston first stopped was near Webbers Falls; letters from army officers at
Fort Gibson definitely fix the location of the store three miles from that post
(Foreman, *op. cit.*, pp. 167, 195).

[54] Houston to Secretary of War, "Wigwam, October 3, 1829," AGO, ORD.

[55] The Indians had a council ground at a spring a quarter of a mile east
of Bayou Menard about six or seven miles east of Fort Gibson on the road
now running from that village to Tahlequah. Buildings constructed here by
Byrthelet and Heald for a trading post were purchased in 1837 by Gov. Mont-
fort Stokes for the Cherokee Agency. It was continued here with short inter-
ruption until 1851, when Cherokee agent George Butler sold the buildings and
removed the agency to a point three miles from Tahlequah. The exact location
of this spring and agency is in Section 12, Township 15 North, Range 20 East.

ries in revenge for the killing of the Cherokee hunters. This meeting was attended by Sam Houston who had come from the home of Chief John Jolly; as Jolly was too ill to attend, he bore from that chief a message to the warriors urging them not to engage in another war expedition. But instead of heeding the words of peace, they lent themselves to the warlike mood of a leader named Captain John Smith, who had great influence over them. Houston was mortified

> to witness in despite of all my efforts the raising of the Tomahawk of War, by seven Cherokees. The Creeks did not join and I trust that you may by attending their council be enabled to prevent them at any future day. Tho' I am sensible that Smith will use every persuasion in his power with them to unite with him and his partizans in this unjust and impolitic war against the Pawnees & Kimanchies. It is the project of a few restless and turbulent young men who will not yield or listen to the Talk of their Chiefs.[56]

Houston's hopes were vain, however. The party, with recruits from the Choctaw, Shawnee, and Delaware, living on the Red River and numbering about 250 to 300, proceeded to another conflict, in which the Cherokee lost five warriors but from which they claimed to have brought home sixty scalps of Tawakoni, Waco, and Comanche enemies.[57] The immigrant tribes had become so exasperated by the hostility of the western Indians, who would not permit them to hunt in peace on the prairies, that a formidable war expedition in the autumn of 1830 was planned.

A party of hunters composed of one Creek and six Cherokee Indians were hunting in Texas when they were attacked by a much larger band of Tawakoni who killed three of the visitors; the others made their escape. After scalping the slain Cherokee the Texas Indians dragged the bodies into their town. Three stakes were driven into the earth around the camp fire, to

[56] Houston to Arbuckle, July 8, 1829, OIA, RCF.
[57] *Texas Gazette* (Austin), June 12, 1830, p. 3, col. 1; *Cherokee Phoenix,* September 18, 1830, p. 2, col. 5.

which the naked and scalpless bodies were fastened in an
upright position facing the dance ground where as if in mock-
ery they remained as spectators of the derision of their own
scalps, celebrated in the scalp-dance of the victors.

This ingenuity plumbed the depth of insult, and a report of
the infamy was carried to the colony of Texas Cherokee Indians by members of another tribe who witnessed the scalp-
dance. It was soon after verified by the survivors of the disaster
when they reached their kinsmen. The Texas Cherokee then
wrote in the Sequoyah characters a letter to their brothers living on the Arkansas River disclosing to them the depths of
infamy visited on their tribe. The latter boiled with rage and
swore to be revenged. No ordinary punishment would atone
for the outrage.

They waited for the arrival of spring when the grass would
sustain their horses and make a war expedition possible. They
nursed their wrath and made plans. The punitive expedition
was headed by John Smith, a powerful Cherokee warrior who
lived near Fort Gibson; associated with him were his brother
Moses Smith and James Derrisaw, a Creek Indian. With their
command they marched forth and in five days reached Red
River where the grass was beginning to cover the earth.

"The forest was ornamented with the early leaves of spring,"
said their chronicler;[58] "all was peace, but the hearts of the
sorrowful warriors, the bones of whose friends lay bleeching
unburied in the prairie, & whose scalps hung in triumph on the
Warpole of the enemy's village, the scorn of the boastful warriors, & the ridicule of the women of the Grand Prairie."

The sun declined to the west eight times and as many times
did they sleep, they reported, before they reached the settle-

---

[58] An extended account of this expedition was written by the Cherokee John
Ridge as he heard it from John Smith, one of the leaders of the party. Ridge's
manuscript is in the Huntington Library where Carolyn Thomas Foreman discovered it and prepared it with footnotes for publication in *Chronicles of
Oklahoma*, Vol. IX, p. 233. See also Arbuckle to Brooks, July 20, 1830, OIA.

ment of the Texas Cherokee near the Sabine River. There they were welcomed by the great warrior Dutch, who entertained them in his home. Runners were sent out with word of their arrival and other Cherokee came to greet the visitors. Dutch and nineteen warriors joined them and went to the village of Boiling Mush where a dance was held. The "night was devoted to dancing—it passed happily away, the song, the whoop, the rattle of the tarrapin shell were heard. We danced with them also. No one slept. The next day the great council was convened to which we stated the nature of our journey." Another night of dancing followed and the war expedition was agreed upon. The visitors returned to Dutch's town where they danced the war dance for four nights and the women prepared food for the men on the march; they parched corn and pounded it into meal, then gave each warrior a bagful. Dutch shaved his hair close to the skin, leaving only a small tuft on the top of his head in which to fasten his headdress made of the short feathers of the hawk. He painted his shaved head red and half the length of the feathers, leaving them tipped with white in the original color.

When the party was organized it contained 63 warriors, some of whom were mounted and some on foot. After a journey of about ten days to the west they came to the village of the Indians for whom they were seeking. Early in the morning they approached before the Tawakoni were awake. The Cherokee tarried while they applied their war paint, adjusted their red and white painted feathers and discarded nearly all their clothing. They then attacked the villagers of whom they killed a large number with guns and tomahawk. Many of them were burned in their wigwams when the Cherokee fired their town and destroyed it.

The slaughter of men, women, and children was completed about ten o'clock in the morning and the revenged invaders departed on their return to the Cherokee settlements. As they came to the neighborhood Dutch sent a runner in advance to carry the news of their arrival and to enable the villagers to make preparations for a fitting reception. The warriors cut a long pine sapling, peeled the bark off and painted it red, leaving on the end a bunch of green leaves. On this pole they strung the scalps of the hapless Tawakoni which they had dried and now combed out and painted red with vermilion, like the pole. They then painted themselves the same color.

They were now ready to present themselves to the village. Though hungry and exhausted from their long march they were obliged to lend themselves to the pomp and ceremony of a triumphal entry before they could eat. As they came in sight of the village Dutch sang the war song and gave as many whoops as they had scalps. In an open square were assembled all the people with an abundance of food for the victors; it was steaming in vessels sitting on the ground guarded with men armed with switches to keep the greedy dogs away. The odor was enticing to the hungry men whose eyes wandered to the food while they were obliged to shake hands with all the men and women present and to relate boastfully if briefly of their exploits. At last the ceremony ended and the warriors were permitted to eat.

XIX

DEPREDATIONS ON WHITE SETTLE-
MENTS BY PRAIRIE INDIANS
1828-29

THE prairie Indians sometimes ventured into the settlements protected by Fort Gibson and Fort Towson, where
they caused much alarm; in August, 1826, near Fort Gibson, a
white man was killed and another wounded by arrows that indicated "Pawnee Indians." Colonel Arbuckle sent troopers
after the offenders.[1] The four houses provided by treaty for
the Osage chiefs were completed and delivered to the agent,
who came late in August, 1827, to put them in possession in
the presence of all the Indians of their respective villages. Near
the Little Osage village on the Neosho were some Pawnee Indians who were looking for horses, and they took refuge from a
storm in a house not yet occupied by the chief. In the morning,
when they were discovered, they were pursued by the Osage,
who returned in the evening with three scalps, without loss or
injury.[2] During the summer, according to their agent, J. F.
Hamtramck, the Osage "attacked a Pawnee town in which were
two frenchmen; one of the frenchmen was killed after he had

[1] Arbuckle to Adjutant General, January 10, 1827, AGO, OFD, 12 A 27;
Arkansas Gazette, September 4, 1827, p. 3, col. 1.

[2] Hamtramck to Clark, September 1, 1827, OIA, RCF. Rev. R. P. Charles
Van Quickenborn, a Catholic Priest of St. Louis, was in this village baptizing
some of the Indians the day the intruders came; he was invited to spend the
night there and occupy the new home provided for the chief and his family;
but as he was in a hurry to reach another town, he declined the invitation,
and he believed he thereby providentially escaped death at the hands of the
savage Indians. He says the Osage killed three Pawnee and fatally wounded
another (Rev. R. P. Charles Van Quickenborn to Mgr. R. P. Rosati, March
10, 1829, *Annales de l'association de la Propagation de la Foi,* III, IV, 572).

killed two Osages—the Osages lost 5 men & killed 7 & took one prisoner who is now in the hands of White Hair."

The Indians near home continued to make life miserable for the people of Miller County. In March, 1828, a large number of citizens of that county petitioned the governor for relief; they

> represented the unpleasant situation in which they were placed by the outrageous deportment of a considerable assemblage of Indians, principally Shawnees and Delawares, at Pecan Point on Red River, who lived near them and pilfered from their houses and corn cribs, killed their hogs, and drove off their horses and cattle. .... The statement was confirmed by the certificates of the grand jury, for the March term of the 1st judicial district, and by a communication from Major Pierson commanding the militia of Miller County. Col. W. Rector, Adjutant General of the Arkansas Militia was immediately instructed to proceed to that part of the county to order the Indians to depart, and if resistance was offered, to provide such a force as would oblige these intruders to leave our territory. This has accordingly been effected by the firmness and activity of the Adjutant General, aided by a body of volunteers, under Maj. Pierson.....[3]

Captain Hyde and troops at Cantonment Towson refused to help, and sixty-three citizens volunteered; with this show of force the Indians agreed to remove within twenty days as soon as they could "call in several hunting parties who were absent."[4]

On August 31, 1828, six soldiers from Fort Towson were fishing in the Kiamichi River, when a band of "Pawnee" Indians attacked and killed two of them, Corporal Thomas Gloyd and Musician Glenn, who were in advance of the others.[5] Their companions hastened to the garrison and gave the alarm; ".... and a detachment of 20 men ordered out by Major Birch under

[3] *Arkansas Gazette,* April 16, 1828, p. 3, col. 1; *Ibid.,* May 14, p. 3, col. 1.

[4] *Ibid.,* May 7, 1828, p. 3, col. 1.

[5] Birch, Cantonment Townsend, to Adjutant General, September 3, 1828, AGO, OFD, 243 B 28; *ibid.,* September 7, 1828, 244 B 28.

L. Casey returned with the corpses of Gloyd and Glenn the former being marked with ball and many arrows and the latter with arrows only." There were not enough troops at the post to risk a battle with the Indians, and the sutler rode all night rousing the white citizens of the neighborhood. The next day they joined a party of soldiers and friendly Indians and the whole party, numbering about forty men, set out in pursuit of the murderers.[6] Overtaking them on the fourth day, about ninety miles away on the banks of the Blue River, within what is now Bryan County, Oklahoma, they discovered them dancing around the scalps of their victims.[7] The detachment rushed in, and after a fierce battle only a few of them escaped through the thickets.[8] The avengers returned to the garrison with the scalps of the soldiers and of three Indians, and with the bows and equipment of the wild Indians. Among the Indians who aided the soldiers in punishing the murderers was Natcoming, a Delaware, who in the battle on the Blue River received a poisoned arrow in his thigh. He was subsequently rendered blind and helpless from the effect of this wound, and the officers at Fort Towson and Fort Gibson united in recommending that he be given a pension in recognition of his service. This was done on March 2, 1833, by a special act of Congress.[9]

This raid caused great alarm among the white settlers in Miller and Hempstead counties; it appeared "that the immediate cause of the invasion was a repulse these savages had met with in attacking Austin's Settlement in Texas, and that they vowed revenge upon all the Settlements on Red River."[10] While

[6] *Illinois Gazette* (Shawnee-Town), October 25, 1828, p. 3, col. 1.

[7] *Cherokee Phoenix,* December 14, 1838, p. 2, col. 3; *Missouri Republican* (St. Louis), October 14, 1828, p. 3, col. 1; *Missouri Intelligencer,* October 14, 1828, p. 3, col. 1; *Arkansas Gazette,* September 23, 1828, p. 3, col. 1.

[8] The hostile party numbered eleven men; seven were killed by the force from Fort Towson, and two were subsequently killed by a small party of Cherokee (Arkansas Gazette, October 21, 1828, p. 3, col. 2).

[9] *U. S. Statutes at Large,* IV, 637.

[10] Izard to Secretary of War, September 21, 1828, AGO, ORD, WDF.

it was understood that the Tawehash could bring only about three hundred warriors in the field, their Comanche allies numbered thousands, and it was feared they might join in a raid on the white settlements.[11]

After the troops and citizens had driven out of the community the Indians who killed Glenn and Gloyd, there was another Indian menace that "created so much alarm among the people, that a large portion of the population of Miller county south of Red River (including the Jonesborough settlement, which is said to be entirely deserted) have removed across the river, and are now residing on this side." Friendly Shawnee and Delaware Indians crossed over also for protection and aid to the whites.[12]

Major Pierson, in command of thirty-seven members of Miller County militia, left the vicinity of Fort Towson and went as far west as the Blue River, where the murderers of Gloyd and Glenn had been punished, without encountering any of the enemy.[13] Fort Towson had ceased to give a feeling of security to the whites; the post was reduced to forty men, and ". . . . it is likely to need protection from citizens instead of giving them protection."[14]

However, the situation improved later in the year; the alarms were subsiding, and the inhabitants on the Red River were venturing

a considerable distance into the large prairie, beyond the settlements—some for the restoration of their health, and some for the purpose of catching wild horses &c. The settlers in that part of Miller County ceded to the Choctaw Indians, are daily leaving it. A number of good citizens have gone to the Province of Texas, and have left the United States with great disgust, at the manner in which they have been treated by the government, in depriving

[11] *Ibid.*
[12] *Arkansas Gazette,* October 21, 1828, p. 3, col. 1.
[13] *Arkansas Gazette,* p. 3, col. 2.
[14] *Ibid.*

them of their homes, and all the comforts of life with which they were surrounded, and making them no remuneration for the great losses which they have sustained.[15]

In the spring of 1829, while the removal of the troops from Fort Towson[16] was under consideration, Major Birch gave an account of the Indians subject to the influence of the post:

> The nearest hostile tribe to us are the Pawnees whose summer residence or town is about three hundred miles west of us; they are a wandering tribe, mostly go in small parties on hunting and horse stealing expeditions. In winter they reside on the headwaters of the Sabine in Texas—they amount to about 400. It was one of those parties which committed the murder in August last on two of our men; but as they have been properly punished we apprehend no further difficulty on that account. The Comanches belonging to Texas frequently join the small parties of Pawnees in the summer at the above named residence and assist them in committing depredations. The Pawnee Pics are still further N. W. of us— we have not been troubled by them. There are also Pawnee Loops, but we do not know about them, and seldom hear of them. The friendly tribes are generally located on Red River below us, and are as follows: The first are about 15 miles, are the Cherokees, about 30 in number. The next are Shawnees about 30 miles, consisting of about 250—the next are the Delawares about 60—there is a small party of Kickapoos who generally reside on the Sabine in Texas. Still lower down are the Caddos and the Choctaws.[17]

The next year Colonel Arbuckle reported that there were from five to seven hundred warriors on and near the Red River

[15] *Ibid.*, December 9, 1828, p. 3, col. 1.

[16] Among the reasons urged for the abandonment of Fort Towson, one was the difficulty of navigation of the Red River, caused by recent additions to the Great Raft. A wagon road from Fort Towson to Natchitoches had been authorized, but it was not constructed until after the post was reëstablished in 1831.

[17] Maj. George Birch to Acting Assistant Adjutant General, April 9, 1829, AGO, OFD, 152 B 29.

belonging to the Caddo and Quapaw tribes, and bands of Cherokee, Koasati, Choctaw, Delaware, Shawnee, and Kickapoo.[18]

Fort Towson was finally abandoned in June, 1829, to the great indignation of the white people in the vicinity, who then prepared to leave also; for, they said, the frontier would be left "in a deplorably helpless condition—exposed on two sides for a distance of upward of 300 miles, to numerous hostile Indians."[19] And after the troops had gone they complained that they were "left to the mercy of merciless savages."[20] The Territorial Legislature memorialized the President

> . . . . that since the removal of the troops from Fort Towson on Red River, the inhabitants of our Southwestern border have been greatly disturbed and kept in considerable alarm by the incursions and depredations of hordes of Indians residing upon that frontier. That the citizens are almost daily subject to every species of outrage by the numberous tribes of Cumanchie and Pawnee indians, who reside for half the year within the limits of the United States, as well as from the revenged Cherokees, Shawnees, Delawares, and Kickapoos. That they are constrained at their own expense to keep scouts continually employed to repel minor agressions and give notice of the approach of more formidable parties; that many of our citizens, hopeless as to the future, are abandoning their property and seeking places of more security.[21]

The Legislature asked that the Federal Government authorize them to raise two companies of rangers to police the border.

One of the trading parties came to grief during the winter. A man named Whitesides and four others had gone on a trading expedition with the Comanche; the Indians received them in a friendly manner, but for some cause not related, attacked and killed four of them, including Joel Dyer of Hempstead County.

18 Arbuckle to Macomb, May 31, 1830, OIA, RCF.
19 Account from *Arkansas Gazette,* in Cherokee Phoenix, July 15, 1829, p. 1, col. 5.
20 *Cherokee Phoenix,* June 5, 1830, p. 2, col. 3.
21 Memorial of Legislature, November 5, 1829, AGO, ORD, WDF.

Whitesides made his escape by leaping down a high bluff, and concealing himself in a thicket until night, when he returned and saw the bodies of his murdered companions. He picked up scraps of meat (having no gun) on which he subsisted sparingly ten days, after which he was five days without provisions before he reached our settlement

where he brought the account of the massacre.[22]

The hostilities of these western Indians were the occasion for furnishing a military escort, under the command of Major Bennet Riley, for the protection of the Santa Fe traders in the summer of 1829. General Atkinson had received orders to protect the frontier, and the Osage offered eight hundred warriors for service against the western Indians, through their agent, Hamtramck.[23] After the troops had abandoned Cantonment Towson, prairie Indians invaded the adjoining settlements; on January 22, 1830, one band of fifteen Pawnee killed Isaac Murphy, who was at work in his field about three miles from Miller Courthouse. A company of forty armed citizens pursued them as far as the Blue River. The white people on the Red River became much alarmed,[24] and called on Acting-Governor Fulton for authority to raise a body of volunteers for protection of the settlement against an anticipated attack by the wild Indians.[25] Colonel Arbuckle said he believed the apprehension of the people of Miller County was well founded, and recommended the employment of some woodsmen as spies to investigate and give warning of impending danger.[26] This precaution was accordingly authorized by Governor Fulton, who directed Colonel Clark of the militia to order all the soldiers

[22] Letter from Miller County, February 16, 1829, *Cherokee Phoenix,* February 25, 1829, p. 1, col. 5.

[23] *Ibid.,* p. 2, col. 1.

[24] *Ibid.,* March 17, 1830, p. 2, col. 1.

[25] John Clark to Fulton, February 20, 1830, OIA, RCF.

[26] Arbuckle to Fulton, April 8, 1830, *ibid.*

under his command to prepare themselves to take the field at a moment's warning to repel invasion by the Indians.[27]

The shadow of the hostile Indian menace still hung over the settlements on the Grand and Verdigris rivers.

> The Pawnees with the Comanches are becoming hostile to the Whites. Two [whites] were killed last fall near Fort Gibson, and lately four have been killed, who were among them to trade. And before all this some had been killed from Missouri—Then the Osages, all know, have had perpetual war with these people, so that they do not sooner shoot a bear than a Pawnee and so *visa versa in toto;* and within a year the Cherokees have had a skirmish with them and bro't home some of their scalps so that the motives for an invasion on their part are increasing. We have had two seasons of alarm on account of these people fearing they were coming in upon us like a flood—and we are quite sure that it was the Pawnee who killed Ols Swiss a Frenchman, near Mr. Chouteau's trading house summer before last; and last summer Col. Arbuckle sent us an express that he had understood that there were 1500 hundred Comanches approaching, so that we do not know what to expect. Should they come with a double layer of wrath in their breasts—one for the Indians—another for the whites—we should of course be in great danger.[28]
>
> There was an Osage wounded a few days ago near the center of the Cherokee settlements, supposed to be by a party of Pawnees; and a few days afterwards there was a Creek Indian killed . . . .

on the south bank of the Arkansas north of the site of the future city of Muskogee. This killing just at daybreak on June 18, 1830, created great excitement in the neighborhood. The Indian had gone out of his cabin to build his morning fire to cook breakfast when he was attacked by a number of wild Indians, who shot him with balls and arrows, scalped him, and made off with his two horses. His wife, who lay on a pallet in the cabin looking out between the logs, witnessed the murder,

---

[27] Fulton to Clark, April 9, 1830, OIA, RCF.

[28] American Board of Commissioners for Foreign Missions, Manuscript Library, Vol. 200, No. 199, Vaill to Evarts, Union Mission, February 21, 1829.

and with their little son made her escape and gave the alarm. At a conference attended by the Indians and the military it was decided that the attackers were from the Red River. The Creeks organized a party of 150 men, under Chilly McIntosh; with a military contingent under Captain Wilkinson ordered out by Colonel Arbuckle, they took up the trail of the marauders in the direction of the Kiamichi.[29] Arbuckle said that because of their friendship of the Osage, the Creeks were disliked by the Indians on the Red River.

In 1829 the Osage were visited by severe punishment at the hands of their exasperated neighbors, the Choctaw and Cherokee. The former had lost a number of horses, and the credit for the robberies was given to the Osage. Coming on one of their hunting camps on the Canadian River, the Choctaw attacked and killed seven of them.[30] In November, 1829, eight Osage were killed by a party of fifteen Cherokee from the Red River,[31] and in the following May a conference was held at the Creek Agency to adjust their claim for the loss of their tribesmen.[32] Captain Pryor, acting subagent for the Arkansas Osage, Colonel Arbuckle, and Colonel Chouteau, managed the affair. Sam Houston had been asked to assist; but as he was in Washington in connection with the Indian ration contracts, he was unable to be present. The Osage said that the tears of their

[29] Arbuckle to Macomb, June 23, 1830, AGO, ORD, WDF; Blake to Secretary of War, June 20, 1830, *ibid.*

[30] *Cherokee Phoenix*, February 24, 1930, p. 2, col. 2. "In one of my visits among them (the Osage) last fall, I found many weeping, and mourning, and crying vehemently, on account of the destruction of six or seven of their family connections. The slain were all the relatives of Tally, the second chief, and had been cut off a little before by a Red River party, while sitting peaceably in their tents. The party was supposed to be Choctaws, avenging themselves for some previous losses by the Osages" (Vaill reporting from Union Mission, *Missionary Herald*, XXVI [September, 1830], 285).

[31] Arbuckle to Adjutant General, December 24, 1829, AGO, OFD, 162 A 29; "A war party of the Osages is said to be in pursuit of the Cherokees . . . . The bands of different tribes on the upper Red River are all hostile to the Osages" (*ibid.*).

[32] Arbuckle to Macomb, May 31, 1830, OIA, RCF.

people could not be dried for less than $800 and it required 136 yards of blue stroud,[33] 80 pairs of mackinaw blankets, 397 yards of domestic plaid, 12 butcher knives, 4 pounds of vermilion, and a few other items to appease them.[34]

The Osage, finding the hazards of combat in the south and east uncomfortably increased by the militia and the co-operation of the well-armed Indians there, directed their attention to their enemies in the west, where they hunted buffaloes.[35] An account came from the Western Creek Agency on the Verdigris, on February 10, 1830, of the return of the Osage from a war expedition against the Pawnee on the upper Arkansas River.[36] The report stated that the Osage, three hundred strong, attacked the Pawnee

> .... and drove them after a short but bloody battle into a large lake, where the Osage laid down their guns and chased them in the lake with the tomahawk and massacred them before they could make their excape..... It is asserted by them, that since their knowledge of the Pawnees, they never have as yet had a fight where so much blood was spilt. It is remarkable that the

[33] Stroud, a coarse cloth about a foot in width, used by the Indians for breech-clout, or flap, tied around the body and the ends or flaps hanging down before and behind. Probably from Stroud, England, celebrated for its manufacture of cloth.

[34] Arbuckle to Macomb, May 21, 1830, OIA, RCF.

[35] During the early days of the residence of the Cherokee Indians in Arkansas the Buffaloes were hunted within the limits of the present state of that name and in eastern Oklahoma, though they were found in greater numbers on the western prairies. But with the location of the Indians from the East in their country and the unbridled slaughter of the buffaloes by white hunters, that source of food and raiment was exhausted in the eastern country and the Osage were obliged to travel hundreds of miles to the Cross Timbers, and beyond, and contest with the western Indians to secure their supply of game, so that their families might be saved from starvation. The scarcity of buffaloes in what is now eastern Oklahoma began to be noted in the twenties, and by 1834 it was reported that there were not enough of them east of the Cross Timbers to sustain traveling bands of Indians.

[36] *Cherokee Phoenix*, March 17, 1830, p. 2, col. 1.; *Niles' Weekly Register*, XXXVIII, p. 48; *National Intelligencer*, March 8, 1830, p. 3, col. 5.

Osages did not lose a single man. The number of Pawnees[37] killed is about 80 or 90—five women taken prisoners, and they brought in 84 horses which they stole from the Pawnees.

The Osage brought home sixty or seventy scalps, and were so elated over their victory that they were considering an expedition against the Choctaw on the Red River.

In December, dressed as an Indian and accompanied by Walter Webber and John Brown, Houston went to Washington and pressed his charges against the Indian agents. The removal of several of them followed. At the same time he was engaged in promoting his own interests. He endeavored to secure a contract to ration the Indians who, it was supposed, would be removed under the terms of the Indian Removal Act. His proposal was referred by President Jackson to General John H. Eaton, secretary of war, who declined to let a contract except after advertising for bids. When the bids were received, charges of collusion between some of the bidders led to a refusal by Eaton to let a contract to anyone.[38]

Houston departed soon afterward for the Verdigris with an assortment of goods to retail in the West. When he reached the White River in Arkansas, he addressed a letter to General Eaton making application for the post of sutler at Fort Gibson on the supposition that General John Nicks, then sutler, was to be removed. Houston arrived at the Verdigris ahead of his boatload of merchandise, and learned that Nicks was to be retained; and hearing also rumors at Fort Gibson that, by authority of General Eaton, he had been charged with an attempt to impose on the Government in the matter of the ration

---

[37] While contemporary custom of speaking of Kiowa, Wichita, and Pawnee Pique as Pawnee, gives rise to some confusion, the Osage were actually at war with the Pawnee of the Platte. Col. A. P. Chouteau relates (Choteau to Commissioner of Indian Affairs, June 28, 1838, OIA, RCF) that his nephew E. L. Chouteau encountered a war party of Pawnee Republicans about seventy-five miles west of Fort Mason, who in company with a number of Pawnee Loups were in quest of the Comanche, Osage, and their allies.

[38] For a fuller account of this affair see Foreman, *op. cit.*, pp. 185 ff.

contracts, he wrote an intemperate letter to the Secretary of War violently assailing him for the charges of fraud. He also said he would not have the post of sutler if it were offered to him by Eaton, and announced that he was going to begin a series of letters over the signature of "Tal-ohn-tus-ky" in the *Arkansas Gazette*.[39] Eaton denied that he had made the statements attributed to him.[40]

In the spring of 1831, the Cherokee held their election for national officers. Since the enactment of the treaty of 1828, several hundred Cherokee, among whom white blood predominated,[41] had emigrated from the old nation east of the Mississippi; and the new arrivals managed to have themselves elected to the most important offices; Joseph Vann as President of the Committee; Andrew Vann and Alexander Saunders as members of the Committee; Richard Rowe as Clerk to the House of Representatives; and Edward Hicks as Clerk of the Committee.[42]

In October, 1829, the autumn after Houston's arrival in the West, a certificate of admission to the tribe was issued to him, and he proceeded to live and dress as one of them. He contracted marriage in some form with Diana Gentry, widow of David Gentry, formerly Diana Rogers, the comely niece of the Cherokee chief, John Rogers.[43] At the spring election in 1831, as a

[39] Houston to Eaton, "Wigwam," June 13, 1830, AGO, ORD, WDF.

[40] *Ibid.*, Eaton to Houston, July 28, 1830.

[41] *Cherokee Phoenix*, March 10, 1830, p. 2, col. 3. One muster roll in 1829 accounted for 113 white men with Indian families and 237 Indian men and their Indian families who traveled from Tennessee in twenty flatboats, bringing 122 slaves, 99 guns, 324 blankets, and 103 kettles furnished by the Government, beside their other personal effects; of another party enrolled in June, 1829, and waiting for the next high water, 90 families were from Georgia, 173 from Alabama, and 70 from Tennessee (OIA, RCF); 500 emigrant Cherokee arrived at Fort Gibson during 1830 (Vashon to Secretary of War, August 28, 1830, *ibid.*).

[42] *Cherokee Phoenix*, May 28, 1831, p. 2, col. 4.

[43] For a more detailed account of Houston's life in Indian Territory, see Foreman, Grant, *op. cit.*, pp. 179 ff.; Marquis James, *The Raven, a Biography*

member of the tribe, he was a candidate for a seat in the Cherokee Council, but to his great mortification he was defeated. To
find his fervid interest in the Indians so little appreciated,
chagrined and "exasperated him so much, that he has abandoned his Indian wife, among them, and has signified his intention to banish himself to the Choctaw Nation."[44] However his
mind was concentrated on plans concerned with the region
south of the Choctaw country. The next year he visited Texas
and afterward interested himself in the efforts of the Americans
there to set up a government for Texas, independent of Mexico.
In these plans Houston counted on the Cherokee and Creeks
for assistance; and through his acquaintance and the influence
he had established with them, a few became involved in his
schemes.

of Sam Houston. "Some New Light on Houston's Life Among the Cherokee
Indians," by Grant Foreman, *Chronicles of Oklahoma,* IX, p. 139.

[44] *Cherokee Phoenix,* May 28, 1831, p. 2, col. 4.

XX

CREEK IMMIGRANTS ARRIVE IN THE SOUTHWEST, 1828

BY a cession procured in 1805, millions of acres of Creek lands were transferred to Georgia. The people of the state constantly clamored for fulfilment by the Government of its compact of 1802; and the Creeks, alarmed at the prospective wholesale alienation of their ancient domain, made a law in general council in 1811, on the motion of William McIntosh,[1] forbidding the sale of any of the remaining land under the penalty of death. McIntosh was an able and prominent member of the Lower Creeks, who had taken a leading part in the War of 1812 as the head of the Creek allies of the Americans.

Following the Creek War of 1812, a large part of the territory of the conquered tribe was confiscated and opened to white settlement. In 1828 more lands were acquired by treaty, and in 1821 the fifth treaty was negotiated by Georgia citizens, acting on behalf of the United States, with McIntosh, who was in the pay of the whites, and a dozen other chiefs controlled by him. Thirty-six other chiefs who were present refused to sign and made clear to the commissioners the irregularity of a cession arranged with a party representing only a tenth of the nation, which to be legal required the consent of the entire nation assembled in council. After an attempt by McIntosh to convey more land in 1823, the law punishing with death any Creek who offered to cede their land was re-enacted in 1824;

---

[1] William McIntosh was the son of a Scotch trader and a Creek woman. His principal residence was on the Chattahoochee where he had two wives, Susannah and Peggy, one a Creek, the other a Cherokee; fifty miles away on the western branch of the Tallapoosa he had another plantation where resided another of his wives named Eliza. She was the daughter of Stephen Hawkins, and sister to Samuel and Benjamin Hawkins. Samuel Hawkins, who was married to Jenny, the daughter of William McIntosh, also had a second wife on another plantation (OIA, RCF, "1825 Creeks, D. G. Campbell").

fifteen million acres had already been transferred, and ten million acres remained in the possession of the Creeks.[2]

John C. Calhoun, secretary of war, appointed James Meriwether and Duncan G. Campbell of Georgia on July 16, 1824, as commissioners to negotiate with the Creeks for the extinction of their title to all their lands, with the injunction that "the feelings and wishes of the state of Georgia should be particularly attended to in any treaty that may be made with the Creek Nation." John Ross, of the Cherokee tribe, advised and actively encouraged the Creeks to oppose the efforts of the Georgia commissioners to effect a treaty with them, and proposed that the two tribes stand together in opposition to further cession of their lands.[3] The influence of Ross was doubtless partly responsible for the failure of the commissioners to effect the treaty desired by them. In January, 1825, they reported to the President their failure to secure a treaty with the chiefs of all of the tribe, but informing him that they could get McIntosh and his following to sign. They complained to the President that Ross was actively opposing their efforts. They had previously reported to Governor Troup of Georgia, that "for sometime past the Cherokee have exerted a steady and officious interference in the affairs of this tribe." In February the commissioners renewed their negotiations, which were limited to the comparatively small part of the tribe represented by McIntosh; and by working on his avarice[4] were able to induce McIntosh and his chiefs on February 12, to set their names to

[2] They said they were resolved not to sell one foot more of land. As evidence that they were progressing in the arts of civilization the Creeks cited the fact that thirty thousand yards of cloth had been manufactured by those living on Coosa and Tallapoosa rivers during the year 1824 (*Public Advertiser* [Louisville], December 25, 1824, p. 2, col. 5).

[3] *American State Papers*, "Indian Affairs," II, 574.

[4] Calhoun informed the commissioners that $50,000 would be at their command for expenses of the negotiations including "Presents" (*ibid.*, p. 565). Drake says (Samuel G. Drake, *The Aboriginal Races of North America* [New York, 1880], pp. 392 ff.) that McIntosh not only accepted a bribe for signing the treaty, but, two years before, had acted as agent in the offer of a bribe to

a treaty[5] ceding what remained of the Creek Nation and agreeing to the removal of the tribe to the country lying between the Arkansas and Canadian rivers. Although Secretary Calhoun had declared that he would not recognize a treaty in which the chiefs of the Creek Nation did not acquiesce, President Monroe laid it before the Senate and after the accession of President Adams, it was approved on March 7. The Creeks did not rise in rebellion, as was expected; but in accordance with the tribal law already mentioned, formal sentence of death was passed on McIntosh. It was executed at daybreak on April 30, 1825, by a party of Oakfuskee warriors sent for that purpose, under the command of Manawee, who surrounded his house and shot him as he tried to escape. They killed also the Chief Etome Tustunnugge; and later in the day they hanged Colonel Samuel Hawkins, son-in-law of McIntosh, in the town square; Hawkins' brother Benjamin escaped.[6]

These events produced such bitterness between the factions of the tribe that the partisans of McIntosh expressed a determination to migrate to the country west of the Mississippi. President Adams, convinced of the fraud committed in the execution of the pretended treaty of 1825, directed Secretary Barbour of the War Department to enter into negotiations with the tribe for the execution of a new treaty. This was accomplished on January 24, 1826,[7] in the office of the Secretary of

John Ross and other Cherokee to secure the cession of the Cherokee land. "I will make the United States Commissioners give you two thousand dollars, A. McCoy the same, and Charles Hicks 3000 dollars for present, and nobody shall know it . . . . The whole amount is $12,000 and you can divide among your friends exclusive $7000 (Wm. McIntosh to John Ross, Newton, October 21, 1823, OIA, RCF, "1825 Creeks"). Ross, however, was not to be bribed.

[5] *U. S. Statutes at Large,* VII, 237; Kappler [ed.], *op. cit.,* p. 151.

[6] *Handbook of American Indians,* I, 782; *American State Papers,* "Indian Affairs," II, 563, 768; *Louisville Public Advertiser,* June 11, 1825, p. 2, col. 1; *ibid.,* September 3, p. 3, col. 2; *Missouri Advocate,* June 8, 1825, p. 2, cols. 2, 3, and 4; *Arkansas Gazette,* June 21, 1825, p. 2, col. 3. The name of McIntosh's executioner is spelled "Menewa" in the *Handbook of American Indians;* other authorities spell it "Manawee" and "Ma-nah-wee."

[7] Kappler [ed.] *op. cit.,* II, 188.

War, between him and the chiefs of the tribe. This treaty admitted the wrong committed by the one of the year before and abrogated all its terms; it provided for an exploring party, composed of five of the McIntosh following, to examine the country west of the Mississippi and determine upon a location; provided for the removal of the McIntosh Indians; and agreed that if as many as three thousand of them would go within two years, the sum of $100,000 would be given to them, or a like proportion for a smaller number. Each warrior so removing was to have one rifle and ammunition, one butcher knife, one brass kettle, and one beaver trap, and they were all to have rations on the journey and for one year after. An agent with a salary of $1,500 annually was to go and live among them for two years to look after them. As an inducement to the representatives of the majority of the tribe for the cession of part of the land of the tribe, the sum of $217,600 was offered[8] to the chiefs and warriors upon ratification of the treaty.

In the Creek treaty of 1826, members of the Cherokee tribe again seem to have been concerned. As John Ross had used his influence against the one of the year before, the Cherokee, John Ridge, Major Ridge, and Joseph Vann were interested in the success of the second. John Ridge was secretary of the Creek delegation to Washington.[9] As soon as the new treaty was signed by the Creeks, Ridge and Vann submitted to the Bureau of Indian Affairs a list agreed to by the Creek chiefs designating the manner in which $159,700 of the sum mentioned in Section 3 of the treaty should be paid, reading as follows: John Ridge, $15,000; Joseph Vann, $15,000; Opothleyaholo, $10,000; John Stedham, $10,000; Manawee, $10,000; Charles Cornells, $10,000; Mad Wolf, $6,000; Paddy Carr, $500; Tippee, $200; to the remaining members of the delegation, each $5,000, or $35,000 in all; Little Prince, $10,000; Tookenehaw of Tuckabatchie, $10,000; Tuskenuggee Mallow,

[8] In Section 3 of the treaty.
[9] OIA, RCF, "1826 Creeks, Deputation."

$10,000; Major Ridge of the Cherokees, $10,000; Tuckabatchie Tuskenuggee, $1,000; Tuskenehaw Cusseta, $2,000; Hubi Hujo, $1,000; McGillivray, $4,000.[10]

The treaty was proclaimed on April 22, but the appropriation authorized by Section 3 was not voted until May 22. The House and Senate disagreed on this measure; and Senator Benton, for the conferees, charged that the method of paying the money, which seemed to have the tacit acquiescence of the Secretary of War, was a gross fraud on the rights of the Creek Nation. The Secretary wrote to the conferees:

> Whatever has been done, or is proposed to be done, is contained in the treaty; for, although I was advised, as Col. Benton is aware, to approach the influential chiefs, with secret gratuities, justified, as it was urged, by the usages of the government, I peremptorily refused to do so; and determined that whatever was given as the price of the land, should appear on the face of the treaty. Its distribution at their own instance is considered no affairs of this government, except so far as humanity was concerned in preventing disturbance.[11] [The appropriation as finally adopted provided that the bribe money should be] paid to the Chiefs of the Creek nation, to be divided among the chiefs and warriors of said nation, and that the same be done under the direction of the Secretary of War in a full council of the nation convened upon notice for that purpose.

Colonel David Brearley, who had been an agent to the Arkansas Cherokee, was appointed on May 13, 1826, as agent to the McIntosh Creeks, with direction to accompany the exploring party, select a place for an agency in the western country convenient to the section chosen by the Creeks, and superintend the removal of the Indians, for which two years' time was allowed. Funds were provided, and Brearley was directed to purchase rations for the Indians on their way and after their arrival in the West.

[10] *American State Papers*, "Indian Affairs," II, 667.
[11] *American State Papers*, "Indian Affairs," II, 665.

Brearley and his exploring party of five Creeks traveled by steamboat from New Orleans up the Arkansas to the Dardanelle; and from there they went overland, reaching Fort Gibson in the early part of May, 1827. Here they procured an interpreter, guides, and additional horses, and proceeded up the north side of the Arkansas River about sixty miles, then crossed and passed southwest to the Canadian River, thence down that river to the road at that time traveled from Fort Gibson to Fort Towson, by which they returned to Fort Gibson.[12] Both the Cherokee and the Osage of Clermont's Town exchanged beads and tobacco with them as a token of their friendship.

The delegation returned to Alabama and on August 1 reported to the National Council at Wewoka, giving a favorable account of the country in the West. They recommended settlement on the heavily-timbered land on the north side of the Arkansas River, lying west of the Grand and Verdigris rivers.[13] In those days of the rail fence and log house, prairie land was considered worthless for agricultural purposes, not only by the Indians but by the government officials; they reported that the prairies between the Arkansas and Canadian were barren and sterile.[14] Speeches were made by Arbeka Tustenuggee, the leader of the exploring party, who gave a lucid description of the features of the country, depicting the water courses, the character of the land, and the variety of game. His account was confirmed by members present who had hunted over the western country many years before. Other speeches were made by Little Prince and Mad Tiger, to which responses were made by Chilly McIntosh and others, and they parted in a friendly spirit—the McIntosh faction to organize their own council at the Falls of the Chattahoochee, to make their own plans for

---

[12] *U. S. Senate Document No. 512,* Twenty-third Congress, first session, "Indian Removal," II, p. 633; Brearley to Barbour, July 20, 1827, OIA, RCF, "1827 Creeks."

[13] OIA, RCF, May 28, 1827. [14] *Ibid.*

emigration, to listen to the report of their exploring party, and to receive the emblems of friendship sent by the Osage and Cherokee in the West.[15]

Brearley recommended, for a Creek agency in the West, the purchase of the buildings of Colonel A. P. Chouteau, used as a trading post on the east side of the Verdigris about three miles above its mouth, and on August 30 of that year he was authorized to make the purchase. By November he had 739 members of the McIntosh party, under the leadership of General Chilly McIntosh, enrolled for the journey, and by November 25 they had arrived at Tuscumbia on the Tennessee River, to embark on boats that would carry them to the West. But they had not been permitted to depart in peace.

> On our way to our location west of the mighty river, we stopped and stationed ourselves at Harpersville in the State of Alabama, and tarried there many weeks for some of the emigrants to come up, who were then behind. We received no hospitality from the citizens of that place, but were harrassed with attachments upon our property, and thrown into confusion with fake accounts. After we had taken up our line of march from Harpersville, at a late hour of the night for our long journey, we were still disturbed by persons laying claim to property in our possession, which had been obtained by us properly.
>
> Hoping to march our people along peaceably, we were troubled with constables every few miles, with false papers, and we did not enjoy any peace until we came down the mountain; then we marched along with peace and harmony—passed through many villages, and arrived at Tuscumbia, where we encamped for a few days, intending to take boats down the waters of the Tennessee, and so on to the Mighty River. Here we have remained several days, and have received all kind of hospitality and good treatment. The citizens of Tuscumbia have treated us like brothers and our old helpless women were furnished by the good women of the town with clothing. On Tuesday the 29th of November, the Law of our Great Father above was explained to us; and our people were

---

[15] *Arkansas Gazette*, September 25, 1827, p. 3, col. 1.

glad to hear it. As long as our nation remains upon the earth, we will recollect Tuscumbia.[16]

In the following February, Brearley ascended the Arkansas and Verdigris rivers in the steamboat "Facility," with two keel boats in tow, having on board the vessels 280 men, women, and children who were landed at the agency. The "Facility" had overtaken the two keel boats and assisted them up the river. Brearley returned on her to Fort Smith, where he met some of his Indians, who were traveling by land, and conducted them up to the agency. When this land party reached Little Rock it contained four hundred persons, two hundred horses, and twenty baggage wagons. Emigrants who were traveling by land were scattered all along the Arkansas from the Dardanelle to Fort Smith to be collected by Brearley.[17]

Soon after the arrival of the first Creeks who came by boat, Brearley undertook to reconcile his party with the Osage, the whole of Clermont's and Tallai's party being at the mouth of the Verdigris. They were somewhat sour of temper at first, and the small party of Creeks were in some fear of them. Colonel Arbuckle, however, with his usual firmness, gave the Osage distinctly to understand that the Creeks were under his immediate protection and that any offense committed by them would be followed by the severest punishment. At the same time he advised the Creeks not to pass up the Arkansas even through the land allotted to them, as it was coursed by the warpath of the Osage who might find an excuse to attack them. The next night Clermont sought a council with Brearley, in which he manifested a great desire to be on friendly terms with the

[16] Statement by Chilly McIntosh, Tuscumbia, Alabama, November 30, 1827, in *Tuscumbia Patriot,* copied in *Niles' Weekly Register,* December 29, 1827; it was preceded by the following in the *Patriot*: "For the last four or five days, our town has been thronged with Indians. About 739 Creeks, a part of the McIntosh party arrived on their way to Arkansas, under the superintendence of Colonel Brearley. General McIntosh, son of the famous chief of that name, and who is now the principal warrior of the tribe, is in the company . . . . ."

[17] *Arkansas Gazette,* January 30, 1828, p. 3, cols. 1 and 2; *ibid.,* February 13, 1828, p. 3, col. 1.

whites and proposed that the bonds of good will might be
strengthened with the other nations by intermarriage.[18] While
the Indians were in council, "a war party of Osage returned
from excursions against the Pawnees, bringing with them 8
prisoners."[19]

Colonel Brearley returned to Alabama in April and began to
organize a second emigrating party; but he met with much
opposition from designing whites[20] and Indians, who prevented
the Creeks from going to the rendezvous at Fort Strother. The
report was circulated that his Indians were deserting; this
statement was made by an intelligent Creek named Paddy Carr
who was, when seen, on his way to Choctaw Academy in Kentucky with seven Creek boys.[21] The Indians were said to be
in a most miserable condition, bordering on starvation. Instead
of the fifteen hundred who were expected to emigrate, Colonel
Brearley succeeded in organizing only a small party, and in
November he returned to the West with some five hundred
more Creeks who joined the first arrivals in their settlement
on the land at the junction of the Arkansas and the Verdigris.
They had divided into two parties at Creek Path.[22] Three hundred of them went overland with thirty loaded wagons and a
drove of one hundred horses;[23] and the old men, women, and
children traveled by boat down the Tennessee, Ohio, and Mississippi, and up the Arkansas,[24] 268 of them being landed at

18 Brearley to Barbour, July 14, 1828, OIA, RCF.

19 *Arkansas Gazette,* February 13, 1828, p. 3, col. 1. In the summer the
Creeks "were visited by a deputation of Delaware Indians who did not fail
to tell the Creeks what they proclaimed wherever they went, that they were
the grandfather of all the other Indians" (*Cherokee Phoenix,* October 22, 1828,
p. 4, col. 5).

20 The Indians were detained until their annuity was received; this was then
taken from them to pay the debts which they had been induced to incur.

21 Account in *Cherokee Phoenix,* October 8, 1828, copied in *Arkansas Gazette,* November 4, 1828, p. 3, col. 3; *ibid.,* November 18, 1828, p. 3, col. 2.

22 *Cherokee Phoenix,* November 5, 1828, p. 2, col. 2.

23 *Arkansas Gazette,* November 11, 1828, p. 3, col. 1.

24 *Ibid.,* November 18, 1828, p. 3, col. 1; Brearley to Secretary of War,
December 12, 1828, OIA, RCF, "1828 Creeks."

the agency on the Verdigris on November 28. Some of the wealthier ones went independently; Colonel Hawkins, a half-breed, with his family and thirty or forty slaves, reached Little Rock in August on his way west.[25]

With these emigrants came Luther Blake, conducting an exploring party of Creeks not of the McIntosh faction,[26] who carried back to their people such favorable reports of the land at the mouth of the Verdigris that many of them began to organize for removal. And the white people of Alabama congratulated themselves, "We may now confidently look forward to the speedy acquisition of the delightful and valuable territory possessed by this miserable race."[27] By September, 1829, twelve hundred of those Creeks of the majority faction had migrated, under the supervision of the Creek agent, Crowell, and his subagent, Luther Blake. Part of them crossed the Mississippi at Memphis and went overland, and the remainder traveled by Tuscumbia and the waters of the Tennessee and the Mississippi to the White River, where they embarked on the "Virginian," which could not ascend higher than Little Rock[28] because of the low stage of water in the Arkansas.[29] About four hundred emigrating Creeks "passed up through the Big Prairie about a week since, on their way to the country assigned them on the Arkansas"; one hundred were on the "Virginian," which ran aground in the Arkansas.[30] Passage thence to the Western Creek Agency was accomplished partly by keel

[25] *Arkansas Gazette,* August 20, 1828, p. 3, col. 1.

[26] Brearley, December 1, 1828, OIA, RCF.

[27] *Cherokee Phoenix,* July 1, 1829, p. 2, col. 3.

[28] "Those who came here while in camp near by were orderly and of correct deportment, neat looking and clean" (From *Arkansas Gazette,* copied in *Cherokee Phoenix,* September 30, 1829, p. 3, col. 1).

[29] *Cherokee Phoenix,* September 30, 1829, p. 3, col. 1.

[30] Account from *Arkansas Gazette* in *Cherokee Phoenix,* September 16, 1829, p. 2, col. 2.

[31] *U. S. Senate Document No. 512,* Twenty-third Congress, first session, "Indian Removal," II, 44.

[32] *Ibid.*

boat and partly by land.[31] Crowell removed a total of 1,200, and 1,203 went under the direction of Brearley.[32]

According to Sam Houston, the conduct of this emigration

.... was enough to shock humanity..... Between fifty and a hundred Uchees were left in the swamps of Mississippi and I believe have not arrived. A considerable number of the emigrating party I heard of on the Illinois River about eighteen miles east of Cantonment Gibson; they were nearly all sick, famished, and most of them unable to turn themselves on their blankets. They subsisted principally upon what fish they could catch, and Mr. Flowers, a Cherokee Indian countryman, furnished them some provisions on his own responsibility.[33]

These early immigrants settled compactly for a distance of ten or twelve miles along the Arkansas and the Verdigris, where they were conveniently near their agency and under the shelter of Fort Gibson. Here they were found by the Cherokee when the latter began removing under their treaty of 1828. Both tribes had valid claims to this fertile land, and much controversy and bitterness grew out of this blunder of the Secretary of War.

The Creeks had a number of other complaints; they were harassed and terrified by the aggressions of the wild Indians to the south and west of them; but most of all they were suffering from the failure of the Government to redeem its promises to them. Notwithstanding the fact that, by the treaty of 1826, the Government promised them a sum of money and rifles, guns and ammunition, blankets, kettles, beaver traps, and butcher knives on their arrival in the West, this pledge was not kept even in part for more than two years after they migrated; and it was November, 1831, before they saw a dollar of the money so much needed by them. In the meantime the chiefs had to devote their slight funds to keep their hunters[34] in

33 Houston, "Wigwam, Cherokee Nation 3d October, 1829," to Secretary of War, AGO, ORD, WDF.

34 "General Chilly McIntosh and 27 of our Creek Indians have been on

ammunition so that, at the risk of their lives from hostile prairie Indians, they might secure food to relieve the distress of the poor immigrants.[35]

Without traps they could not catch the beaver whose furs they expected to barter for the necessities of life; in the summer of 1831 the Creek agent, Campbell, made inquiries about these traps and other much-needed personal property, and an investigation was started. More than a year later, on August 29, 1832,[36] the Secretary of War replied. He said that the rifles and beaver traps promised in the treaty of 1826 were shipped from Philadelphia in the fall of 1830 to New Orleans, where part of them were reshipped to Fort Gibson in April, 1832, and the remainder were still held for storage charges in New Orleans. At this late day the quartermaster at New Orleans was directed to pay the storage bill and forward the beaver traps to Fort Gibson at such time as the state of water would permit. In desperation the Creeks had employed Colonel A. P. Chouteau to endeavor to secure these things that they so greatly needed.[37] This indifference of the Government to promises given the Indians may seem amazing at first, but Indian history is full of such instances. What wonder that the Indians distrusted the promises of government officials!

a buffalo hunt, and after an absence of twenty days returned with the meat of 24 buffaloes which they killed. They saw about 600 buffaloes and an immense number of deer, while out and would have killed more but had not the means of bringing the meat home, every horse having as much as he could carry. A second party will go out next month" (Letter from Creek Agent Thomas Anthony, Fort Gibson, July 1, 1828, in *New York Evening Post,* copied in *Arkansas Gazette,* October 14, 1828, p. 3, col. 3; *Cherokee Phoenix,* October 22, 1828, p. 4, col. 5).

[35] *U. S. Senate Document No. 512,* Twenty-third Congress, first session, "Indian Removal," II, 647.

[36] *Ibid.,* p. 914.

[37] The Creeks said of this trader with whom they did business: " . . . . we have full confidence in his integrity and knowledge of the Tribes, languages, manners, customs &c . . . . " of the Indians (*U. S. House Document No. 116,* Twenty-third Congress, first session).

XXI

EFFORTS TO REMOVE THE CHOCTAW AND CHICKASAW TO THE WEST, 1827-30

THE running of the eastern boundary line of the Choctaw Nation was completed on January 1, 1826. John P. Pitchlynn of the Choctaw Nation had accompanied the commissioners and assisted in the survey. On his return home he carried favorable reports of the country to his people; he wrote the Secretary of War that he was so much pleased with the western country that he would move there, if he could get pay for his improvements, and would take with him as many of his fellow countrymen as he could prevail on to go, if the Government would make a contract with him to ration them.[1] With the help of such influential men as Pitchlynn, the Government was trying to arouse in the tribe a sentiment favorable to removal.

There was already some movement of emigrant Choctaw, or anticipation of it, in the minds of those hoping to profit thereby. Colonel Phillips of Arkansas had built a ferryboat to carry the Choctaw across the Mississippi, and opened a road for them; he proposed to build some houses on the Choctaw lands east of the river to shelter them while they were detained, if the Government would pay for them.[2]

Talk of removal soon stirred the bitterest animosities between opposing partisans in the tribe. Mushalatubbe, of the Northeast District, who was favorable to the plans of the Government, was deprived of his office, and David Folsom was

---

[1] Pitchlynn to Barbour, February 26, 1826, OIA, RCF, "1826 Choctaw Emigration."

[2] Conway to Barbour, February 4, 1826, *ibid.*

appointed in his place. Robert Cole, of the Northwest District, who also supported the views of the Government, was likewise removed, and Greenwood Leflore succeeded to his post. Folsom, who explained to Mr. McKenney the removal of Mushalatubbe, said the ". . . . warriors thought best to do so on account of his intemperance, tyrannical disposition, ignorance and his manner of disposing of the annuity . . . . the warriors . . . . were determined that a second McIntosh should not rise up among them and dispose of their lands." He said that while there was some commotion, as yet there had been no bloodshed.[3]

The first agent for the Choctaw living west of the Mississippi was George Gray, who was appointed on March 27, 1821, in anticipation of the expected removal of other Choctaw under the recent treaty. He located his agency at Sulphur Fork near Long Prairie.[4] Soon after the execution of the Choctaw treaty of 1825, Major William L. McClellan of Mississippi was appointed agent to the western Choctaw and directed to establish his agency at the western limits of Arkansas.[5] In the spring of 1826 Major McClellan arrived at Fort Smith, where he was instructed to locate his agency and with his blacksmith and interpreter to occupy some of the old buildings. His first duty there was to unpack and repair a shipment of arms which he brought with him, intended for the Choctaw Indians.[6] He found the buildings in a dilapidated condition, the troops on moving to Fort Gibson having carried off the floors, doors, and windows.

In the following January, McClellan began the erection of new buildings for his agency fifteen miles above Fort Smith, near a fine spring.[7] Arrangements were made to receive there

[3] Folsom to McKenney, June 27, 1826, OIA, RCF, "1826 Choctaw Emigration."

[4] Gray to Calhoun, June 16, 1821, *ibid.*, "Choctaw, Sulphur Fork."

[5] Secretary of War to Governor Izard, July 1, 1825, *ibid.*

[6] Izard to Secretary of War, April 15, 1826, *ibid.*, "1826 Arkansas."

[7] In later years this was known as Skullyville.

a number of Choctaw who were understood to be emigrating
on their own resources; but after they were heard from on their
arrival at the Mississippi, no further news was received from
them for several months. A thousand Choctaw were living in
scattered bands in the western part of Louisiana and Arkansas,
and an effort was made to reach and get them to remove to
their new home convenient to Fort Smith; but some were too
poor to leave their little settlements and fields and undertake
so long a journey.[8] Others were fearful that outrages would be
committed on them by the whites if they undertook to settle
on the choice land in their new home, which the squatters had
refused to vacate.[9] McClellan found a large number of white
citizens living on the Poteau and Arkansas rivers near Fort
Smith, and they were told they might cross the Arkansas to
Lovely's Purchase.[10] Many of them refused to go,[11] but in
1829, McClellan reported that some of them were leaving the
Choctaw lands and that 150 Indians had moved up to occupy
the improvements vacated by the whites.[12] McClellan said also
that the Choctaw exploring party had called at his agency, and
told him that many of their countrymen in the East were so
destitute as to be living on acorns and by stealing hogs and
cattle and could easily be induced to migrate if the Government would furnish them food on the march.[13]

The whites of Arkansas were resentful of the consideration
shown to the Choctaw by the Government, and lost no oppor-

[9] McClellan to Secretary of War, February 15, 1827, OIA, RCF, "1827
Choctaws West."

[9] McClellan to Barbour, December 28, 1826, *ibid.*

[10] By an act of Congress of April 5, 1826, the land districts of the Territory
of Arkansas were extended; this was understood to look to the settlement and
sale of land within Lovely's Purchase, and the inhibition against settlement
was thereupon withdrawn (McKenney to Barbour, March 26, 1827, AGO, ORD,
WDF).

[11] McClellan to Secretary of War, February 15, 1827, OIA, RCF.

[12] McClellan to Secretary of War, OIA, RCF, March 12, 1829, "1829 Choctaws West."

[13] *Ibid.*

tunity to visit their displeasure on them. What proved to be a wholly fictitious report of misconduct on the part of some Choctaw near Arkansas Post was made, and a force of militia was sent to drive them from the country. This was accomplished, after the killing of two of the Indians.[14] The Choctaw fled to Clark County, where they insisted on remaining, to the displeasure of the inhabitants who reported to Governor Izard that the Indians were annoying them. The Governor then sent Colonel Wharton Rector to summon a force of militia to drive them from the country and order them to report to their agent.[15]

As McClellan began the construction of his agency, he granted a license to "young Peter Folsom" to operate a ferry at Fort Smith. "He has a fine boat and has commenced setting citizens over the River."[16] The Cherokee were already operating a ferry which they kept on their side of the Arkansas. Colonel Arbuckle made some objection to Folsom's ferry, as he said that Fort Smith was still in charge of the military authorities,[17] and thus probably began the controversy that continued for many years between the Choctaw and the Government, involving title to the land formerly occupied by the post.[18]

Through General Clark as intermediary the Choctaw east of the Mississippi had made overtures of peace to the Osage,[19] and sent word to their people on the Red River to commit no more hostilities against their enemies. McClellan reported that some of the Choctaw on the Red River had Osage prisoners; and in order to restore peace between the tribes he proposed

---

[14] Izard to Secretary of War, September 21, 1828, AGO, ORD, WDF. A Choctaw named Richmond Peeler belonging to a village on the Bayou Bartholomew was killed by the whites in June (*Arkansas Gazette,* June 11, 1828, p. 3, col. 2).

[15] Izard to Rector, August 8, 1828, OIA, RCF, "1828 Delaware."

[16] McClellan to Arbuckle, February 2, 1827, *ibid.,* "1828 Choctaws West."

[17] Arbuckle to McClellan, February 9, 1827, *ibid.*

[18] McClellan to Secretary of War, February 16, 1827, *ibid.*

[19] *American State Papers,* "Indian Affairs," II, 717.

that Nathaniel Pryor be appointed agent for the Osage; and that Pryor accompany him and some of the Osage chiefs to the Red River for the purpose of securing these Osage captives. By thus restoring peace between the tribes, McClellan believed the greatest obstacle to Choctaw emigration would be removed.[20]

The treaty of 1826 with the Creeks having been effected, Governor William Clark, Thomas Hinds, and General John Coffee were appointed commissioners to negotiate with the Chickasaw and Choctaw for the purpose of extinguishing their title to land within Mississippi and securing their consent to remove west of the Mississippi. The commissioners arrived in the Chickasaw country on October 15, 1826, but the conference did not begin until the twenty-second. The Chickasaw were represented by chiefs and commissioners including Levi Colbert, Martin Colbert, J. McLish, Tishomingo, and many other well-known members of the tribe. The conference continued from day to day until November 2, but the Indians flatly refused to consider the sale of any part of their land. The commissioners proposed that the Government pay the expenses of an exploring party of Chickasaw to the western country, if they would go and examine it, and this also the Indians rejected. The commissioners then proceeded to the Choctaw Nation. The tribe appointed a delegation of thirteen members to meet the commissioners in their country; and the meeting convened on November 10, 1826.[21] The Choctaw delegation included such prominent members as Joel Nail, Israel Folsom, and Peter P. Pitchlynn. The conference continued in session for a week; but while a few of the Choctaw were favorable to the plans of the commissioners, the majority were unalterably opposed. The meeting broke up with nothing accomplished except

---

[20] McClellan to Clark, May 25, 1827, OIA, RCF. General Clard in the following summer appointed Pryor subagent to the Arkansas Osage at a salary of $500 annually.

[21] *American State Papers*, "Indian Affairs," II, 709.

overtures of peace, through the mediation of the commissioners, by the Choctaw to their hereditary enemies west of the Mississippi, the Osage, and Delaware.[22]

Governor Clark having previously demanded of the Choctaw satisfaction for several murders committed by members of their tribe upon the Delaware Nation, Colonel Daniel Folsom at this time addressed the Governor. He told him that by mistake some of his warriors had killed some Delaware, who were their grandfathers, that he regretted it and the nation regretted it; that there had been war for a long time between his nation and the Osage; and that his warriors had killed the Delaware thinking they were Osage. After they found out their mistake, they threw away the scalps, "and returned home without any honors." He asked Governor Clark to bear to the Delaware their messages of regret and friendship.[23]

Greenwood Leflore wrote: ".... wee are anxious to become sivillize Nation if our father lets us rest few years but wee have been pastered for land so much wee dont know what to do hartly, but I hope wee will rest now a while."[24]

In 1827 Thomas L. McKenney, the head of the Indian Department, was directed to visit the Choctaw and Chickasaw nations and urge upon them the necessity of their removal to the West. He went first to the Chickasaw nation. A council was held at the home of Levi Colbert on October 9 and 10, with a large number of leading men of the tribe; a committee composed of Tishomingo, William McGillivray, Levi Colbert, and others, submitted their answer, in which they agreed to an exchange of lands provided the Government would defray the expense of an exploring party to be composed of twelve mem-

[22] The Choctaw and Delaware had been at war for more than half a century (Clark to Secretary of War, January 4, 1827, OIA, RCF), and in a recent war excursion the former had killed five Delaware (*ibid.*); the Choctaw in council admitted this to General Clark, who, however, does not tell us where the killing occurred.

[23] *American State Papers*, "Indian Affairs," II, 716.

[24] Leflore to McKenney, December 15, 1827, OIA, RCF.

bers of the tribe with three white men and a doctor, and provided also the members approved of the land in the West.[25]
They agreed to go the following May, 1828, by steamboat from
Memphis to St. Louis, and thence overland to the western
country.

McKenney then went to the Choctaw Nation, and held a
council with a number of chiefs at the Choctaw Agency on
October 17. The Choctaw, through their chiefs Greenwood
Leflore, David Folsom, and others, refused to agree to remove
on any terms, but said they would send six of their people with
the Chickasaw to examine the western country, without committing themselves to anything. McKenney found that the
chiefs Mushalatubbe and Cole had been displaced by their
constituents in favor of Folsom and Leflore, on the express
understanding of resistance to any proposal made to the nation
for an exchange of their land. They, however, were secretly
favorable to removal and told McKenney they would probably
consider the subject after the return of the exploring expedition.

Congress made an appropriation of $15,000[26] to defray the
expense of the exploration; and the Government employed
Isaac McCoy to conduct the party from·St. Louis. He received
his commission at Carey, Michigan, whence he went to St.
Louis, accompanied by three Ottawa and three Potawatomi
who wished to examine the western country. He reached St.
Louis on July 16 and installed his Indians in camp across the
river, while he took lodgings in the city hall.[27] On July 21,
since none of the southern Indians had arrived, he sent a messenger to learn when they were coming. On August 13, Luther
Blake arrived with Coe Marthla and two other Creek chiefs,[28]
and on the sixteenth the messenger returned and reported that

[25] Thomas L. McKenney, *Memoirs, with Sketches of Travels* (New York,
1846), 1, 316 ff.

[26] *U. S. Statutes at Large*, IV, 315.

[27] Kansas Historical Society, Journal of Isaac McCoy (unpublished manuscript).

[28] Tuskeneha and Choeste.

the Chickasaw and Choctaw had decided to postpone their journey[29] until the following March. McCoy sent a messenger back to tell the Indians that the excursion could not be postponed and that they should come at once. While he was waiting for them, he left St. Louis with the Ottawa and Potawatomi Indians for an examination of the country within what is now eastern Kansas. After an absence of forty-nine days he returned to St. Louis on October 9, and on the thirteenth the Chickasaw and Choctaw arrived.[30]

The party then departed on October 17 and 18 from St. Louis for the West.[31] It was composed of Captain G. H. Kennerly, as leader, Lieutenant Washington Hood and John Bell, topographers, Doctor Todson, surgeon, and Isaac McCoy, fiscal agent; the Chickasaw, headed by Levi Colbert, who was accompanied by his black servant, numbered thirteen[32] beside George B. Duncan, subagent, and three other white men chosen by themselves; the Choctaw, including Peter P. Pitch-

[29] The Indians complained that the expedition was starting too late in the year; they wisely urged that spring and summer would be a better season to judge of the quality and character of the soil than fall and winter (Colbert to Clark, August 2, 1828, OIA, RCF, "1828 St. Louis").

[30] After the departure of the Chickasaw an observer in their country wrote: " . . . . The Indians generally are in the greatest suspense. They have no confidence in each other, particularly on such an occasion as this. The people are unanimous in their opposition to a removal.

"The nation has recently formed some wholesale laws, and to our astonishment they are strictly enforced. Whiskey is banished from the country. A thief is punished with thirty lashes, without regard to color, age or sex" (Letter in *Missionary Herald*, copied in *Cherokee Phoenix*, February 18, 1829, p. 2, col. 2).

Levi Colbert and other friends of the Government were suspected of trying to sell their lands for bribes, and they were threatened with the fate of McIntosh (Levi Colbert, Tishomingo, and others to McKenney, March 11, 1828, OIA, RCF, "1828 Chickasaws").

[31] Clark to McKenney, October 23, 1828, OIA, RCF, "1828 St. Louis"; Kennerly and McCoy did not start until the twenty-first (*ibid.*).

[32] Isaac Love, Charles Colbert, and Benjamin Love were included, the latter as interpreter; Garland Lincecum, James Davis, and William D. King were the other white men (Bell and Duncan to Clark, List of Members, October 13, 1828, *ibid.*).

lynn, numbered six[33] with D. W. Haley in charge; there were three Creeks, with Luther Blake; as interpreter to the Osage went Noel Mongrain, a half-breed Osage.[34] The party numbered in all forty-two and traveled with sixty horses.

After crossing from Missouri into what is now eastern Kansas, they stopped at White Hair's village near the site of Parsons, Kansas,[35] where the Osage, on the one hand, and the Choctaw and Chickasaw chiefs, on the other, confirmed the peace[36] that had been signalized by the exchange of pipes at long distance two years before, in the presence of Governor Clark, putting an end to the war that had raged between those tribes for many years. A few miles brought them to Riviere du Bete or "River of Reptiles,"[37] now called "La Bête" or "The Beast," because, according to Washington Irving, the Indians once saw a great and terrible animal there, the like of which they had never seen before or since.[38] Soon they crossed the headwaters of Planche Cabin, or "Plank Cabin Creek," near the site of the modern town of Vinita, Oklahoma, the name probably celebrating the presence of a cabin made of boards. The topographers noted the celebrated salt spring near Colonel Chouteau's house, where Salina, Oklahoma is now, and on Thanksgiving Day crossed Pryor's Creek; a few miles farther

[33] "Tuppenhoma, Chief, Daniel Nail, interpreter, Peter Pitchlynn and Captain Kincade of Folsom's District, Capt. Red Dog of Leflore's District and Captain Auittatomas of Tuppenhoma's District" (Haley to Clark, October 15, 1828, OIA, RCF).

[34] Isaac McCoy, History of Baptist Indian Missions (New York, 1840), pp. 349 ff.; *U. S. House Document No. 87,* Twentieth Congress, second session, pp. 6 ff. Mongrain was a well-known Osage interpreter; he was frequently mentioned by Pike (Coues [ed.], *op. cit.,* pp. 393, 566, 579) who called him Maugraine or Noel.

[35] White Hair had moved there from the Little Osage River in 1822.

[36] Library of Congress, Manuscript Division, House of Representatives Collection, "Second Series," Box 192, Kennerly to Secretary of War, February 4, 1829.

[37] *U. S. House Document No. 87,* Twentieth Congress, second session, p. 37.

[38] William P. Trent and George S. Hellman, *The Journals of Washington Irving,* The Bibliophile Society, III, 126.

on they came to Union Mission[39] on the bank of the Neosho, and the next day brought them to the Creek Agency.

> The agency is situated immediately on the eastern bank of the Verdigris, three or four miles from its mouth; there is a high sandstone bluff or hill just below, and on the same side as the agency .... this is the highest point to which steam or keel boats ascend, the navigation being interupted by a fall in the river 6 or 700 yards above this point; the fall is from five to six feet.[40]

Here and at Fort Gibson the party remained until December 2. The Creek delegation visited here a few days, and renewed friendships with the resident Creeks, numbering over one thousand, who for the time overlooked the bitterness they cherished against the faction responsible for the killing of their leader, William McIntosh. In fact, McCoy says, they held a council and preparing a writing which they entrusted to the delegation, inviting the eastern Creeks to join them and assuring them that old grudges would be forgotten.

From Fort Gibson the party proceeded south and crossed the North Fork, near where Eufaula is now, and in the vicinity, on December 5, killed two buffaloes; they then crossed the Canadian River and started up that stream to examine the country in that direction. They had gone only a few miles when they saw a moccasin track; they thereupon faced about and traveled rapidly on a hunter's trace toward Fort Smith until they reached approximately the point where Webbers Falls now is. Here they ended their explorations. The Choctaw proceeded home by way of the Red River to see some of their countrymen living on that stream; the Chickasaw also departed for their home; McCoy and the remainder of the men returned

---

[39] "The Choctaw, Chickasaw and Creek delegations in pursuit of a country, passed us 3 days ago accompanied by Mr. McCoy the missionary" (Vaill to Evarts, November 30, 1828, Congregational House (Boston), Manuscript Library, Vol. XXXIV). The exploring party traversed the well-used trail which passed Union Mission, over which Washington Irving traveled in 1832.

[40] *U. S. House Document No. 87,* Twentieth Congress, second session, p. 41.

to Fort Gibson, and from there went to St. Louis. Before separating, McCoy pressed the Indians for some expression as to their impressions of the country they had examined, but they refused to commit themselves. They had come reluctantly, and declined to express any views favorable to the removal of the tribe, merely saying that if after their return home they found affairs with the Government satisfactory they would make their report to the President.

Thus, by 1830, part of the Cherokee, Choctaw, and Creek tribes had found their way west of the Mississippi, to a land of strife and lawlessness, bitter jealousy, and bloodshed, in the midst of an elemental struggle for existence. Some of these Indians had come as stragglers, hunters, and adventurers in response to a roving, restless spirit, others with the definite purpose of finding a place where they could sustain their families by hunting, and a very considerable part of them in quest of good farming and grazing lands where they could pursue peaceful, pastoral lives free from the rapacity and cruelty of white neighbors. The total constituted a considerable part of the tribes; some came by their own efforts and others with a small measure of ill-considered assistance by the Government. But the whole result had been achieved in a haphazard manner, wholly detached from any definite policy or plan on the part of the Government.

The pressure of the people of the states east of the Mississippi for the removal of their Indian neighbors continued unabated. In 1828, Andrew Jackson, who was committed to the policy of removal, was elected President, and on the following March 4 he was inaugurated. In July of that year gold was discovered in the Cherokee country in Georgia. On December 19, 1829, the Legislature of Georgia incorporated the Cherokee lands in the territory of the state and declared all tribal laws to be inoperative after June 30, 1830. Governor Gilmer proclaimed that the state had the "title in fee simple" to the

Cherokee lands and "entire and exclusive property" in the gold and silver therein.[41]

The Cherokee appealed to Jackson for protection, but he warned them to expect no assistance from him. In the President's first message to Congress, on December 7, 1829,[42] he recommended legislation looking to the removal of the Indians from the southern states, whose sovereign rights he said were menaced by the attempt to keep the Indians there on their own lands secured to them by treaty.

Bills were then introduced in the House and Senate providing for Indian removal and there followed one of the bitterest debates in the history of Congress. The whole country was aroused over the subject; mass meetings were held in New England and other sections of the North, and resolutions protesting against the proposed legislation were showered upon Congress. But Jackson's bill was passed on May 28, 1830,[43] and the Government was for the first time committed to something like a definite policy of removal of all Indians in the East. The bill authorized the President to cause the lands west of the Mississippi to be surveyed and divided into districts, and to offer these tracts to Indians living within the limits of any state or territory in exchange for the lands there held by them. Provision was made further to aid the emigrant Indians to remove and to maintain them after their removal, and the sum of $500,000 was appropriated to carry the act into effect. The President was further authorized

> solemnly to assure the tribe or nation with which the exchange is made that the United States will forever secure and guaranty to them, and their heirs or successors, the country so exchanged with them, and if they prefer it, that the United States will cause a patent or grant to be made and executed to them for the same.

[41] *U. S. Document No. 512,* Twenty-third Congress, first session, "Indian Removal," II, 231. Alabama had extended her laws over the Creeks and Mississippi hers over the Choctaw and and Chickasaw (*ibid.,* p. 290).

[42] James D. Richardson, *Messages and Papers of the Presidents,* II, 458.

[43] *U. S. Statutes at Large,* IV, 411. Grant Foreman, *Indian Removal.*

So closed a period of preparation of this southwestern country for its participation in a dramatic experiment with a race of people, unsurpassed in interest and pathos in our history. A wild and lawless expanse of beautiful country, hunted and fought over by the Indians, was on the eve of a great change. A decade then just beginning was to witness the immigration of more than sixty thousand Indians of fixed and domestic habits. These Indians, torn from their homes in the East and forced to move to this wild country, were to dot the landscape with farms and settlements, and establish new homes, governments, and schools; and their habits and achievements were to win for them the name of The Five Civilized Tribes.

BIBLIOGRAPHY

SOURCE OF MANUSCRIPTS

THIS book has been written in the main from unpublished manuscript material found in archives, the majority of which are in Washington, D.C. These manuscripts are usually records of official intercourse, the statements of persons in possession of information about the country and people which it was their duty or interest faithfully to convey to others. As they are contemporary accounts of scenes, conditions, and events observed by the writers, they are the best authority, and in many cases the only testimony in existence, concerning the matters described. In those early days of slow transportation, when postal service was almost unknown in the West, infrequent official intercourse provided practically the only enduring source of information concerning this frontier country. Intensive research has disclosed, sometimes in different places, numbers of documents relating to the same subject, which supplement and verify each other. The archives referred to are as follows:

WAR DEPARTMENT

ADJUTANT GENERAL'S OFFICE. The office of the Adjutant General possesses several archives which contain vast collections of manuscripts of great interest to the historian. Of first importance to the subject in hand is the department known as the "Old Files Division," located in the old library on the fifth floor of the State, War, and Navy Building in Washington. Reference to these files for the period covered by this book is afforded by a series of indexes which contain, in chronological and alphabetical order, the names of the writers of letters to be found there. These letters were usually written by officers at their stations over the country to the Adjutant General; and their value lies not only in the contents of the reports themselves, but also in the frequent and often voluminous enclosures of accounts of military expeditions and Indian forays, letters, complaints, reports, memorials, testimony, and maps from other officers, civilians, and Indians. These files, known as "Adjutant General's Office, Old Files Division," for brevity and convenience are referred to as AGO, OFD.

In the same building, another series of files and reports belonging to the Adjutant General, which have been consulted with profit by the author, are the Post Returns and Regimental Returns.

Of next importance in the Adjutant General's Office is the "Old Records Division," located in the Munitions Building, constructed during the late War. The catalogue of its contents is extensive, but for the purpose of this book reference is made to only a part—a series of letters and reports known as "War Department Files." They were written to the Secretary of War by army officers, officials, and civilians over the country; and many of them contain enclosures and detailed accounts of the Indians and their movements, and descriptions of people and events that contribute to the background of historical periods of the country. The files are classified as "Adjutant General's Office, Old Records Division, War Department Files"; for convenience, reference is to AGO, ORD, WDF.

The "Old Records Division" includes also Letter Books, Order Books, and other post records of Fort Gibson and Fort Smith which contain copies of letters and orders of great interest, written at those posts. There are also letter books of the department and division headquarters in the West and Southwest, Cincinnati, St. Louis, Louisville, Memphis, and New Orleans, in which are preserved copies of letters to officers at the remote army posts and to the War Department at Washington; these records are rich in historical material. Reference here is to AGO, ORD.

QUARTERMASTER GENERAL'S OFFICE. The Quartermaster General's Office is the repository of an extensive series of files located in the Hall of Records at Fort Myer, Virginia. Here are arranged, in chronological and alphabetical order, letters and reports dealing with construction of army posts and roads, movements and supply of troops and garrisons, and much detailed information related to those subjects; many of these files were first examined by the author while they were stored at the Schuylkill Arsenal at Philadelphia, whence they were removed to Fort Myer as room became available after the demands of the late War had relaxed.

COMMISSARY GENERAL'S RECORDS. In the Hall of Records are also the Commissary General's Records, a series of letters and reports, many of which concern the movement and provisioning of western troops, including collateral matters of historical interest.

THE DEPARTMENT OF THE CHIEF OF ENGINEERS. This department contains old records and maps made by the topographical engineers on their explorations of the West and Southwest that have been examined with profit.

DEPARTMENT OF STATE

In the "Department of Publications" of the Department of State, are preserved extensive records of events and conditions in the Territories of the United States, which contain much historical information. As the region which is now Arkansas and Oklahoma was, after it passed from French and Spanish sovereignty, successively part of Indiana, Louisiana, Missouri, and Arkansas territories, it is obvious that a varied documentary history must have survived. By authority of an act of Congress of March 3, 1925, the State Department has been engaged in collecting, arranging, and compiling these records, not only in that department, but also those relating to territorial periods which are now in the archives of other departments. A bill providing for the publication of these records was enacted in February, 1929, so that in time they will be accessible to the student without his being obliged to visit Washington to examine them. Departmental references employed are "Bureau of Rolls and Library," and "Bureau of Indexes and Archives," which are abbreviated to "BRL" and "BIA" respectively.

DEPARTMENT OF THE INTERIOR

OFFICE OF INDIAN AFFAIRS. In this office is a vast collection of letters relating principally to the Indians, though collateral matters of historical significance are often included; they were originally entered by letter and number in the form of folded files. This system recently has been changed, however, to a flat filing system; reference is not by indexes, as formerly, but only by date and subject noted on the folder. These were originally part of the files of the War Department, but, upon the transfer of the Indian bureau to the Interior Department in 1849, these files were transferred also. Reference is made to them as "Office of Indian Affairs 'Retired Classified Files,'" abbreviated here to OIA, RCF.

GENERAL LAND OFFICE. In this department are old records which have furnished some valuable information about the old salt works and early surveys.

POST OFFICE DEPARTMENT

The early records of post offices in the Southwest contribute part of the history of that region.

LIBRARY OF CONGRESS

In the monumental and well-organized Manuscript Division of the Library of Congress the author has found valuable material in the Senate Files, House of Representatives Collection, Jackson Papers, and Transcripts and Facsimiles from Papeles de Cuba in Archivo General de Indias, Seville; the Map Division of this Library has also been drawn upon.

Much material was obtained from the letters and reports of the missionaries in the archives of the American Board of Commissioners for Foreign Missions at Boston. Outside of the War Department and Indian Office the author has derived most assistance from the Missouri Historical Society in the Jefferson Memorial at St. Louis. Other archives in which material for this book has been found are the Missouri State Historical Society, at Columbia, the Wisconsin Historical Society, the Texas State Library, the University of Texas Library, the Oklahoma Historical Society, the Kansas Historical Society, the St. Louis Mercantile Library (Chouteau Manuscript Collection), the Bancroft Library at the University of California, the Huntington Library at San Marino, California, and the Louisiana Historical Society.

AUTHORITIES

The author has drawn freely upon old newspaper files for a considerable amount of the material used; while he found the most assistance in the Newspaper Division of the Library of Congress, he was aided also by research among the old files in the Missouri Historical Society at St. Louis, the State Historical Society of Missouri at Columbia, the University of Texas Library, the Texas State Library at Austin, the Louisiana Historical Society, the New Orleans City Hall, the Reading Room of the British Museum in London, and the Bibliothèque Nationale in Paris.

The following is a list of the books and newspapers consulted:

ABEL, ANNIE HELOISE, ed., *A Report from Natchitoches in 1807, by Dr. John Sibley* (Museum of the American Indian, New York, 1922).

American Historical Association, *Annual Report for 1904* (Washington, 1905).

————, *Annual Report for 1906:* Annie Heloise Abel, "The History of Events Resulting in Indian Consolidation West of the Mississippi River" (Washington, 1908).

————, *Annual Report for 1919:* Vol. II, "The Austin Papers," ed. by Prof. Eugene C. Barker (Washington, 1924).

American Historical Review, Vol. XXIV, Documents from Office of Indian Affairs concerning Nathaniel Pryor, compiled by Stella M. Drumm.

American Missionary Register.

American State Papers (Washington, 1834): "Indian Affairs," Vols. I, II, III.

Annales de l'Association de la Propagation de la Foi.

Arkansas Gazette (Arkansas Post and Little Rock), November 20, 1819—December 31, 1845.

Arkansas Territory, Acts of Territorial Legislature.

BANCROFT, HUBERT HOWE, *History of the North Mexican States* (San Francisco, 1884), Vols. I, II.

BERQUIN-DUVALLON, *Travels in Louisiana and the Floridas in 1802* (New York, 1806).

BOLTON, HERBERT E., *Athanase de Mézières and the Louisiana-Texas Frontier* (Cleveland, 1914), Vols. I, II.

———— and MARSHALL, T. M., *The Colonization of North America* (New York, 1920).

BOSSU, N., *Travels through That Part of North America Formerly Called Louisiana*, trans. by J. R. Forster (London, 1771).

————, *New Travels* (Amsterdam, 1777).

BROWN and BARCROFT, Map of Arkansas Territory, Library of Congress, Map Division.

BROWNE and LEE, *American Atlas*, Map of Arkansas Territory (Philadelphia, 1822).

Cherokee Phoenix (New Echota, Georgia, 1828-31), file in British Museum.

CORNELIUS, ELIAS, *The Little Osage Captive*, an Authentic Narrative (Boston, 1822).

CORTAMBERT, LOUIS, *Voyage Au Pays Des Osages* (Paris, 1837).

COUES, ELLIOTT, *The Expeditions of Zebulon Montgomery Pike*, Vols. I, II, III (New York, 1895).

————, ed., *The Journal of Jacob Fowler*, Narrating an Adventure from Arkansas through the Indian Territory, Oklahoma, Kansas, Colorado, and New Mexico, to the Source of Rio Grande del Norte, 1821-22 (New York, 1898).

Courrier des Natchitoches (Louisiana, 1827).

Daily National Journal (Washington, D.C.), February, 1825.

DEWEES, W. B., *Letters from an Early Settler of Texas*, compiled by Cara Cardelle (Louisville, 1852).

DOUGLAS, WALTER B., ed., *Three Years among the Indians and Mexicans*, by Gen. Thomas James (Missouri Historical Society, 1916).

DRAKE, SAMUEL G., *The Aboriginal Races of North America* (15th ed.; New York, 1880).

DUBROCA, LOUIS, *Itinerary of the French in Louisiana* (Paris, 1802).

DUMONT, M., *History of Louisiana, Translated from the Historical Memoirs of M. Dumont*, "Historical Collections of Louisiana" (New York, 1853), Part V.

Dwight Mission Journal, unpublished manuscript, Congregational House, Boston, Manuscript Library.

ELLICOTT, ANDREW, *The Journal of Andrew Ellicott, Late Commissioner for Determining the Boundary between the United States and the Possessions of His Catholic Majesty in America* (Philadelphia, 1814).

FLINT, TIMOTHY, *Recollections of the Last Ten Years in the Valley of the Mississippi* (Boston, 1826).

FOREMAN, GRANT, *Pioneer Days in the Early Southwest* (Cleveland, 1926).

————, "Red River and the Spanish Boundary in the United States Supreme Court," *Chronicles of Oklahoma* (Oklahoma City, 1924).

Fort Smith (Ark.) *Herald*, 1848.

GOULDING, REV. F. R., *Sal-o-quah; or Boy-life among the Cherokees* (Philadelphia, 1870).

HATCHER, MATTIE AUSTIN, "Background of Colonization of Texas," *Southwestern Historical Quarterly*, Vol. XXIV.

HODGE, FREDERICK W., ed., *Handbook of American Indians* (Washington, 1912), Vols. I, II.

HOSMER, JAMES K., *History of the Expedition of Lewis and Clark* (Chicago, 1902), Vols. I, II.

HOUCK, LOUIS, *History of Missouri*.

————, *The Spanish Régime in Missouri*.

HUNTER, JOHN D., *Memoirs of a Captivity among the Indians of North America* (London, 1823).

Illinois Gazette (Shawnee-Town, 1828).

IMLAY, GILBERT, *A Topographical Description of the Western Territory of North America* (London, 1797).

JAMES, GEN. THOMAS, *Three Years among the Indians and Mexicans*, ed. Douglas, Walter B. (Missouri Historical Society, 1916).

JEFFERSON, THOMAS, and DUNBAR, WILLIAM, *Documents Relating to the Purchase and Exploration of Louisiana* (Boston, 1904).

Journal de la Société des Americanistes de Paris (Paris, 1921), Tome XIII.

Journal of Arkansas Mission, unpublished manuscript, Andover-Harvard Theological Library.

KAPPLER, CHARLES J., ed., "Indian Affairs," "Laws and Treaties," Vol. II (*U. S. Senate Document No. 452*) Fifty-seventh Congress, first session (Washington, 1903).

Kentucky Gazette (Lexington, 1824).

Laws of the Cherokee Nation, passed during the years 1839-67 (St. Louis, 1868).

LE PAGE DU PRATZ, ANTOINE S., *Histoire de la Louisiana* (Paris, 1758), Vols. I, II, III.

LEWIS, ANNA, "Du Tisné's Expedition into Oklahoma in 1719"; "French Interests and Activities in Oklahoma"; *Chronicles of Oklahoma* (Oklahoma City, 1924, 1926), Vols. II, IV.

Louisiana Herald (Natchitoches, 1821).

Louisville Public Advertiser, 1824.

McCOY, ISAAC, *History of Baptist Indian Missions* (New York, 1840).

————, Journal of, unpublished manuscript, Kansas Historical Society.

McKENNEY, THOMAS L., *Memoirs, with Sketches of Travels* (New York, 1846).

———— and HALL, JAMES, *History of the Indian Tribes of North America* (Philadelphia, 1854), Vols. I, II, III.

McLAUGHLIN, J. FAIRFAX, *Matthew Lyon the Hampden of Congress* (New York, 1900).

MARSHALL, T. M., ed., *Life and Letters of Frederick Bates* (St. Louis, 1926), Vol. II.

MARTIN, FRANÇOIS-XAVIER, *History of Louisiana* (New Orleans, 1882).

Missionary Herald (Boston, 1818-26).

Missouri Advocate and St. Louis Public Advertiser (1825).

Missouri Gazette (St. Louis, 1817).

Missouri Intelligencer (Franklin, 1821).

Missouri Republican (St. Louis, 1828).

Missouri Territory, Acts of the Territorial Legislature, 1813-18.

MONETTE, JOHN W., M.D., *History of the Discovery and Settlement of the Valley of the Mississippi* (New York, 1848), Vols. I, II.

MORSE, REV. JEDIDIAH, *A Report to the Secretary of War on Indian Affairs,* Comprising a Narrative of a Tour Performed in the Summer of 1820 (New Haven, 1822).

Natchitoches Courier (1825).

National Banner and Nashville Whig (Nashville, Tenn., 1828).

National Intelligencer (Washington, 1830).

Nebraska Historical Society, Addison E. Sheldon, *Nebraska History; the Battle at the Forks of the Loup and the Platte*, August 11, 1720 (Lincoln, 1923).

————, "Massacre of Villasur Expedition" (Lincoln, 1924).

New York Spectator (November, 1826).

Niles' Weekly Register, containing political and historical documents, essays, and facts, with notices of the arts, Vols. I-LXXIV. Baltimore (from July 5, 1848, Philadelphia), 1811-48.

O'HANLON, JOHN, *Life and Scenes in Missouri* (Dublin, 1890).

Oklahoma Historical Society, *Chronicles of Oklahoma* (Oklahoma City, 1924, 1926), Vols. II, IV.

————, Grant Foreman, "Red River and the Spanish Boundary in the United States Supreme Court," *Chronicles of Oklahoma* (Oklahoma City, 1924).

RICHARDSON, JAMES D., *Messages and Papers of the Presidents,* 1903.

ROYCE, CHARLES C., *The Cherokee Nation of Indians* (with *Fifth Annual Report of the Bureau of American Ethnology* [Washington, 1887]).

St. Louis Enquirer, 1824.

SAUER, CARL O., *The Geography of the Ozark Highland of Missouri.*

SCHOOLCRAFT, HENRY R., *Tour into the Interior of Missouri and Arkansaw* (London, 1821).

SHEA, JOHN GILMARY, *Early Voyages Up and Down the Mississippi* (Albany, 1861).

SHELDON, ADDISON E., *Nebraska History; the Battle at the Forks of the Loup and the Platte, August 11, 1720* (Lincoln, 1923).

SHINN, JOSIAH H., *Pioneers and Makers of Arkansas* (Little Rock, 1908).

SIBLEY, DR. JOHN, *A Report from Natchitoches in 1807*, ed. Abel, Annie Heloise (Museum of the American Indian, New York, 1922).

Smithsonian Institution, "The George Catlin Indian Gallery," *Annual Report to July, 1885* (Washington, 1886), Part V.

STODDARD, AMOS, *Sketches, Historical and Descriptive of Louisiana* (Philadelphia, 1812).

Texas Gazette (Austin, 1830).

THOMAS, A. B., "The Massacre of the Villasur Expedition at the Forks of the Platte River, August 12, 1720," in Nebraska State Historical Society, "Publications" (Lincoln, 1924).

————, "Spanish Reaction to American Intrusion into Spanish Dominions, 1818-1819," in *West Texas Historical Year Book, 1928.*

————, "Spanish Explorations of Oklahoma," *Chronicles of Oklahoma* (Oklahoma City, 1928).

THWAITES, R. G., ed., *Early Western Travels,* 1748-1846 (Cleveland, 1904-08).

Vol. XIII, Nuttall, Thomas, *Journal of Travels into Arkansas Territory,* With Occasional Observations on the Manners of the Aborigines, October 2, 1818—February 18, 1820, reprint of original edition (Philadelphia, 1821).

Vols. XIV, XV, XVI, and XVII, James, Edwin, *Account of an Expedition from Pittsburgh to the Rocky Mountains,* Performed by Order of Hon. J. C. Calhoun, Secretary of War, under Command of Maj. S. H. Long of U. S. Topographical Engineers; compiled from the notes of Maj. S. H. Long, Mr. T. Say, and other gentlemen of the party, March 31, 1819—November 22, 1820. Text reprinted from the London edition, 3 vols., 1823; Preliminary Notice, Long and Swift's calculations of observations; and Say's vocabularies of Indian languages, from Philadelphia edition of same year.

TRENT, WILLIAM P., and HELLMAN, GEORGE S., *The Journals of Washington Irving,* The Bibliophile Society (Boston, 1919).

Union Mission Journal, unpublished manuscript, Oklahoma Historical Society.

United States House of Representatives:
Document No. 263, Twentieth Congress, first session.
Report No. 87, Twentieth Congress, second session.
Report No. 549 Twenty-fifth Congress, second session.

United States Senate:
Document No. 23, Twenty-fourth Congress, first session.
Document No. 512, Twenty-third Congress, first session, Vols. I, II, III, IV, V.

United States Statutes at Large, Vols. II, III, IV, VII (Boston, 1846-50).

United States v. Texas, "No. 4 Original," United States Supreme Court Printed Record, Vols. I, II, III.

View of the Spanish Colony of the Mississippi, 1802, by a Resident Observer on the Premises.

VILLIERS, BARON MARC DE, *La Decouvérte du Missouri et l'histoire du Fort d'Orleans (1673-1728)* (Paris, 1925).

WASHBURN, CEPHAS, *Reminiscences of the Indians* (Richmond, 1869).

YOAKUM, H., *History of Texas* (New York, 1855-56).

INDEX

INDIANS AND PIONEERS
by GRANT FOREMAN, has been composed in Lino-
type Old Style No. 7. In essential details this face
was modeled on a series originally cut by the Bruce
Foundry during the decade following the Civil War.
The Bruce cutting appears to have descended from
a type cast by the famous Edinburgh founders,
Messrs. Miller and Richard. Old Style No. 7 presents thought with exceptional candor and sin-
cerity. It is unpretentious and unadorned with
graces, but it possesses to an unusual degree
the first requisite of type—ready legibility.
A slight contrast between the heavy lines
and hair lines relieves the printed page
of what otherwise might be
tiresome monotony

THE PRINTED PAGE IS   EVERYMAN'S UNIVERSITY

UNIVERSITY OF OKLAHOMA PRESS
PUBLISHING DIVISION OF THE UNIVERSITY
NORMAN